the PACK of WOMEN

ROBYN ARCHER • DIANA MANSON • HELEN MILLS • DEBORAH PARRY • ROBYN STACEY

Hessian Books
10 Belgrave Street
Petersham, New South Wales, 2049 Australia

Penguin Books Australia Ltd,
487 Maroondah Highway, P.O. Box 257
Ringwood, Victoria, 3134, Australia
Penguin Books Ltd,
Harmondsworth, Middlesex, England
Penguin Books,
40 West 23rd Street, New York, N.Y. 10010, U.S.A.
Penguin Books Canada Limited,
2801 John Street, Markham, Ontario, Canada
Penguin Books (N.Z.) Ltd,
182-190 Wairau Road, Auckland 10, New Zealand

First published by Hessian Books
in association with Penguin Books Australia Ltd, 1986

Copyright © Black and Blue Inc Pty Ltd, 1986

Typeset by Anna Pappas Typographics Pty Ltd, Sydney.
Made and printed in Australia by Valentine Graphics
Designed by Deborah Parry Graphics Pty. Ltd.
FRONT AND BACK COVER PHOTOGRAPHY: ROBERT McFARLANE

CIP

The Pack of Women.

Bibliography.
ISBN 0 14 008634 X.

1. Feminism. 2. Women's rights. I Archer, Robyn,
1948—
305.4'2

CONTENTS

THANKS

The authors wish to thank the many people who have been driven mad in one way or another working on this book — Cate Anderson, Maureen Barron, Ben Evans, Phil Gerlach, Maureen Kelleher, Deborah Owen, Anna Pappas, Diana Simmonds, Robert Thompson and Carmen Warrington.

And to our editors at Penguin — Jackie Yowell, Clare O'Brien and Bruce Sims.

The Pack of Women was first produced at The Drill Hall, London, in 1981. Starring Robyn Archer, Margo Random and Jane Wood with Andrew Bell, Irita Kutchmy and Jeremy Wesley. Directed by Pam Brighton. Musical Director Andrew Bell. Produced by Diana Manson and Dianne Robson for Diehard Productions.

The Pack of Women was first produced in Australia at the Downstairs Theatre, Seymour Centre in 1983. Starring Jane Clifton, Judi Connelli and Michele Fawdon with Andrew Bell, Dianne Spence and Jeremy Wesley. Directed by Robyn Archer. Designed by Roger Kirk. Musical Director Andrew Bell. Produced by Sue Hill and Chris Westwood for Understudies Pty Ltd.

The Pack of Women has also been made into a television program for ABC-TV. Starring Robyn Archer, Judi Connelli, Tracy Harvey, Jo Kennedy and Meryl Tankard with Andrew Bell, Sandy Evans and Maree Steinway. Directed by Ted Robinson. Designed by Roger Ford. Musical Director Andrew Bell. Produced by Diana Manson for Sideshow Alley Limited.

The program is available on videocassette through ABC Marketing and on soundtrack album through Festival Records.

INTRODUCTION
THE WOMEN SIT DOWN TO PLAY

Robert McFarlane

THE WOMEN SIT DOWN TO PLAY

THE WOMEN SIT DOWN TO PLAY
ROBYN ARCHER

DEALER:

Have you watched a woman deal?

It's different, look at her hands
Look at her hands, look at her hands;
Less of a game, more of a game
The cards are electric
The stakes are high; they couldn't be higher,
But no woman here packs a gun.
Age-old shame will be enough to send a deceiver packing,
The shame shared round will bring her back again,
Her credit is extended.

HONKY TONK PIANO IN THE BACKGROUND.
THE WOMEN PLAY SILENTLY.

The game goes on for days;
The endurance of women surpasses that of your average
cowboy.
As you watch, bear in mind,
This deck could be dangerous.

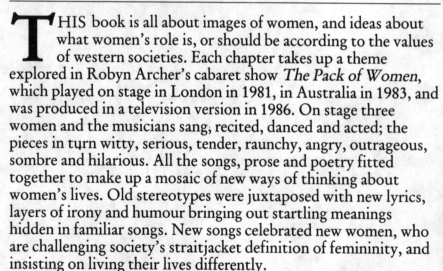

THIS book is all about images of women, and ideas about what women's role is, or should be according to the values of western societies. Each chapter takes up a theme explored in Robyn Archer's cabaret show *The Pack of Women*, which played on stage in London in 1981, in Australia in 1983, and was produced in a television version in 1986. On stage three women and the musicians sang, recited, danced and acted; the pieces in turn witty, serious, tender, raunchy, angry, outrageous, sombre and hilarious. All the songs, prose and poetry fitted together to make up a mosaic of new ways of thinking about women's lives. Old stereotypes were juxtaposed with new lyrics, layers of irony and humour bringing out startling meanings hidden in familiar songs. New songs celebrated new women, who are challenging society's straitjacket definition of femininity, and insisting on living their lives differently.

The Pack of Women got its name from the theatrical image of a deck of playing cards in the hands of women — women cutting the pack, women dealing out the cards, women with the aces up their sleeves, women taking chances and gambling for high stakes. As a metaphor for living life according to new rules, the image of the card-playing women takes off into all sorts of interesting associations: the pack of women —the women's movement; a game with new players, questioning the rules, women taking their futures into their own hands, changing the luck of the draw. . .

MUSIC
How do you stick out a game
When the rules keep changing?
The strategy's clear
You gotta keep re-arranging:
Re-assessing is the only attack
And once you've started playing
It's a trick to look back. . .

The cabaret worked by playing with familiar images of women, turning them on their heads, holding them up to the light for a good hard look. Sitting in the audience watching it unfold was for many people something like the first encounter with feminist thinking — and indeed very like seeing feminist thinking take shape. It was a process of beginning to see familiar things in a new light, seeing suddenly (and then it all becomes so painfully obvious, that we can't understand why we never saw it before) how these pictures of women are concealing another level of reality — the level of women's own experience of their lives, which is not usually given a form of expression in our culture. On stage this shock of recognition came about through the unexpected juxtaposition of themes, or by singing a love song with an irony of voice or musical setting.

Jane Wood, Irita Kutchmy, Margo Random
(writer of THE GIRL ON THE WALL),
& Robyn Archer in the London production.

It's a challenge to reproduce this process in a book. Books aren't like stage shows, where the director and the actors can create the environment for the audience. Readers can be more selective, escaping the framework intended by the authors, fast-forwarding through the parts that don't appeal, going back to savour an earlier page; so we knew we should cheerfully accept reader anarchy, and fill the pages with as many illuminating insights into the themes as could be linked together.

And so the book comes to represent a sort of map of contemporary culture, throwing into high relief the changes in the cultural landscape brought about by feminism. But maps aren't guides or 'how-to' manuals. They can only draw a picture of what the terrain looks like. They show the gasworks next to the highway, and the location of the traffic lights and the parks and swimming pools, but a map doesn't show the way that particular bit of the highway next to the gasworks looks and feels when you're stuck in the car at an interminable red light on a sweltering afternoon before the storm clears the air of the stench of fumes. If you think of our culture — the ways we express our interpretations of life through fashion, films, books, art, stories, newspapers, television, customs and routines of everyday life — as the ordinary map, and think of feminism as adding that extra dimension of experience, you will see what sort of map we are trying to draw. It's a map which shows the bits that other maps show, but adds a new perspective.

We have tried to make sure that all the signposts point in more or less the same directions, but to be honest, feminism adds many different perspectives. After a decade of intense debate, political action, organising and thinking, and reacting to the society around, many different feminist ways of thinking have developed. But all of them have in common the idea that in western industrial societies, and probably in most other forms of society past and present, women are subordinated to men, and women's full potential as human beings is limited by social arrangements which advantage men. Feminist thinking comes up with explanations for why this should be so, how it came about, what it is that keeps things this way, and how women might go about changing things. All feminist thinking adds to the culture a new dimension: that men's and women's interests are not identical, and that society on the whole looks out for the interests of men. The tabloid newspapers write dismissively of the 'sex war', trivialise it and pretend it's all a game. Feminism is a critical theory, saying that on the whole the world looks and feels worse for women than for men — but feminism also celebrates the delight of women's realisation that it doesn't have to be like this for ever. That it is neither nature nor fate which ordains women's place, but only cultural arrangements, which can be changed.

MUSIC
You do have a choice about entering this game
But then most games are a matter of choice.
The problem with this game is
If you choose not to play

You might one day
Find yourself wishing you had
learnt the rules
taken a risk earlier
perhaps for those who come after.

And if you also choose to play
Then you could
Seem to lose,
Sometimes almost as bad as losing itself.
And the rules are difficult
For there are many variations within the generic group of cards
And there is no doubt that the games and the rules keep
Changing quite dramatically. . .

Thinking about how women are represented in visual images is a good way of thinking about women's position in society.

Wyatt Earp, Doc Holiday and the dealer
sat down to play
(Annie Oakley, Calamity Jane, and the Madam
were practising their aim),
It could have been, for what didn't need to be re-thought
re-assessed, or
re-arranged,

a scene amongst three men in Roman times.
That men have leisure to game together is seen as
Something socially correct
Something one can probably detect
In any place from time immemorial.

But look now as the women sit down to play
(What's wrong with this picture?),
If the women are dressed as men it's unimportant,
not just Sodom & Gomorrah in the twentieth century,
there have always been transvestites. . .
No, it's not that.
Just watch a moment and listen.
NOISES OF THE WOMEN PLAYING CARDS.
BAND PLAYS CHORUS IN BACKGROUND

Shouldn't the women wear feathers,
sit themselves on the randy knees of
Yosemite Sam toothless goldminers?
Aren't they better placed in serving at the bar
and at your tables,
Or disporting bits and pieces on the tatty stage?
Serving in the dining room
or on the brass beds in the rooms above the saloon?

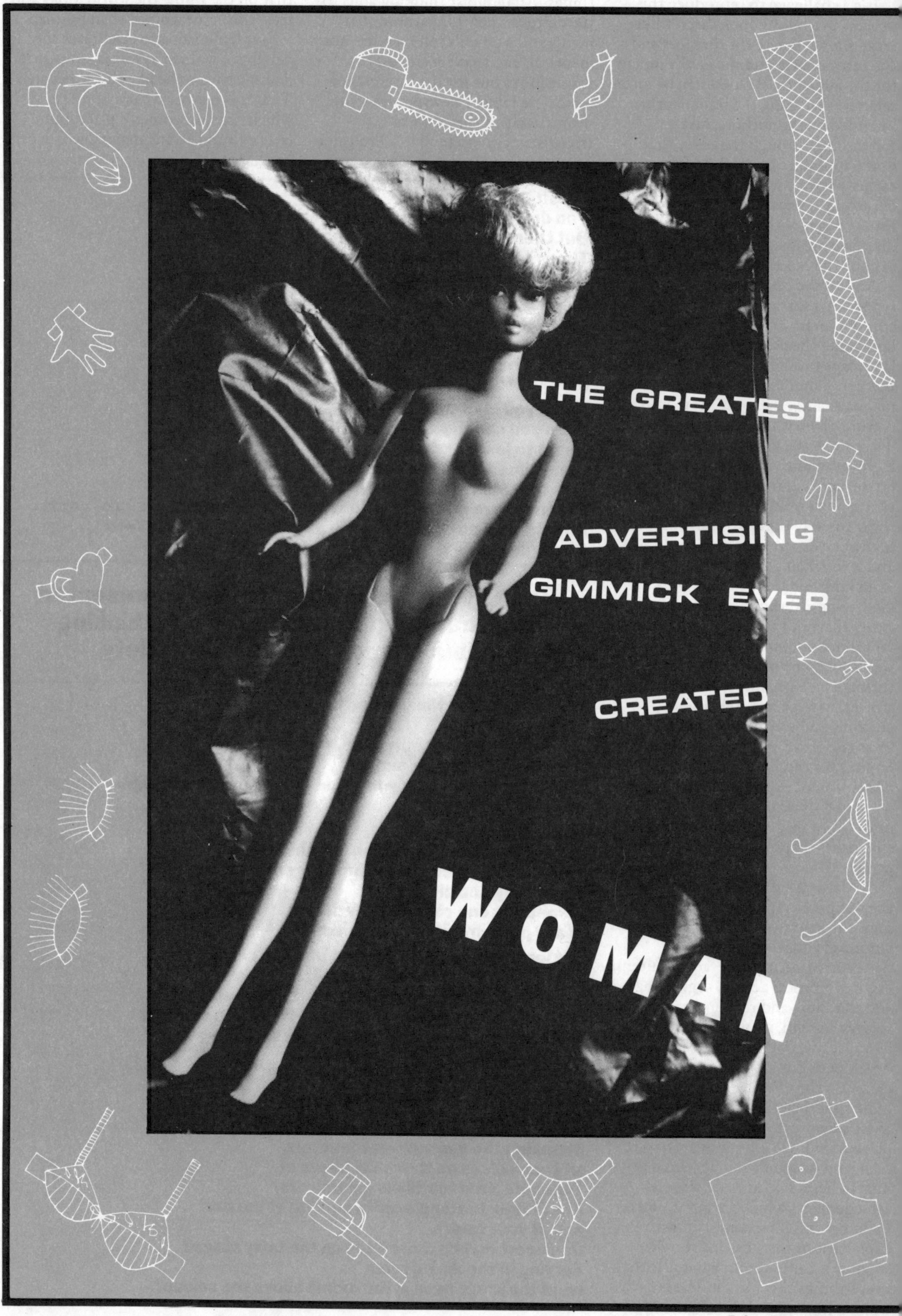
THE GREATEST
ADVERTISING
GIMMICK EVER
CREATED
WOMAN

Robyn Stacey & Jenny Clark

Women are the sex which is constantly on display; women are looked at, in the flesh and in a ceaseless flow of pictures. The fashion industry is organised around the assumption that women express their personalities and moods through clothes, that women are always alert to nuances of style, that women endlessly care about how they look. Advertising works on the principle that there are commonly agreed ideal images of women — ideal bodies, ideal relationships, ideal feminine attitudes — that most women accept and aspire to. Our society regards women as aesthetic objects, to be gazed at, admired, yearned for and possessed.

Ironically, our society also condemns and ridicules women for the very self-obsession that fashion, advertising and women's magazines have worked so hard to promote. Go too far in the pursuit of the ideal body, the essence of style, and a woman becomes a symbol of vanity and smallmindedness. Guilt lies all around; guilt that you have let yourself go, guilt that you should be devoting so much energy to passing fads, guilt that you care so much about appearances.

Whatever their individual feelings about these ideal images of women, women as a sex are made to feel very conscious of being the sex which is looked at. Sometimes this can bring a sense of power and strength, for the woman who is confident of her appeal; but for women conscious of their ' failure' to match the ideals of beauty, charm and 'feminine' behaviour, or irritated by the need to try, there is anxiety or defensiveness. At its most destructive extreme society's preoccupation with putting women on display can make women into scapegoats, blamed by society for the uglier manifestations of male sexuality. Later in this book we show how women can be made to feel profoundly guilty and responsible for male sexual behaviour — for example, young women said to have 'invited' rape by their style of dress, or outgoing manner, or to be responsible for sexual harassment in their workplace, simply by being female in the wrong place at the wrong time.

This is just one example of how the process of looking at images of women through feminist eyes gives us a new perspective on our society, gives us a way into understanding how it all works, how the contradictory images of woman as mother, whore, guardian of respectability can be held all at the same time. And these are not just images of women in the minds of men: *The Pack of Women* showed, through songs and prose, how we all, men and women, live with these ideas about women, how they shape our imaginations, run through our literature and popular songs, and shape our ideas about sexuality and love.

Having a feminist perspective means far more than putting a sense of female grievance into words (though that too is an important task of feminism).

The cabaret and this book aim to demonstrate his point. Feminism takes up questions about the nuts and bolts of life — love, sex, jealousy, work, our physical bodies, motherhood, fatherhood, ageing — and shows how they should be seen as more than just personal concerns, but underpin, like foundations, all social arrangements.

Feminism points out that we 'see' things as we have been taught to see them, and that in our society we have been taught a male vision of the world. We are taught to see and evaluate through men's eyes. The point has already been made that women are the sex which is looked at, discussed, preached to, sold ideas and fantasies. This puts women at a disadvantage, makes them the object of society's thinking, not the subject.

Consider how different the world would look if the reverse were accepted as the norm, if all the images of physical perfection were male bodies, if men were encouraged to have a constant concern for the details of their appearance, to the extent of taking out pocket mirrors to check for straying hairs or smudged lipstick in restaurants. We would probably assume that in a world organised like that male homosexuality was the norm — because we are totally unused to imagining that the desiring person might be a women, and the desired object a man. We are used to thinking that men desire, women respond. Men are the subjects, women the objects. It takes a real wrench to think of women as the subjects, the doers.

See Lily Tomlin desiring John Travolta in 'Moment by Moment' — no marks for guessing why the movie was a box office flop.

All our social arrangements including language reflect this male perspective. So the word 'man' is used to stand for all humanity, and when we say 'he' we often mean he and she (or at least we pretend that we mean women as well, in contexts like this one: 'the successful applicant will be a highly motivated individual. He will have a strong sense of his own worth. . .' Will *she*?)

Quite ordinary words like 'manager' or 'actor' can sound odd applied to women — we have to mark the fact that they are being applied to women by changing them, to 'manageress' (which sounds more like running a canteen than presiding in the boardroom), and 'actress'.

Because men are the subjects and women are the objects, history, politics, customs, ideas and theories have been written and recorded by men. **See Sheila Rowbotham's *Hidden From History.*** What we are accustomed to define as 'art' has been, on the whole, produced by men, to be purchased by other men. Historically, the art which women have produced has been called 'craft', or 'decorative art' and has never been important in the art market. **See Germaine Greer's *The Obstacle Race.*** Language, recorded history, and our definitions of culture make women their objects; women as producers are invisible.

When asked to state what was the most important philosophical development this century, Herbert Marcuse, the German-American philosopher, author of ONE DIMENSIONAL MAN, replied 'Feminism'.

'Big Boys Don't Cry' *Preston*

9

And the images of women which appear everywhere, saturating our culture, are fantasies of women. Women and their bodies are the subject of countless metaphors and symbols.

Women appear in advertisements for anything from breakfast cereals to power tools; women's bodies keep the huge pornography industry profitable; figures of women adorn public buildings and ceremonial occasions, symbolising justice or mercy or beauty or grace or the mother of god; women are the source of powerful emotions of joy, or more usually pain, which give point to popular songs, great novels, and sensational family tragedies in the Sunday papers. Women fill up the news as victims ('among the dead were Brian Hogg and his wife, daughter and mother-in-law'), innocent bystanders, or social problems — prostitutes, single mothers, shoplifting housewives. Women rarely appear as individuals in their own right, unless they are exceptional or odd, like the first woman in space, or Princess Diana. By contrast, men in the news are there for doing things. Statues of male figures are usually representations of real men — governors, generals, poets, statesmen — with names and histories. Even the unknown soldier stands for real dead soldiers. But women in these public representations have their qualities abstracted from them. Their images represent ideas about women in general, or abstract ideas given feminine qualities.

Feminists ask the question: what sort of society is it that uses images of women to stand for noble values and deep emotions, while real live women are underpaid as workers, undervalued as mothers, ridiculed as activists? How do these everpresent images of unreal fantasy women feed into men's and women's ideas of differences between the sexes? Why indeed does our society insist that women and men are so different?

Feminists have been confronting images idealising women for generations, recognising their potential to shape and constrict the lives of women. Suffragettes fighting for the right to vote in the late 19th century poured scorn on male opponents who glorified women's virtues as the conscience of society, while refusing them any say in the running of that society. Women in the socialist movement pointed to the hypocrisy of factory owners who revered women for their delicacy and charm, but found nothing unfeminine in the sight of a woman on all fours scrubbing their floors.

In 1968 the current feminist movement made the headlines in an ironic battle of images. As Anna Coote and Beatrix Campbell tell the story, a group of American women had organised a protest against the Miss America pageant. They were arguing that beauty contests degraded all women, and set up false standards of beauty which forced women to push and pull their bodies into unnatural shapes, in order to please men. To make their point forcefully the protesters organised a dumping of bras and girdles (it *was* 1968) into a rubbish bin.

UPI

'Imaginary flames were added later by a news agency reporter and the idea caught on in a big way. The media loved it. Sexy and absurd, it neatly disposed of a phenomenon which would otherwise have proved rather awkward to explain.'

The idea of burning a bra was so ludicrous that people made an easy slide into saying that the ideas of feminism were ridiculous. One of the strongest criticisms made of feminists is that they have made themselves ugly, that they are out to destroy all beauty in women and all harmony in the home. Many women who want to say something feminist have been unnerved by this seemingly unanswerable claim, and feel the need to distance themselves from the women's movement. Thus as always do men control women through the power of an image of woman.

But in the battle over images there have been significant gains for women. Many of the insights on which current feminist theory are built came directly from the experience of women looking closely at the way image and reality didn't quite match in their own lives. In 1963 Betty Friedan's book *The Feminine Mystique* showed many women that the misery, loneliness and lack of purpose that they felt as they tried to live out the all-American dream of the super-sexy, super-efficient housewife, was something they shared with countless other women. Women realised that they had been conned. They realised that the ubiquitous pictures of women as sexy, maternal, efficient and self-effacing (all at once) were the propaganda of a social system which denied them real status, destroyed their potential for economic independence, and channeled their lives into a single stream. The images sold them on the ideal, then confronted them with feelings of personal inadequacy when they failed to measure up.

**Yes of course that's what's wrong with this picture,
But the rules are changing.
Now you must watch a moment and listen,
For the women are sitting down to play.
They're using a loaded pack the game's tougher than you imagined,
and this deck could be dangerous. . .**

All through this book we will introduce the ideas of many different feminist thinkers; this book is about feminism, as well as about women. It will become obvious that not all feminist thinkers start from the same point, and certainly don't all reach the same conclusions about the nature of women's oppression, the causes for it, or the nature of the cure for it. We have decided that it would not do justice to the sheer excitement and range of feminist thinking to try to pull everything together into one consistent line. But, to avoid confusion, it is necessary to sketch out the sort of ground that feminist thinking covers.

We can illustrate this by looking at the different meanings given to the basic feminist slogan 'the personal is political'. For some feminists, all this means is that in our personal lives we are living out patterns of 'femininity' and 'masculinity' which conform to the roles we have been taught. That is what 'sex role stereotyping' means. For some feminists it is enough to point out that the roles can change, and should be changed, to make women more assertive and successful, and men more tender and thoughtful, for the good of society. So their 'politics' is about changing sex roles, by education and example.

But there is a much deeper truth being expressed by other feminists. They are saying that there is more to it than boys being taught to be tough, while girls are taught to be tender. They are saying that the difference in the way that men and women experience life is the most fundamental difference in our society, and that society is structured so that men have advantages at the expense of women. Women are not just 'held back' by society's expectations of them, but are oppressed and subordinated to men.

So both sets of feminists agree that sex role stereotyping exists. The first group says it is unnecessary, out of date, a hang-over from history. The second group says it is the basic building block of our society, that far from being unnecessary, without it society would change its shape. And therefore we as feminists have to accept that our politics involves changing society — feminist politics is revolutionary.

But what sort of revolution do feminists want?

On the one hand there are those who, with Mary Daly in her book *Gyn/Ecology*, argue that society is so deeply marked with a woman-hating attitude that the only hope for women is a total withdrawal, and the revolutionary development of women's communities based on women's principles of personal and social relationships. This style of feminism is called radical separatism. Radical separatists say that male ways of thinking are about power and domination, and will doom the earth to destruction. Survival for women depends on discovering their true female selves hidden beneath the layers of lies, contempt, denigration and ignorance of women which male culture teaches us all. On this side of the revolution, feminist women should seek out their true womenselves, live independently of men, and root out all traces of male thought from their imaginations.

On the other hand there are feminists who say that we can and must begin the process of revolutionary change within the society as we know it, that feminist politics involves outward-looking attempts to change laws and social practices, working with our own flawed selves towards the great transformation of society.

Put bluntly, and a bit too simply, the greatest division in feminist thinking is between those who see the process of change as one for women alone, a sort of spiritual adventure, liberating the 'essential woman' trapped inside the doll-like creature which society calls 'woman'; and those who argue that we cannot change ourselves like this without also bringing about changes in work, in education, in ways of bringing up children, in imagination and culture — because we shape our society as it shapes us.

From the separatist vision of the feminist future we can take inspiration, a sense of solidarity with other women, and the sheer poetry of this vision of a world of women. From the social activist vision and analysis we can take a cool and rational line on the tasks to be done in bringing about change, as well as a passionate politics of action. This book cannot reconcile the conflicting visions of feminism, and does not attempt to do so. We can only present the insights. The women's movement has started to seep into our culture, challenging the old certainties about 'human nature'. You don't have to be a feminist to be interested in what women are becoming. . .

Thanks to feminism, advertisers have discovered a whole new market and a new way of selling. Women, they announce, should be seen as the Moving Target. A woman is not just a housewife, or just a career girl — no, all women are on the move between different stages of life, sometimes home oriented, sometimes career oriented, but not either/or. So now its official. It is now counter-productive to aim advertising messages at women on the assumption that their needs are primarily domestic, chained to the kitchen sink and the dinner table. We are solemnly assured that advertisers will want to use these new insights to 'identify new product opportunities that address the real needs of women, such as domestic help (!) and financial packages.'

Somehow the slogan of the 'moving target' undermines the sincerity of these good intentions to improve the lot of women. They've aimed at women before, told us how we wanted to look, how we really felt and what we really needed — and that's been a large part of the problem. Sometimes there is a sickening feeling that it's just more of the same, that this constant barrage of discussion about who women really are is reinforcing the tendency to see the world from a male point of view, where women are the sex which needs to be explained, where women are 'the other'.

But at least, as *The Pack of Women* said, now we are looking to our own questions, and our own answers.

Ida

ROSEMARY FLORIMELL

Washing dishes, as expected,
you said shyly
'I don't have time to read'.
I turned the glossy pages for you
as I would for a child
and we came to a photograph
of the world's most beautiful
jewels.
'Would you murder for those,
Ida',
and firmly adjusting your apron,
you said 'yes'.

THE MoVing TARGeT

Robyn Archer & Jenny Clarke, adapted from Philippe Halsman

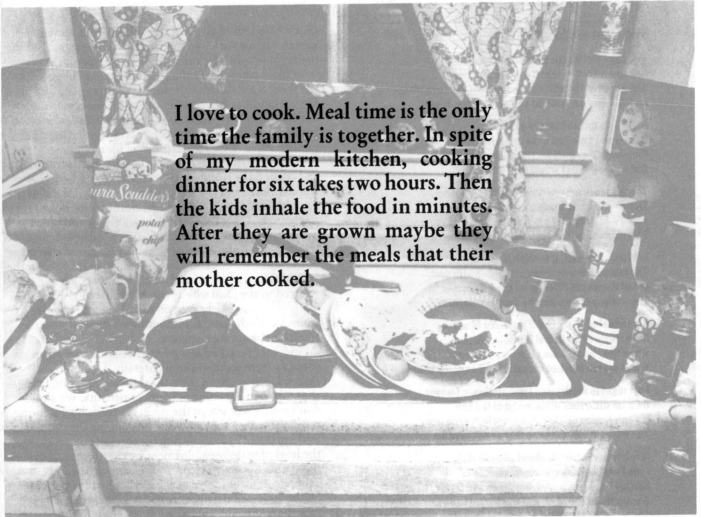

I love to cook. Meal time is the only time the family is together. In spite of my modern kitchen, cooking dinner for six takes two hours. Then the kids inhale the food in minutes. After they are grown maybe they will remember the meals that their mother cooked.

Bill Owens, SUBURBIA

SUBURBAN *Sonnet*

ALL women are housewives — whether they're married, single, widowed, in paid work, unemployed, with children, without children. A woman is supposed to have an almost mystical relationship with a house, turning a house into a home by being there, cleaning it, making it comfortable, giving it her personality.

An unemployed woman is rarely completely idle, and no woman living with a man and children can be idle. Our society has no special compassion or care for a woman who has no paid job, but who does have a man to bring home a wage; she has after all, a 'career' — indeed, the one career that offers continuous prospects, that has no interruptions. From helping out mum after leaving school, while looking for a first job, or a man; to her first home, looking after the children while they're little, then back to work (still looking after the home); to her late middle years, with the children off her hands, but perhaps an aged mother or mother-in-law to care for; to her own old age, fiercely resisting her family's pressure to put her into a nursing home, wanting to stay among all the familiar household things — looking after a home is a lifetime's work.

The Housewife's Lament   (trad)

One day I was walking I heard a complaining
And saw an old woman the picture of gloom.
She gazed at the mud on her doorstep, 'twas raining,
And this was her song as she wielded her broom.

O, life is a toil and love is a trouble,
Beauty will fade and riches will flee.
Pleasures they dwindle and prices they double
And nothing is as I would wish it to be.

There's too much worriment goes to a bonnet,
There's too much ironing goes to a shirt,
There's nothing that pays for the time that you waste on it,
There's nothing that lasts but trouble and dirt.

In March it is mud, it is slush in December,
The mid-summer breezes are loaded with dust.
In fall the leaves litter, in muddy September
The wallpaper rots and the candlesticks rust.

It's sweeping at six and it's dusting at seven.
It's victuals at eight and it's dishes at nine.
It's potting and panning from ten to eleven.
We've scarce finished breakfast, we're ready to dine.

Last night in my dreams I was stationed forever
On a far little rock in the midst of the sea.
My one chance of life was a ceaseless endeavour
To sweep off the waves as they swept over me.

Alas! 'twas no dream; ahead I behold it,
I see I am helpless my fate to avert,
She lay down her broom, her apron she folded,
She lay down and died, and was buried in dirt.

Song from North America (1861–65) in the Civil War period. Author unknown.

Our whole idea of civilisation has been built around the idea of a home with a woman in it. We have measured the march of progress by the gradual separation of the workplace from the dwelling place, putting the cows in the shed, the loom into the factory, keeping the dirt of the coalpit out of the house; and in the process turning our homes into expressions of our personalities, and the focus of family life. In the 20th century we in the industrialised West have created an ideal of home ownership as the most basic of the democratic freedoms, and created the world of the ideal home — where every woman cleans and tends for her own home, instead of the bad old days when many women cleaned and cooked for the households of the wealthy few. Privacy and home ownership are the hallmarks of wealth. Although we no longer build a sort of household religion out of the image of the homemaker caring for her family, as they did in the 19th century (a famous and much-quoted poem in 1855 referred to the ideal wife as the Angel in the House, and married love as like heaven on earth), we still identify women with the home, without much sense of how the traditional ways are changing.

And once attached securely to her house, a woman vanishes from sight — almost literally. Unemployed married women don't show up as social statistics, because they may not claim unemployment benefits. We simply don't notice women on the streets in the suburbs during the day, because the sight of women doing the shopping, walking the baby is so absolutely normal; but we can *see* the level of male unemployment by the number of men in the streets during working hours, hanging around shopping centres, down at the TAB, up at the pub. Men on the streets in daylight are very visible; women merge into the landscape, unnoticed.

The other side of the comforting normality of women's identification with the home is the jarring abnormality of men at home. One of the most compelling images of the purposelessness of unemployment is a picture of a man in his thirties slumped in front of television at midday, while *Days of Our Lives* grinds out its seventh hundred soothing episode. Why is it so natural for a woman to spend her days like this, and so 'unnatural' to complain about it?

The layout of our cities and suburbs, and the rhythms of daily life, reflect the identification of women with home, and men with work.

Ringing the metropolis, spreading far out into the quiet countryside, the neat suburbs, bounded by ramparts of backyard fences, encapsulate the ideal of privacy, and the home as the emotional centre of life. Most public transport connects the suburbs with the centre of the city, designed to funnel workers in and out. The suburbs are not connected to each other by transport systems, so that most social movement in the daytime takes place along the home-city axis; movement from your home to someone else's is not in the transport plan. People on public transport are travelling from home to work and back again. Visiting is done in cars, mobile extensions of the home environment.

Shopping hours are organised on the assumption that it is women who do it, and that they are there to do it in the daytime. Look around the city streets in the lunch hour, crowded with scurrying women, far outnumbering men. They are the working women, who still have the responsibility for provisioning their families, rushing around using up their mealbreak to buy for their (or their bosses') families.

And it seems somehow symbolic of the stubborn persistence of the old order that butchers' shops still keep to the old shopping hours. Meat, the food which must be cooked, which cannot be eaten straight out of the shopping bag, is only available in the housewife's shopping time.

Daytime television is, on the whole and especially in the hours around midday, a cheap and trivialised version of nighttime programming. Instead of drama, we have melodrama, banal predictable plots revolving around the stock figures of women's romantic novels (doctors, nurses); instead of news and current affairs, we have the studio chat shows, nothing too hard, a bit condescending, homey and familiar. The pace of television, and the frequency and glossiness of the ads, picks up as the children (little consumers) come home from school; accelerates again as working people return home, and is at its paciest while mum is seeing to the dinner (early evening news time). Daytime television assumes a female audience who expect little from it except a familiar presence, something to keep the toddlers quiet, a voice in the house.

Talkback radio successfully assumes that women at home are longing to participate in the life of the community outside, even if it is only indirectly, by way of ringing up the station to offer an opinion on politics, or the news. Talkback comperes are almost never women: all those smooth-voiced authority figures with the lightest touch of insincerity are offering women the dream that never comes true in real life — a man who will listen, take a woman seriously, answer in a mellow and intimate tone, make a woman feel important.

NEUROTICA SUBURBIA
ROBYN ARCHER

My life's role is all mapped out.
It makes me want to scream and shout
With satisfaction as a real housewife,
I'm married to a building for the rest of my life.

CHORUS:
Neurotica suburbia, you're quite a girl.
Your life's so full, it's such a whizz and a whirl,
With your babies and your unit and your old T.V.,
Well, hell! how happy can one woman be.

When my husband goes to work each day he takes the car
And it's a good seven miles to the shopping centre
There ain't a shop or a cinema or a park that smiles
Just concrete home units for miles and miles and miles and miles and miles
CHORUS
So all there is to do all day is stay inside the flat
There ain't no garden and we can't have a cat
Don't like the people next door and we can't afford a phone
But who's gonna complain about the simple joys of home
CHORUS
My husband leaves, I feed the kids and put 'em all to sleep
A largish dose of aspirin knocks them out so long and deep
Then I can sit and watch the programs about love and life
And that's the way I get contentment as a mother and a wife
CHORUS
Of course if that don't work and I occasionally get depressed
I get my sherry and my pills and they put my mind at rest
I've had ten swigs and twenty pills by quarter to nine
And by the time my husband's home Neurotica's feelin' fine
CHORUS
You see I can't walk or talk by then, the babies all are cryin'
My sweet hubby thumps 'em, gives me peace of mind
He eats his fritz and drinks his beer, passes out 'til six a.m.
And I keep starin' into the goggle box until the bitter end
CHORUS
That's a day in the life of a suburban wife, my dear
And it's exactly the same every week every year
But please don't cry too hard for me when you hear my woeful song
Cos at this rate of existence there's no way I can last long

'The best thing on this week was an American documentary about *Clotheslines* by Roberta Cantow on *The Eleventh Hour: Women Direct* (Channel 4). Why was it so agreeable to look at all those shots of other people's washing blowing in the wind in different parts of the world? "They're like sculptures," said a woman on the finely edited voice scrapbook of remarks and reminiscences. "The pleasure I take in sun-dried clothes goes beyond. . .there's always a fresh beginning.". . .I had never realised what deeply felt traditions and habits of self-expression were involved in the hanging up of coloured and white clothes. "You went out on the roof with your washing," said a New York woman, "and it was like a new beginning, a fresh start. It was sort of like when I gave birth. I was connected to all other women. . ." (I got points at home for liking this film. Worth having in this weather.)'

from a television review by Hugo Williams in the New Statesman, 18 January 1985

This little item brings to the surface many ambivalent feelings about housework. On the one hand, there is the delight in everyday, simple, familiar routines, which people share across different cultures. In Western societies, the simple and familiar are a defence against the pressures of a competitive, fast-lane social system. On another hand, the piece brings to mind the confidence being shown by women filmmakers influenced by feminism, who are insisting that the humble and unremarked routines of women's domestic lives are worthy subjects for cultural commentary, can become the basis of a new art, and anyway must be taken seriously because they occupy so much of women's time and energies. But yet again, there is a sense of unease when you realise that women feel connected with other women in rituals of service like washing — and that there is probably a hint of smugness in the male reviewer's feelings of satisfaction contemplating the agreeable forms taken by the work of women. Somewhere lurking in the review is nostalgia for an earth-mother. But there's also somewhere a hint of envy that feminists have to find an antidote for: men and women must be convinced that there are better ways to find their way back to simple feelings than by romanticising housework.

Mary Leunig

Women have a large emotional investment in housework, often bordering on the obsessional. It is a fact that housewives appear to have more likelihood of becoming depressed than women who work outside the home, and unmarried women. Prescriptions of tranquillisers for women accounted for more than 1 in every 20 prescriptions written in New South Wales in 1983, and many of these were for housebound women.

Ninety-five per cent of sufferers from agoraphobia —fear of leaving the house — are women. These women are prisoners in their own homes, bound there by inexplicable feelings of dread and panic should they step outside the boundaries of the house.

Obsessional anxieties revolving around housework are common. Sometimes it is an obsession with cleanliness, with sweeping spotless floors and scrubbing the saucepans over and over. Sometimes it is an overwhelming anxiety about things being forgotten, so that a woman keeps having to rush home to check that the iron wasn't left on, that the windows were locked; a fear that it will all fall apart if not carefully watched.

Ann Oakley *(Taking it Like a Woman)*, describes the irritation she felt contemplating her mother's life, its 'search for glory reflected off the polished table-tops and in the achievements of [her] husband,' and hoped there would be more to life than that.

Domestic work is somehow regarded as coming 'naturally' to women. Women who can't make the the grade, that is, those who don't take too much care about it, are criticised as lacking in femininity; men who can perform the simpler household tasks are praised as paragons. Of course there's nothing 'natural' about it; girls are trained from childhood to be more alert to dirt and disorder, encouraged to help mummy in the kitchen, learning the virtues of painstaking care, learning the complexities of co-ordinating all the tasks that make up the job of making other people's lives comfortable.

Feminists have pointed out over and over how this expectation that certain work comes 'naturally' to women is used to confine women in the paid workforce to the type of work that most closely resembles housework and mothering — minute, painstaking environments, managing the office, serving food, nursing, looking after children, cleaning — all the lower paid jobs, with no career structure and no prospects. In this way the division of labour between men and women in the family, which is said to be natural, underlines and helps to perpetuate the division between men's work and women's work in the workforce, keeping wages unequal. And women's jobs are often the ones most at risk of being replaced by new technologies, as word processors take over from typewriters, computers replace the armies of ledger machine operators, automation takes over the assembly line.

Interestingly enough, technological advances in the home have not made housework and the housewife obsolete. In fact, as new labour-saving devices were invented for the home, the expectations on women increased, not decreased. Clothes were expected to be washed more often once you had a washing machine, cooking expected to be more elaborate with advances in kitchen technology.

And of course, no one argues that housewives should be able to take advantage of economies of scale, and combine with the other mothers on the block to cook together, or shop collectively, or take turns in doing the neighbourhood washing. Housework has never been completely industrialised like other things have been (e.g. manufacturing); it has remained an individual activity, each home a self-contained little consumption unit, buying its own washing machine, refrigerator, microwave, blender... Housework has remained an isolated activity, so that the wheels of commerce and industry can keep turning. The organisation of the modern family, our ideas of femininity, and the needs of industrial society complement each other admirably.

Housework is also discipline.

Women on the margins of society — alcoholics, delinquent girls — who do not conform to their expected domestic role are punished for this failure. Far fewer women than men are convicted of criminal offences. Most women in prison are there for relatively minor offences, often involving drugs, alcohol, theft, and prostitution. Studies of women who end up in prison show that the magistrates saw them as 'bad mothers' or 'rootless', the sort of women who would benefit by being taken in hand and rehabilitated. In women's prisons what little rehabilitation there is consists largely in disciplining women in domestic tasks. The idea is that by instilling strict standards of hygiene, and teaching household skills, these women will be learning how to behave as women. Good housewives caught shoplifting don't get sent to prison; they are sent home to discipline themselves. But the message that housework is discipline comes across most clearly when we look at the circumstances in which men are forced to do it. All-male institutions like army barracks and men's prisons have routines of discipline built on obsessive attention to detail, and demeaning physical work, like scrubbing floors, polishing brass buttons, or extremely monotonous tasks like peeling potatoes. When men are forced to do it, domestic work assumes quite a different aspect, and becomes a means of breaking a stubborn will, or inflicting humiliation.

Why aren't women paid for doing housework?

The answer is not that housework is not **work** — if you send the kids down the street for a carton of milk, you will happily reward them with pocket money, in clear recognition that you have been provided with a service, which has a value, and involves effort.

And in property settlements after a divorce the Australian Family Court will count a woman's contributions towards the total property of the marriage, by giving a value to her work as homemaker and parent.

But while the marriage lasts, society stubbornly refuses to put a money value on housework. It has to do with sustaining the idea of the family as a special unit whose members offer each other services out of affection, outside the cold economic calculus. And any unit that looks like a family is expected to behave like one. Under the 'cohabitation rule' a woman is not eligible to receive social security benefits while she is in a sexual relationship with a man; he is expected to support her. If this rule did not exist, we **would** see wages for housework, as the state paid a woman to stay at home, out of the workforce, to look after children and home, regardless of her marital status.

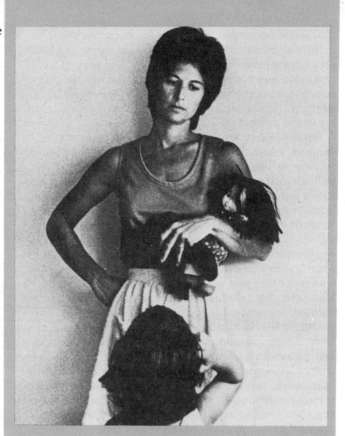

Self-portrait as the mother of two small children
ETHEL DIAMOND

This image occurred to me when I was in the middle of cleaning. I felt so overwhelmed by the endless drudgery of housework; I thought if I just stood in front of the camera as I felt then, this feeling might show through. As I was about to take this self-portrait, my son walked up to me, demanding my attention.

"It is a truism to say that the channeling of female energy into domesticity can produce overprotectiveness, overscrupulosity, martyrdom, possessiveness disguised as sacrifice, and much repressed and displaced anger. We can expect such distortions when nurturance is a tiny enclave in a harsh and often violent society."

Adrienne Rich, from an essay "The Antifeminist Woman", in ON LIES, SECRETS AND SILENCE

Women's domestic labour (that is, housework in industrialised societies, and women's gardening and food preparation in less developed societies, and sewing, and childrearing in both societies) is estimated worldwide to contribute the equivalent of $4000 billion — that is, 1/3 of all the world's production. But women do not own 1/3 of the world's property.

But if domestic work was paid, as some feminists demand, would this be a real improvement in the position of women? The first problem is that paying each individual woman to stay at home would make no change to the isolation, monotony and silent desperation of the housebound woman's life. In the second place, wages for housework would only reinforce the link between what women do at home and what they do in the paid workforce; housework would take on all the trappings of a real 'career' for girls, without raising the status of women's other paid work. It would reinforce the argument about the 'natural' division of labour between men and women within the family.

During the Russian Revolution, and in the years just after, Russian revolutionary feminists like Clara Zetkin and Alexandra Kollontai argued that the solution to women's low social and economic status lay in socialising housework, taking it out of the individual home, making it into a communal activity which men and women did together, just like any other work. The experiment did not survive except as one of the West's favourite bogeys about the regimentation of life under socialism...

SUBURBAN SONNET
GWEN HARWOOD

She practises a fugue, though it can matter
to no one now if she plays well or not.
Beside her on the floor two children chatter,
then scream and fight. She hushes them. A pot
boils over. As she rushes to the stove
too late, a wave of nausea overpowers
subject and counter-subject. Zest and love
drain out with soapy water as she scours
the crusted milk. Her veins ache. Once she played
for Rubinstein, who yawned. The children caper
round a sprung mousetrap where a mouse lies dead.
When the soft corpse won't move they seem afraid.
She comforts them; and wraps it in a paper
featuring: Tasty dishes from stale bread.

The idea of a necessary link between femininity homemaking/housework, and 'the family as we know it' runs very deep in our social thinking.

Robyn Stacey

Robyn Stacey

Women on the edge

I n this chapter we are looking at ways in which women try to come to grips with the conflicting demands placed on them by the requirement that they conform to their feminine role. It's a chapter dealing with extreme responses — madness, obsessiveness, jealousy — and although we are saying that these responses have something important to tell us about the damage that can be done by the requirement to conform, we are not pretending that these are typical female responses. But often enough the message from our culture is that these *are* essentially feminine characteristics.

In the process of becoming a woman, a girl is moulded into the shape required by the current definition of The Essential Woman. The required physical shape changes (the bosomy ideal of the 1950s has been replaced by the leaner look of the 1980s), but the list of desirable personal qualities is not much changed. A 'feminine' woman is sensitive to the needs of others, values subjective feelings and intuition, is slightly naive and prepared to believe the best of people, is not cynical, is patient, romantic, eager to please, avoids hurting people's feelings or giving offence by stating strong views, prefers to act indirectly and by suggestion when she wants to influence other people, is reluctant to assert her own interests if to do so would provoke discord...

The same list could be expressed in different terms: weakness, vanity, lack of objectivity, indecisiveness, capriciousness, irrationality, jealousy, deviousness — the familiar litany of complaints about women's character that has come down to us through Shakespeare to Norman Mailer.

Feminist psychology sets out to explain how and why women come to shape their feelings and their behaviour to conform to both the positive and the negative versions of the list of feminine characteristics — and how much damage is done in the process.

Explanations of women's oppression in terms of psychological damage have been around for a long time. In 1972 Phyllis Chesler argued that the social definition of femininity doomed women to a condition of anxiety, obsessiveness and neurotic behaviour not far removed from mental illness, which prevented most women from achieving any sort of independence and a strong sense of themselves.

In her book *Women and Madness* she showed how women who refused

WOMEN AND MADNESS

A more red-blooded feminism turns the definitions on their heads, and argues that the traits for which women have been denigrated and treated with contempt are indeed womanly traits, and should be celebrated for their positive values — more later.

to conform to the expected model of passivity, suggestibility and compliance to the wishes of others could be punished for their nonconformity by being classified as deviant, or mentally ill. Either way, therefore, women have a special affinity with madness. If you conform to the ideal model of femininity you do so at the expense of permanent anxiety — am I desirable, thin enough, coping well enough with husband's and children's demands? Rebel, and you will be classified as maladjusted, hostile, aggressive, lacking in maternal instinct, lesbian. Tip the scales too far either way, and you might really go crazy.

In her fascinating study of the case histories of women admitted to South Australia's mental hospital in the middle years of this century, Jill Julius Matthews shows in case after case how 'proof' of each woman's mental instability was her failure to live up to the expectations about conventional feminine behaviour. So, for example, one woman who found sexual life with her husband unfulfilling was diagnosed as having lesbian tendencies, and therefore deviant, in the complete absence of any evidence either that she was attracted to women, or that if she was, there was any link between that and her emotional distress. Another woman's refusal to feel remorse about having several sexual affairs with men was classified as 'promiscuity', another sign of deviance. These women were in some distress, and not finding life easy; but all the evidence the doctors relied on to diagnose mental illness was social, not medical in character. Even carelessness in dress and refusal to be pleasantly sociable were signs of deviance for the doctors. The idealised version of the happy monogamous heterosexual married woman who dresses to please and always loves her children had become norm for judging sanity.

Moonshine
KATE JENNINGS

Yesterday I was sick, sick
in the head
panic and paranoia,
it's been like that for years, used to say
I was a victim or the victim.
I'm gettin' older now
so I put myself to bed, filled myself
with pills and, after a while,
floated quietly to sleep.
Today I feel all right
(Although I wanted to cry for help,
cry out to you,
it's not that I'm a clinging female,
it's just that I'm ill).

Oh but he comes on tender,
the fucker,
He's a lizard,
he's a lizard with a serrated tail
rasping his way
through a fancy dancing poetess.

Caring and love have
become blood and semen spattered
and coagulated all over
my abused body and my gothic imagination.
I remember my friends,
let me tell you bout them,
And say, and I meant to say and what
could I have said?
I'm not bitter,
I've just got many reasons to sing the blues

n 1970 a group of clinical psychologists showed that a
tandard set of psychological characteristics, which were
sed as the basis for testing people against a standard of
ormal adult development, in fact discriminated against
omen. The normal healthy adult who matched these
haracteristics was in fact bound to be male. Any woman
ho scored highly was regarded as too aggressive,
nfeminine, destined for psychological difficulties. So in
ffect the standard of adult normality was male; a
sychologically well adjusted adult female' scored highly
n those characteristics which would define a man as
nmature, dependent, with weak self-esteem. This made a
onderfully ironic point: society's model of an adult woman
atched the psychological profile of an infantile man.
omen were defined by science as psychologically sick
dults.

Feminist psychologists, scholars and poets have broken
nto this vicious circle (doomed to anxiety and
nmaturity if you conform, classified as mad if you don't)
y re-examining women's discontent and sense of
ienation from a woman's point of view. They use the
sights of a theory which links a woman's individual
evelopment of her sense of herself as a woman, with a
ocial and psychological portrait of a woman's experience
f girlhood, being at school, first encounters with sex,
experiencing her body as the source of her own and
others' pleasure, experiencing her body as a reproductive
being, trying to reconcile her sense of herself as a mature
woman with the state of prolonged childishness she feels
at home for years with small children. This explanation is
nothing less than an alternative psychological and social
history of half the human race. It is saying that women are
different from men in a really profound way — and that
the differences have always been turned against women in
a society based on the subordination of women to men.

The Pack of Women picked up several threads of this
new feminist analysis of femininity and madness: how the
contradictions of living as a woman create particularly
female phobias and obsessions, centred around anxieties
about her body and relationships — jealousy, passion and
romance and madness as rebellion. The theme is the dark
side of the feminine ideal. The argument is that women's
attempts to reconcile in their individual lives the
irreconcilable conflicts involved in this ideal keep many
women close to the edge. Think of all the mad women of
literature, like Rochester's wife in 'Jane Eyre'; and all the
hysterical girls and distraught young women who
drowned their new-born babies in fairy-tales and legends.
But don't go looking just for the injustices they may have
suffered as women dependent on men, denied a life and
choices of their own. The moral is more subtle than that.
Think again about these women's relationships with their
own bodies, as well as with their families and men. And
ask yourself why the image of the crazed young woman
driven to the extremity of grief by jealousy, or slowly
metamorphosing into a vacant-eyed inhabitant of an
impossibly imaginary world of endless romance, should be
so often found in popular songs and novels.

The Ballad of Lucy Jordan
SHEL SILVERSTEIN

The morning sun touched lightly on
The eyes of Lucy Jordan
In a white suburban bedroom, in a white suburban town.
As she lay there 'neath the covers, dreamin' of a thousand lovers
Till the world turned to orange and the room went spinnin' round

Chorus:
At the age of 37, she realised she'd never ride
Through Paris in a sportscar with the warm wind in her hair,
So she let the phone keep ringin', and she sat there softly singin'
Little nursery rhymes she'd memorised in her daddy's easy chair.

Her husband, he was off to work and the kids were off to school
And there were o so many ways for her to spend a day,
She could clean the house for hours, or re-arrange the flowers
Or run naked through the shady street, screamin' all the way

Chorus:
The evening sun turns gently on
The eyes of Lucy Jordan
On the rooftop where she climbed when all the laughter grew
too loud,
And she bowed and curtsied to the man, who reached and offered
her his hand,
And he led her down to the long white car, that waited past the
crowd.
At the age of 37, she realised she'd found forever
As she roared along through Paris with the warm wind in her hair.

Is the heroine of the song a cautionary figure, reminding us not to mistake the ideal for the actual, not to demand that romance and relationships live up to their claims? Why do we need to be told what we all know? How can male songwriters so calmly assume that they can enter the minds of these women? Why are so many of the strongest literary images of women in extremity written by men? All these questions shaped the material for the show.

In the last chapter we described women's relegation to the narrow and confined world of the housewife, and showed how its consequence could be a kind of imprisonment for a woman cut off from society, spending her days in the company of small children. Women's bodies, and their feelings and emotions, can also be a kind of prison. Love and relationships are supposed to be a woman's profession. Her body and her sexuality are her qualifications for the practice of her profession. Constantly prompted to anxiety by the more fashionable bodies of the women on the billboards and in the fashion magazines, young and insecure women who have not had time and experience enough to work out what is really important can become obsessive about their body shape, to a life-threatening degree.

So, what's so specially feminine about that? The 1980s is the era of the obsession with the body (joggers, aerobic addicts, marathon runners). But there is something very peculiarly feminine about the forms that women's body-consciousness take, compared with men's. While it is true that men, probably more than women, take to physical regimes involving quite punishing routines, in order to show that they are in control of their bodies, and therefore in control of their lives, men rarely become the victims of eating disorders as a result. Men may drop dead with heart attacks, or become so addicted to the 'runner' high' that they are unable to distinguish the point of physical exhaustion; but they don't as a rule starve themselves to death.

Men's obsession seems to be directed towards activity, perhaps with the object of staving off the inevitability of age and physical decay; they overdo a socially approved activity. Men (and women) who are obsessed with running or weight training **want to achieve something** — a socially admirable goal — they want to look fit, feel in control. Anorexics, women who cannot make themselves eat normally, want to be thin. Even when their bodyweight drops to below 60% of normal, they can still look into the mirror and see a fat person. They want the flesh to melt away.

Classical   17th Century   1930s   1940s   1980s

ANOREXIA

* Luise Eichenbaum and Susie Orbach, OUTSIDE IN...INSIDE OUT: WOMEN'S PSYCHOLOGY: A FEMINIST PSYCHOANALYTIC APPROACH.

MEDICAL and psychiatric writers all agree that anorexia nervosa is an illness of psychological origin, and that it usually appears in young girls around the age of puberty, although after its onset it can last for decades.

Most of the explanations for the cause of the illness rely on theories about women's sexuality. One theory is that eating disorders are related to a 'desire to be impregnated through the mouth, which results at times in compulsive eating (presumably to achieve pregnancy!) and on other occasions in guilt, and consequent rejection of food'. Another theory is that refusal to eat is a young woman's symbolic rejection of her mother (who stands for nourishment, and hence food), turned onto herself by her feelings of guilt and hostility resulting from her ambivalence about wanting to be free. Other theories see a sexual dynamic, but this time it is the mother herself who is the main actor in the psychic drama: in this version the mother feels sexual anxiety and unconscious rivalry as her daughter matures into a more desirable woman; the daughter internalises these feelings and retaliates by refusing food.

What is striking about all these theories is that they involve an exaggerated reaction by the girl to some aspect of 'femininity'. So for example, the 'oral impregnation' theory harks back to the idea that the desire to bear children lurks in the emotional life of a young girl. The 'mother conflict' theory relies on the idea that women are in constant sexual competition with each other for men —and that this is played out between mothers and daughters, as well as between strangers. It is fascinating to see how these enduring staple themes of drama surface in scientific theories of women's illnesses.

So how do feminist theorists improve on the diagnosis?

Feminist psychologists have tried to fit together all the parts of the picture, including the part of the puzzle which explains why thinness is regarded as desirable in twentieth century women (on this, see chapter 13).

Luise Eichenbaum and Susie Orbach observe that many aspects of women's lives inevitably cause conflicts that are difficult to express, because women are being pressured to live up to an ideal which, if achieved, goes against a woman's sense of herself as an individual. This distress and conflict show themselves in the only part of a woman's life which is under her direct influence — that is, her body. Eichenbaum and Orbach see anorexia as a woman's attempt not to become a woman. So, at puberty she is saying no to breasts, no to menstruation, no to becoming like her mother. 'I will not be like you, mother. I will not reproduce your life and I will not take in your food. I will not take you inside of me, I will make myself into something else, something other than you.' *

See also FAT IS A FEMINIST ISSUE

22

Jill Matthews says that this feeling of ambivalence about mothers and femininity also arises when women become conscious of the injustices of the system of discrimination which defines our life chances for us.

'Who do we blame for this state of affairs?' Externally, various targets can be identified and attacked, ranging from the particularly unjust discriminations of education or employment or law, to more abstract opponents such as capitalism, patriarchy, or all men. Internally, this attack can be undermined by self-doubt, or turned on ourselves. We wonder in anger: 'Why didn't they (our mothers and sisters) tell us about this before and do something to change it?' We become embittered by frustration: 'Why don't they (other women) recognise their own suffering and join us in the struggle for change?' We despair and blame ourselves: 'Why do they, how do we all collude in our own oppression?' We have seen the enemy and he is not only out there but among us and within us.*

Anorexia is also a refusal to have the emotions expected of women. Inside herself the anorexic woman is trying to create a new person who does not have ungovernable emotions or needs which no-one is ever going to satisfy. Anorexia is a strategy for rigid personal control. Compulsive eating, on the other hand, is a strategy for protecting your vulnerable self. Bingeing is giving to yourself the love that you fear no-one will ever give you, symbolised in food. The cover of fat is also a defence against not being desirable, a way of repressing needs. (Fat also gives big women a sense of power, both in the literal sense of physical power and bulk, but also in the sense of freedom from all expectations that you should behave like a sweet little girl.)

'In anorexia and compulsive eating what we see are women trying to change the shape of their lives by trying to change the shape of their bodies.'

Andre Durst

See Kate Grenville LILIAN'S STORY

JEALOUSY

STEAM-YR-LETTER-OPEN BLUES
ROBYN ARCHER

You're bein' warm and lovin', gentle and kind
And I really don't think you'd ever leave me behind
Still I got them ever-lovin'-wanna-steam-yr-letter-open blues

You know it's not upsettin' me or at least not all of the time
And yes I really believe you when you say you're mine
Still I got them ever-lovin'-wanna-steam-yr-letter-open blues

I been livin' in a dream for more than a year
Now I'm admittin' the truth and it ain't nothin' to fear
Still I got them ever-lovin'-wanna-steam-yr-letter-open blues

You got plenty good lovin' for everyone
And your new love's a fine woman and I'm havin' fun
Still I got them ever-lovin'-wanna-steam-yr-letter-open blues

You see the postman came, I read your name
And I'm enjoyin' rediscovery but all the same
I got them ever-lovin'-wanna-steam-yr-letter-open
I got them ever-lovin'-wanna-steam-yr-letter-open
I got them ever-lovin'-wanna-steam-yr-letter-open
Blues, and you know I never had 'em before
Yes, I got them ever-lovin'-wanna-steam-yr-letter-open blues

IT turns out that feminists have written surprisingly little about jealousy.

Could it be that jealousy is so banal, so demeaning, so belittling to the jealous person, that we feel there are no worthwhile lessons to be learned from having a close look at it?

'When jealous, I suffer four times over: because I'm jealous, because I reproach myself for being jealous, because I'm afraid my jealousy doesn't affect the person I'm jealous of, because I'm being carried away by a cliche: I suffer by being excluded, by being aggressive, by being mad, and by being banal.' — Roland Barthes, quoted by Rosalind Coward in *Female Desire*.

Perhaps jealousy is difficult for feminists to deal with because it is so out of step with a philosophy of sexual and emotional freedom. Feminists are accustomed to talking about jealousy as a side-effect of bad old sexist relationships, in which men thought they could own women, and women were forced to tolerate men playing around. Jealousy and possessiveness should begin to disappear, once women assert their sexual rights, and men learn to respect women as equals — or so the theory

Jill Julius Matthews, GOOD AND MAD WOMEN. George Allen and Unwin, 1984.

might go. One way or another, jealousy and sexual fantasies have not come in for their share of attention by feminists (on sexual fantasies, see chapter 13).

But given that jealousy (in women) and revenge (in men) have been such basic elements in the plots of plays and stories from Homer (Greek poet, 800BC) onwards the subject is worth some feminist reflection.

The first thing one feminist researcher wanted to find out was whether the experts — psychoanalytic writers — thought jealousy was a masculine or feminine trait. They were deeply divided on the question, though all agreed that female jealousy was different from male jealousy. Women experience jealousy as intense loss: loss of love, loss of the feeling of singularity, being the most important person for the other, and as a desperate need denied. Not surprisingly, women's reaction is often depression. Jealous men (and men are more prone to delusional jealousy, being convinced of the infidelity of a partner against all evidence) experience intense anger — anger at the rival, and at the supposedly faithless lover. Their reaction is aggression. (Toril Moi, *Jealousy and Sexual Difference*, Feminist Review, summer 1982)

This theory sounds highly plausible, and certainly helps to explain why jealousy in men is more catastrophic for all concerned, and indeed often for anyone who has the misfortune to be in the vicinity. (Remember that the God of the Old Testament often said 'The Lord thy God is a jealous God', as He smote entire tribes with fire or delivered them into the hands of their enemies). But it is wise to be cautious before accepting the theory, because as has been shown, it is always hard to say what is scientific observation, and what is just extrapolation from what people expect of men and women. Women are expected to turn their anger inward, men are expected to be aggressive.

Athough feminists have written little about jealousy, the women's book market thrives on it. As Rosalind Coward points out, jealousy is a vital ingredient in Mills and Boon-style romantic fiction. Almost every story is organised around the idea of the heroine having to overcome all sorts of obstacles — misunderstandings, malicious gossip, real or imagined rivals — in order to reach the ultimate goal, exclusive possession of the hero for ever and ever. Rosalind Coward has the idea that women go on reading these banal and predictable stories, knowing perfectly well that they bear no resemblance to real life, because the obstacles in the path of true love really represent the ambivalence that women feel at the prospect of giving themselves into the sexual power of men. In the stories, obstacles are overcome in the same way that they are in childhood fantasies — the heroine gets her own way, absolutely. Rivals are obliterated, misunderstandings dissolve, the heroine's true virtue and depth of character are revealed for all to see. She takes absolute possession of the man's heart, wins his fidelity, becomes the centre of his world. It's pre-adolescent fantasy, one of a desire for absolute possession. Romantic stories appeal to the wilful child in the grown woman; because in real life it is only through fantasy that a woman can count on having her desires satisfied.

'In pulp romance, the disappointments based on discovering that others have claims on the loved one's attention are obliterated. There aren't really obstacles to total monomaniacal love, only temporary frustrations which the narrative then removes.'
Rosalind Coward, *Female Desire.*

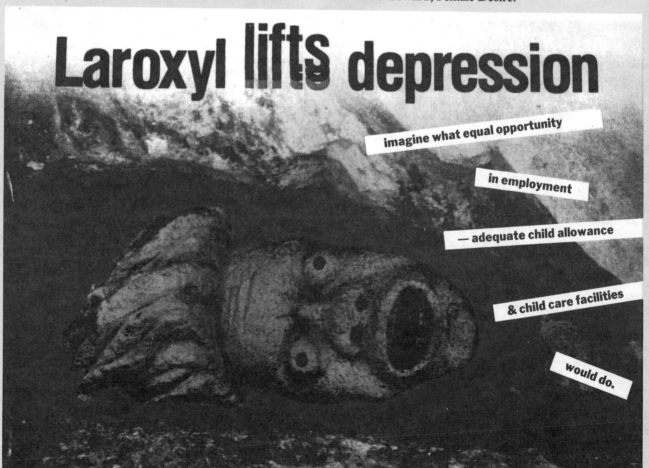

Laroxyl lifts depression

imagine what equal opportunity

in employment

— adequate child allowance

& child care facilities

would do.

Robyn Stacey & Jenny Clarke

So in this feminine fantasy world, jealousy turns out to be just a trial of love. Once love is secured, jealousy becomes unnecessary.

But what happens in the real world? Let us consider the *crime passionel*, the ultimate in jealousy, the lovers' triangle ending in murder. Who does the killing, and who is the victim?

As with all violence, most jealous murders are committed by men. [see chapter 14]

Ann Jones, who made a study of *Women Who Kill*, reports that jealousy is not a very frequent motive in women's killings. And when the one who kills in the jealous triangle *is* the woman, she usually kills the other woman, rather than her lover. The man in a similar situation more likely kills his faithless woman, rarely the other man. Is this because the man feels that the woman is his exclusive property, and killing her is a way of asserting this total ownership, as well as denying her to another man? Whereas the jealous woman kills her rival to protect the romantic relationship, and have her man all to herself?

Luce Irigaray, a French feminist, takes matters further. She says that where two men fight over one woman, in the classic jealous triangle, it is the relationship between the two men which is really the most significant. She argues that any sexual arrangements involving men are in essence homosexual. This does not mean that there is a literal sexual relationship between the two men; but that the men find a connectedness with each other in the jealous triangle, and that the woman doesn't really count. When they have sexual relationships with women, men are experiencing deep feelings of understanding and complicity with other men — 'I am a man, this is what men do'. Sex for men, she argues, is something men do (to women). This is what she means when she calls women 'les marchandises' — merchandise, 'the goods' — exchanged symbolically between men. Through sexual relationships with women, men are engaging in a sort of communion with all other men, and affirming to themselves and each other the reality of male power — that men make the rules.

To test another truth in Irigaray's insights, think how few of the forbidden words for a woman's sexual parts parts are words that women use easily and naturally amongst themselves; whereas men use them at will, in any context. There's more than just modesty or prudery here. It's a question of whose language is it?

Luce Irigaray, WHEN THE GOODS GET TOGETHER

CRIME

PASSIONEL

In 1980 millionaire medico author of the Scarsdale Diet Book, was shot dead in his bed by his mistress of many years, eminently respectable private school headmistress Jean Harris. The motive, they said, was jealous fury, provoked by his flaunted infidelities. Jean Harris always said that she meant to shoot herself, not him; after her conviction for murder she said that if she had intended to kill anyone else, it would have been his new lover.

Ann Jones argues that the trial of Jean Harris became the 'anti-feminist lecture of our day'. With the prosecution alleging murderous jealousy, and the defence claiming that she was suicidally depressed, the moral of the trial was that an educated, successful career woman could not live without the man she loved, and in the face of his manifest lack of love, went over the edge. Her defence lawyer declined to argue the one line which might have seen her cleared: he refused to plead temporary insanity, preferring to play the theme of love gone wrong. The case got immense media coverage, partly because of the celebrity of the victim, but also, Ann Jones suggests, because the triteness and familiarity of the themes in the trial served to reassure men and women made nervous by the advent of feminism:

'It is reassuring to men to know that women, no matter how seemingly independent, simply cannot live without them. It is reassuring to housewives, bedevilled by "women's lib", to know that the real career of the career woman is a cut-throat battle to snare a man of her own.

This reassurance that good girls still love even bad boys was doubly welcome to a nervous public, coming as it did after the highly publicised trials of raped and battered women who killed their assailants and, in a few notorious cases, were acquitted on the grounds of temporary insanity or found to have committed justifiable homicide in self-defence.'

Husband-killer Ruth Snyder, 1928

REBELLION

JUST as there is a long tradition of male fearful fantasy about jealous vengeful women, which serves to comfort while it alarms, so there is a male tradition of sympathy with the pathetic women victims of the illusions of Romance.

It's particularly strong in popular songs like *The Ballad of Lucy Jordan* and *Eleanor Rigby*.

These songs nicely make the point that romance can be a fatal illusion, that a woman who tries to make it come true is doomed to anguishing disappointment, and that it only comes true in the sanctuary of madness.

But in all these songs there is the assumption that the proper target for a woman's despair is her own psyche. Contrast these romantic ballads of women's retreat into catatonia and mental hospitals with all those country and western songs in which male heroes, unhinged by the betrayal of their noble passions, turn their rage on women and the world in general — 'Ruby, don't take your love to town…'

And compare these with the positive assertion of women on the same subject — Bessie Smith's performance of *I Ain't Gonna Play No Second Fiddle — I'm Used to Playing Lead*, or Dory Previn's *Doin' It Alone* in which she claims the right to scream her head off in her own car.

Or Chris Sitka's *Witch Poem*, which takes women's madness as an extreme form of rebellion against the reality of women's oppression, and shows that endurance is the real craziness.

BALLAD OF DANCING DOREEN

RALPH McTELL

See how the lady moves so gracefully across the dance-hall floor,
All eyes upon the 2,000 hand-sewn sequins on the gown she wore
She not only moves but she looks like a queen
Making up for the evenings she's spent at home with her sewing machine.

Brian's a postman by day but tonight he is a king
Lovely Doreen in his arms, no-one will notice him.
Only the lady, turning her head once more
Smiles for the judges, hopes that they'll give her the highest score.
Brian's hair shining, just like his patent leather, potent lover shoes,
Lovely Doreen in his arms, how could they lose.
And after each dance she prettily curtsies
Into the quicksteps, the waltzes, the fox-trots, the tangos.

Wheeling and spinning, weaving and turning, the evening is closing
In a few minutes more they'll hear the names of the winners that the judges have chosen.
But her name wasn't called and Brian fought back his tears,
Doreen didn't move, she just sat there smiling, she did not hear.

And long after all the other dancers had gone home
Out on the dance floor Doreen was dancing alone
And Doreen was dancing when they called the manager
And Doreen was dancing when they phoned the doctor
And Doreen was dancing and no-one could stop her dancing.

Robert McFarlane

WITCH POEM
Child Killed By Freed Madwoman
CHRIS SITKA

Mrs Genevive Parslow, after trying to poison
her own family with me(n)tal poison,
went to the local police station and told them
'I AM A WITCH AND THOUSANDS OF YEARS OLD.'
'I have got to kill everyone in this world, Even babies.'

They told her to go away.

At five o'clock the next morning
she climbed through the window
of a neighbour's house
and took a baby boy.
He was later found dead in a ditch.

They caught her of course.
Where could she go?

In court they said
'She had an unsettled childhood, long history
of mental illness and marital difficulties.'

A 'horrified' judge sentenced her to a mental asylum —
never to be released from strict security.

(This may sound like a poem to you. So let me assure you
sister that this is all taken from a newspaper report —
Melbourne Sun 19.7.1973)

Yes they call her wisdom madness.
And they fear her.

We WITCHES must devise some mental poison
to avenge this sister's imprisonment.

A knifeblade in my throat
keens witches' incantations
to slice through complacency.
I am the black harbinger of
The Bewitched Revolution.

I can no longer bear silence,
inaction.
This knifeblade sanity
shreds my throat with screams.

I will define my Feminism
through a creative, loving violence
which struggles to liberate
our gnarled and knotted souls.

Around this action
my knife carves a circle;
And I am bound within the spell
of a shared sisterhood.

I am bound to the right of women.
I am bound to the rite of women —
Witch women, Feminist Witch Women —
Screaming in agony and joy.

'May we go mad together, my sisters.'

For nine years now
the entire Indonesian Women's Movement
has been in gaol.
Fifteen hundred sisters —
dressed in dirty rags,
every night hungry,
their children crying.

This is not distant from my life.
No, this painful vision
of barbed wire life
rips at my eyes daily.

In Portugal
three courageous Marias —
knowing what they were risking
in that fascist, macho country —
wrote an explicit book about women's oppression.
They were arrested, brought to trial —
then saved from two years gaol
by a male (need it be said) military junta
which abolished censorship.
The newspapers immediately began publishing
photographs of nude women.

Right here in Australia
a woman working in a button factory
for $38 a week —
not speaking English she does not know
that she is legally entitled to more —
two years ago lost two fingers
in an unguarded machine.
She has not received any compensation.

Day after day she returns to that machine
and the murderous boredom of her job
bearing the bruises of her husband's beatings.
Night after night returns home
to screaming children
and yet more, and more, work.

Understand that
she has no choice
but to continue
to suffer.

Yes, I know it has all been said before;
we have all heard about
the rapes, the beatings, the backyard abortions
we women suffer daily.
But because it happens every day
can we afford to feel less angry, less mad?
Isn't it precisely this constancy
of our oppression that should outrage us?

I know that we must not drown in our tears.
Yet how can I not cry whenever I remember
the woman who, pregnant and despairing,
drank a whole bottle of whisky in a gulp
and climbed into a scalding hot bath
which slowly turned red with her own beautiful blood,
and stank from her vomit.

Feeling the reality of this all too clearly,
a volcano erupts in my heart.
Lava flows from my eyes.

But I will not despair
before the enormity of our oppression.
I ask only —
very simply —
that we begin to act
to end all this.

Robyn Stacey & Jenny Clarke

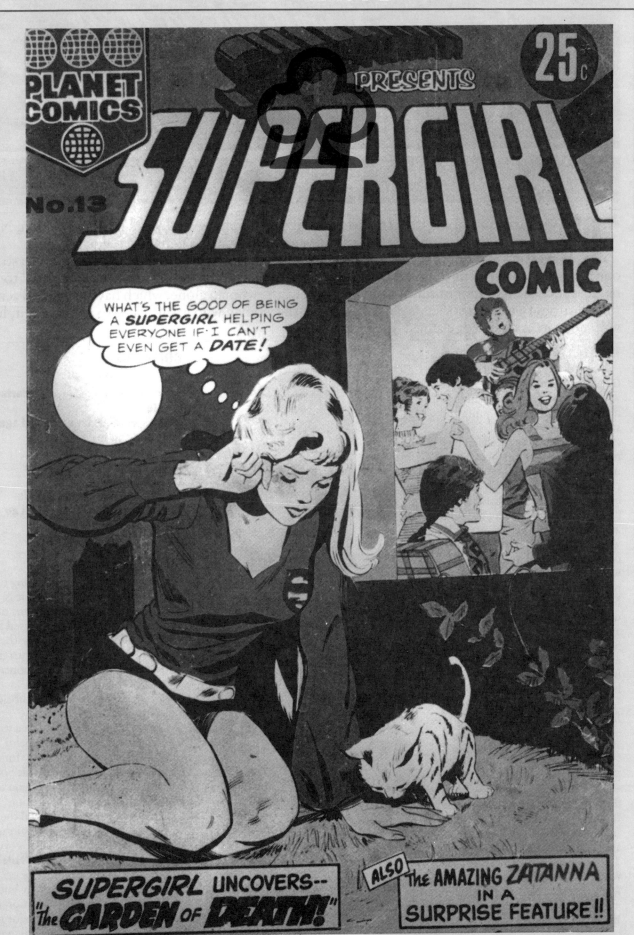

A woman without a man is like a fish without a bicycle

OLD ♠ MAID

THIS brazen piece of graffiti has been raising hackles for several years now, in London, New York and every large city with a feminist community. It's a defiant piece of imagery, suggesting as it does that a woman with a man is as incongruous as a fish on a bicycle; so at one level, it is a statement of sexual independence from men. But it's defiant at another level too, because it challenges a lot of submerged ideas about the woman alone, which have been used across the centuries to express society's deep distrust of the woman who is sufficient to her own self, lives with no man, is owned or claimed by no-one.

THE image of the old maid, the dried-up old spinster, grim and forbidding in children's stories, whiskery and stiff in our childhood memories of unmarried aunts and schoolteachers called Miss, is still current in everyday speech. The old maid is a figure of fun, bequeathed to us by our Victorian forebears, who by the end of the nineteenth century (the century named after Queen Victoria) had totally eradicated all the earlier associations between unmarried women and witchcraft, and the whiff of sexuality which used to cling to the world 'maid', which once meant a marriageable girl. The concept which has come down to us is of a prudish disapproving woman of late middle age, soured by a sense of a wasted life. She is a pathetic figure, the difficult extra person at family celebrations, to be faintly pitied but secretly despised, because she thought she was too good for marriage. But she no longer strikes fear into the hearts of young women, as a reminder of their awful fate if they should fail to marry — not in these days of almost universal marriage...

despite the dire predictions of the pro-family lobby, a decade of militant feminism doesn't seem to have dented the marriage rate. At the time of the 1971 census in Australia, 94% of women had married by the age of 35. At the latest census in 1981, the figure was over 96%. It's a tiny proportion of the brave who never marry.

COUPLING II
ROBYN ARCHER

Scarred and bruised by the efforts to couple,
the desperadoes try again and again.
They cling on to coupling
as if it's the only spar afloat
in the Titanic existence of the twentieth century.
They're such rare brave angels
who've understood it might all go better
as a solo flight.

For more clues to the contemporary cultural meaning of the woman who does not marry, it is useful to look at the definitions of words. Although not much used these days outside legal documents, the term 'spinster' does have current meaning, particularly as contrasted with the word 'bachelor'... There is a marked but subtle difference between these definitions. A spinster is a woman who is still unmarried; a bachelor is simply unmarried. Obviously for women spinsterhood is an inferior social category, from which you are protected by a careful definition which doesn't damn you until the fact of advancing age makes the painful truth too obvious to conceal — you have 'missed out'. You have 'failed to marry'.

Nothing could more subtly but clearly underline the expectation that for women marriage is the major goal in life, not just something which may

According to the Macquarie Dictionary (1981) 'spinster' means 'a woman still unmarried beyond the usual age of marrying; an old maid.' 'Bachelor' means an 'unmarried man of any age.'

or may not happen to you, but something towards which you struggle. On the other hand, a man either is or is not a bachelor; bachelorhood is not defined in terms of failure to reach a goal, nor as a state of suspended animation after the goal has eluded your grasp.

'Bachelor' is culturally a cheerful word, probably because it can be applied to men of any age, and therefore retains a charm for the older man because of its associations with youthful rakishness. For example, in the 1920s the tabloid newspapers were looking for a word to describe independent young women earning their living in the big cities, having affairs and having fun. There was never any question of bringing the old word 'spinster' out of its musty cupboard, dusting it off and giving it the same connotations as the word 'bachelor'. Instead, they called them 'bachelor girls', to underline the fact that this was a new type of woman, or so they thought, who was behaving in a fashion uncharacteristic of women — so they described her in terms used for men. This is a very clear example of how the narrowness of the range of models for women's behaviour means that we have to borrow words and concepts from men's behaviour to describe anything out of the ordinary.

For the Victorians there was no question of finding jaunty descriptions for women who didn't marry. From the 1830s to the end of the century an intense philosophical and political debate raged around what was known as 'The Woman Question'. Although some strands of this debate are very familiar to us today, there was a deep underlying panic which we don't share. During this period there was a marked imbalance between the numbers of men and women in Britain, particularly for people aged between 15 and 45, the marrying and childbearing years. At least 125,000 English women of all social classes, from the aristocracy to the poorest labourers, had absolutely no prospects of marriage. There simply weren't enough men to go around, as a result of emigration to the colonies and, perhaps, different death rates for young men as compared to young women.

To the Victorians, this was a social catastrophe. This was the period during which the idealised role of women as 'the Angel in the House'

had solidified into a recipe for respectable living for the middle classes, while the upheavals of industrialisation had made the harsh nature of working women's lives painfully apparent in the big cities. But for women who could find no man to support them, there was no respectable role model, only the traditional contempt and derision for the ugly old maid, which was in fairness clearly no longer appropriate to everybody. What was to be done with all these surplus women? Very few methods of earning a living were regarded as appropriate for well-born women, apart from governessing, or being a lady's companion, a sort of glorified maid to the upper classes. In addition, some Victorian thinkers saw in this surplus of women a sign that society itself might be in danger of dying out, as the poor and unrespectable would continue to breed without the benefit of marriage, leaving the middle classes exposed and vulnerable to being overrun. A solution to The Woman Question was clearly urgent.

Some progressive thinkers, both men and women, saw the obvious answer — loosen the restrictions on women's role. John Stuart Mill, for example, put forward in his 1869 essay *The Subjection of Women* a sustained and passionate argument for the right of women to education and to work and to participate as equal citizens, so that they would be able to become self-sufficient members of society.

Meanwhile the popular press and novels were full of sensationalised exposes of the plight of 'redundant women,' slipping down the social scale towards poverty and, ultimately, prostitution.

One solution came in the form of a sort of women's self-help. The Female Middle Class Emigration Society set out to assist women to find positions as governesses, teachers and white collar office workers in the Australian and New Zealand colonies. Then, as it would now, this 'solution' gave other feminists serious misgivings. As they saw it, these schemes took it for granted that the only proper destiny of woman was marriage and domesticity, and were really a genteel form of marriage broking, taking the available women to where the men were, and giving the authorities at home an excuse for ducking the question of giving all women access to education and training, which would

OLD MAID
ROBYN ARCHER

Old Maid is a sinister game from
our youth
It showed us the symbol of life's
cruel truth
If you had no profession and you
never got laid
You'd wind up by losing and being
Old Maid

So you pair off the motorist, farmer
and cop
The tenor, the fisherman, the keeper
of shop
The cricketer, postman, the
hornpiping sailor,
The butcher, the baker, the airman,
the tailor

Of ladies there's nothing but dancer
and nurse
And when all pairs are face down,
then nothing is worse
Than to hold the old maid, you try
hard not to choose her
For this game has no winners, dears,
only a loser.

JEZEBEL

MARKED WOMAN

OLD MAID

enable them to live in dignified self-sufficiency.

Out of this uneasy social debate about women, work and marriage grew an interesting tradition of women's writing which extolled the virtues of the single life for women: not as something to be patiently endured because there was no help for it, but as a way of living positively to be enjoyed. In short stories and novels, published in women's journals, there appeared heroines who lived as calm, self-assured free spirits. e.g. *Joanna Trail, Spinster,* by Annie E. Holdsworth (1894). True, they did conform to the expected stereotype of domesticated women, by stepping in to help their married sisters in times of crisis, taking over the education of children, or acting as sisterly housekeeper to the widowed and helplessly grieving brother-in-law. (In some of these stories marriage is shown to be definitely dangerous to women's health, through the hazards of childbirth and the stresses of constant toil and household management, and keeping up appearances.)

GAMES OF PATIENCE
MISS WHITMORE JONES

FORTUNE TELLING PATIENCE

This is a game for three or more players, and is a favourite with young ladies, as being supposed to afford them a glimpse of their future destiny. The four aces are laid in the middle of the board, their significations being: hearts, loved; diamonds, courted; clubs, married; and spades, single blessedness.

Although this picture of useful single women has overtones of self-sacrifice, and indeed exploitation, it was also something positive for Victorian women, because it tied in with the themes of women's right to equality based on a need to be useful, and therefore to be educated and allowed to work and make choices. And these stories also stressed the pleasures of the single state. They showed women able to choose their

Queen Victoria

Florence Nightingale

own friends, and have the time for friendship. They showed women with the leisure to read, paint and cultivate their minds and imaginations through travel and scholarship. And even the impossibly self-sacrificing spinster heroines were at least pointing the moral that a woman's essential womanliness showed in her personality and character, not necessarily through motherhood and status as a wife.

Outside the pages of fiction some eminent Victorian women were living out another version of female self-sufficiency: the spinster as heroine.

Florence Nightingale is a classic example of her type — and what has become of her legend is a classic example of how women's history becomes sentimentalised as its spikier

episodes are integrated into the acceptable version. To us, or at least to our mothers, Florence Nightingale was The Lady With the Lamp, the perfect picture of female solicitude and staunch bravery, soothing the wounded soldiers in the snows and swamps of Crimea in the 1850s, the scrupulous administrator, elevating nursing from a charity to an honourable profession. And never marrying, but answering the call of a higher duty (she believed she had a mission from God).

A closer inspection, and an inquisitiveness pricked by a feminist understanding of the possibilities for women of her time, shows Nightingale to have been an even more powerful figure than her adoring public thought. She saw herself as joining her own life to an heroic destiny, with Jesus Christ and Joan of Arc as her spiritual models. She despised her mother and sister for their opposition to her struggles to train as a nurse; indeed, she despised most women for their ignorance and incompetence. The Victorian expectation that women should fulfil themselves through love, matrimony and the achievements of others was not for her.

'No, there is no whiff of sentimental pathos in Florence Nightingale's spinsterhood, which sprang from her unyielding opposition to the tyrannical trivia of her family. She scorned feminist collectivity, identifying herself instead with her chosen hordes of wounded soldiers, but her proclamation of spinsterhood is the most outspoken defiance we have of the Victorian family.'* We will see more of Florence in chapter 16, when we look at what feminism has made of the tradition of female heroism, but for now she stands out as a self-glorifying single woman, an heroic spinster.

Is it not curious that the two women of the nineteenth century whom most people have heard of were single for most of their lives — Queen Victoria was widowed at a very young age and lived on alone for 40 years — and yet the pathetic image of spinsterhood is a Victorian legacy?

There was nothing pathetic about mediaeval images of the woman alone. The twentieth century has inherited a tradition of deep anxiety about the solitary woman, who lives outside the bounds of men's control. As we have seen, in our time this anxiety has been watered down into a sort of pity, mixed with a sort of contempt for the woman who has no sexual experience. But feminist scholarship has revealed the depth of society's dread of the single woman, stretching back from the seventeenth century, when the last witches were burned or hanged.

Mary Daly, in her astonishing, vast, poetic, infuriating but inspirational study of society's attitudes to women *(Gyn/Ecology)* argues that most of the victims of the dreadful campaigns against witches, (the 'witchcrazes') which preoccupied church and society through the fifteenth, sixteenth and seventeenth centuries, were single women or widows. As she puts it, women accused of being witches (and burned for it) were women who had rejected marriage, and women who had survived it. Mary Daly calls them the 'indigestible elements' of their society — 'women whose physical, intellectual, moral, and spiritual independence and activity profoundly threatened the male monopoly in every sphere.' The activities she talks about, which threatened male monopolies, were probably the practice of traditional herbal medicine, and midwifery. The activities which their accusers alleged were sexual impurities, intercourse with the Devil, child killing, destroying crops by calling up storms, poisoning wells, causing men to become impotent... This is the origin of the figure of the *ugly old hag* which the Victorians bequeathed to us; 400 years earlier she was the consort of the Devil.

... the word spinster is commonly used as a deprecating term, but it can only function this way when apprehended exclusively on a superficial (foreground) level. Its deep meaning, which has receded into the background so far that we have to spin deeply in order to retrieve it, is clear and strong: 'a woman whose occupation is to spin.' There is no reason to limit the meaning of this rich and cosmic verb. A woman whose occupation is to spin participates in the whirling movement of creation. She who has chosen her Self, who defines her Self, by choice, neither in relation to children nor to men, who is Self-identified, is a Spinster, a whirling dervish, spinning in a new time/space.

THE NEW WOMAN

SPINSTERS
ANNE ELDER

Why are the poets so pitiless?
Why is all Art so unkind to be good?
Art is a vulture, it preys, it feasts on life,
points up misadventure, probes with its knife.
Delicious! says Art in an artful way.

Take any poet through and through and finish
not with dislike but pity for self-obsession,
delusion, this passion for being pitiless,
the badness of bending good craft to badness and,
above all, the incorrigible need to express compassion
as though it were compassionate simply to say:
I am compassionate, I feast on death, on life I prey.

Eaten with cancer, abortive in labour,
murderers, victims of all evils — these
all fall victims to the pitiless compassion of poets;
and in particular, I note, the Spinster
calls for their attention. Yes, it is certainly
their noble intention to lighten the burden
of enforced maidenhood by forcing on it
their attentions, for the love of art, its artfulness,
its artless craftiness and, of course, for its good.

Take myself, for instance. I have no pity for spinsters.
I am a poet who finds them glorious.

"Meaning Bronte, Austen, Dickinson?
But they are not spinsters!" you cry. "They have fruits!
Their mind is a womb from which break forth
most passionate speculations. Indeed, being greatly
favoured by posterity they are not eligible
as the brides of pity (meaning the pity of poets)."

You mistake me.
I do not refer to the illustrious blue-stocking
but to the genuine article who, never having
had much time for Poetry
nor for a pitiless poet to fall on her in delicate
rapacity, his cathartic desire
— toddles off happily to the Elderly Citizens Club
to community sing with other elderly citizens and
in due course (unpoetically) expire.

At the still Centre
the audience is small, performance gentler.
The dishes are washed
by golden girls who must, and chimney sweepers
come to do the dusting.

In another re-evaluation of the history of women as written by men, Barbara Ehrenreich and Deidre English *(Witches, Midwives and Nurses: a History of Women Healers)* point out how the height of the witchcrazes in Europe coincided with the beginnings of modern medicine as a profession dominated by men, taught in universities, requiring learning and scholarship. They argue that it was necessary to suppress the older medical practices and traditions, which had largely been the domain of the wise women of the village, and based around herbal lore and carefully guarded female knowledge about birth, abortion and contraception, passed down from one generation of women to another. So they conclude that the witchcrazes were really a struggle over knowledge, and who should possess it — men or women. And the defeat of women's claims to have important knowledge was another step along the road to the complete subjection of women.

Maids & Virgins

ONE of the themes of Marina Warner's history of the cult of the Blessed Virgin Mary is that it was built over the remnants of pagan religious traditions which featured powerful virgin goddesses.

But where the virginity of Mary signifies absolute purity, the 'virginal state' of the Roman goddess Diana, or the Greek Athene, or the middle-eastern Ishtar, meant only that they were not owned by man or god, that there were independent and alone, but not sexless. These goddesses, whose cults celebrated the fertility of nature, retained freedom of choice, to take or reject lovers. Singleness was a sign of their power — sexual power.

In 1905 Miss Hypatia Monk became the first Australian woman automobile driver, and in 1913 entered the first interstate Sydney to Melbourne reliability contest.

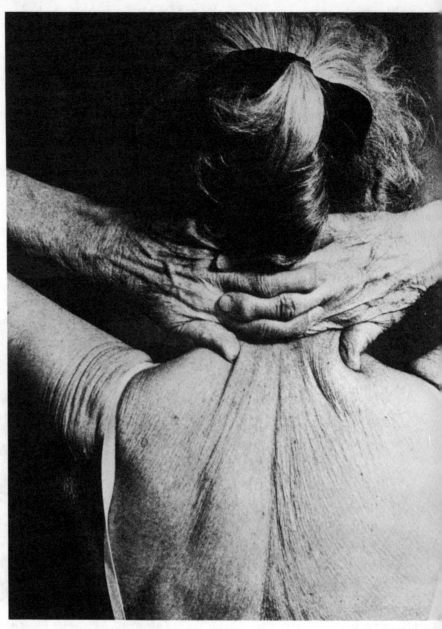

Considering Myself
NINA HOWELL STARR

One of numerous attempts to represent my

knobby arthritic hands in portfolio

(A Room of My Own). Its components: those

lines shooting down my back, the curl of my

ponytail, the twist in the shoulder strap, and

the force of my thumbs and thrust of my

arms, all communicate something of what

I like to consider myself.

Marina Warner's evidence shows that the Christian cult of Mary, mother and virgin, ushered in a new attitude to women and sexuality: over the centuries, it was Mary's purity and chastity for which she was celebrated, as the fathers of the church drove home the association between sexuality, sin and death in the story of Adam and Eve. The powerful virgin goddesses of antiquity became, in the figure of Mary, part of a family of men, mother to one, untouched bride, maternal yet unspoiled. Not like real women, who since the sin of their mother Eve are condemned to sexuality, menstruation and the pain of childbirth.

Marina Warner points out that within the Catholic Church women could only attain influence and respect through imitation of the chastity of the Virgin — by joining religious orders, living the ascetic life of the nun. By withdrawing from men, and giving up sex and motherhood, women would achieve the freedom to study, to teach, to live purposeful lives. But as she says, 'the nun's state is a typical Christian conundrum, oppressive and liberating at once...'

'As an answer to the problem of female equality, the nun's vocation is similar to the lesbianism some members of the contemporary women's movement in America have chosen. By cutting themselves off from the traditional role of women, and by abjuring all relations with men, consecrated virgins established a certain freedom and autonomy that permitted them to lead lives of greater distinction than their married sisters... but at a general level, the solution is completely inadequate. For the foundations of the ethic of sexual chastity are laid in fear and loathing of the female body's functions, in identification of evil with the flesh and flesh with women.'
ALONE OF ALL HER SEX

All these layers of cultural history underlie our contemporary ideas about marriage and spinsterhood. But the puzzle is, why should the figure of the woman alone still cause such social unease, in these days when the thinking of the church no longer holds such sway, and women are able to be economically independent of men and marriage? Why is marriage still so socially important that we keep alive nineteenth century bogeys of dried-up old maids?

The family, based around the married couple, is accorded an enormously privileged place in contemporary society. Nearly all our social arrangements are based on the assumption that people live in families, perhaps more so now than at any point in recent history, as we pointed out in the second chapter. We know this assumption to be false, that only one in three households consists of a married couple with children. But still the myth persists that life outside the bosom of the family is bleak and lonely.

And even feminists have not quite shaken off the fear and anxiety surrounding the idea of the woman alone. For 'the relationship' as the source of a woman's definition of herself...

Me: Myself: I
ELEANOR FASSEL

'Who is your next of kin?' asked the kind lady
When I went to hospital to be admitted —
'So that we can advise them, if it has to be —'
I looked into her kind and sympathetic face
and slowly said, partly ashamed, partly annoyed
to make this intimate confession to a stranger —
'I have no next of kin — no husband, children, father, mother, sister, brother, no aunts and uncles, cousins, nephews — nobody lives to whom I am related — I hang alone, a lonely spider on a thread and only starving cats would miss me —'
But when I saw she was embarrassed, I quickly said
'Of course, there is a friend' and mentioned her address and name
and she wrote that down, relieved, I felt her thoughts:
'Thank God, she's human, after all —'

Not Answering
JUDITH RODRIGUEZ

Times I'm alone
and go to the bed and lie down
and inside me's
grabbing

and times in the subway
I try to send eyes my trouble
all of them busy
not receiving

there's the woman who came on
wretched at 51st and Lexington
holding her burst bag of grief
impossibly

but no-one saw nothing
she never dumped no she went along
with it bubbling and dragging
was it a face

and there's my old aunt
widowed now 3 months asks me
to cuddle up at night
and I don't

Open-Air Pastimes.

Sweet Solitary Blues
ROBYN ARCHER

Sweet solitary blues
Nobody's pushin' me, I don't owe no dues
Sure it's lonesome sometimes
But these days you oughta know that's one of the lesser crimes
Sweet solitary blues

Most blues you hears is mournin' for some other
Someone you never got, or a late lamented lover
But this blues is satisfied blues, hey, I'm gonna blow my cover
My solitude is sweeter to me
Than some foreign body between my sheets

Don't read nothin' between the lines
My heart ain't never been broken, my friends entwine me
I work, I think, I fit myself like dear old shoes
I got them sweet solitary blues

Swimming *Rosalind Moulton*

COUPLING
ROBYN ARCHER

Though living alone makes you feel too frisky
Coupling is risky
Whichever one you choose, you think you're bound to lose

'Cos if I say that I like to live alone
Don't I detect a groan
But if I say this one's my true love without a doubt
Then anyone uncoupled just feels out
Whichever one you choose, you think you're bound to lose

'Cos if you shout it out that your lives are tat for tit
Then the singles just don't go for it
And if you rave too much and spread your tales of love out loud
Then you're certainly going to upset that cynical crowd
And if you should decide on a heterosexual hitch
Then there'll be no hesitation for your gay pals to come out and bitch
(And to speak of the reverse would simply be perverse)

You'd think that life could be more supple
When you go round in couple
I've actually found this theory's without ground

And if you want to play it free and easy
At a certain age, you just look sleazy
But if monogamy's the only double
Shake well before you use or there'll be trouble
You know the facts, of course, 'bout modern day divorce

Though living alone makes you feel too frisky
Coupling is risky
Whichever one you choose, you think you're bound to lose

ANYTHING this book might present on Coupling could be challenged by anyone else, on any number of grounds. We all have our own stories, our own versions of the trials and tribulations, the triumphs and the traps. When it works it's wonderful, no matter what anyone says about the politics. When it starts to founder, it's an all-encompassing worry. Check the bibliography at the back for some good reading about the politics of Coupling ...

What follows is a drop in the ocean of what can, has been, and will be said on the subject. If our particular selection focusses on problems and alternatives, just cast an eye towards the unscalable mountain of published (books, magazines, newspapers), recorded (records, movies, TV, video) and performed (plays, concerts, musicals) material that reinforces the idea that Coupling is only about heterosexual love and romance. In fact, it's hard to avoid the influence of that bias, even when you try — this book has no need to repeat it. And it might just be helpful to know that despite the hefty propaganda about 'normality' and 'happy-ever-after', many of us — women and men, whatever our sexual preferences — find ourselves sharing similar joys when it's great, and the same misgivings when it goes wrong.

ALEXANDRA KOLLONTAI, advocate of free love, member of Lenin's inner party at the time of the Russian Revolution. Writing here at the beginning of the twentieth century . . .

'For thousands of years the capitalist society, based on the institution of property, has been teaching people that love is linked with the principles of property. Bourgeois ideology as insisted that love, mutual love, gives the right to the absolute and indivisible possession of the beloved person. Such exclusiveness was the natural consequence of the established form of pair marriage and of the ideal of "all-embracing" love between husband and wife. Surely it is important and desirable that people's emotions should develop a wider and richer range? And surely the complexity of the human psyche and the many-sidedness of emotional experience should assist in the growth of the emotional and intellectual bonds between people. The more numerous these inner threads drawing people together, the firmer the sense of solidarity and the simpler the realisation of comradeship and unity.

We are talking here of the duality of love, of the complexities of the "Winged Eros": this should not be confused with sexual relations "without Eros", where one man goes with many women, or one woman with a number of men. Relations where no personal feelings are involved can have unfortunate and harmful consequences (the early exhaustion of the organ, venereal disease etc.) but however entangled they are, they do not give rise to 'emotional dramas". These "dramas" and conflicts begin only where the various shades and manifestations of love are present. A woman feels close to a man whose ideas, hopes and aspirations match her own; she is attracted physically to another. For one woman a man might feel tenderness and sympathy, and in another he might find support and understanding for the strivings of his intellect. To which of the two must he give his love? And why must he tear himself apart and cripple his inner self, if only the possession of both types of inner bond affords the fullness of living?

. . . The hypocritical morality of bourgeois culture resolutely restricted the freedom of Eros . . . Outside marriage there was room only for the "wingless Eros" of momentary and joyless . . . sexual relations which were bought (in the case of prostitution) or stolen (in the case of adultery); obliging Eros to visit only the "legally married couple".'

A FAIRY TALE
LEE CATALDI

there was once a princess who fell in love with a handsome young prince, and together they wandered in the wood. but the prince got lost in the pine needles, and the princess searched for him, disconsolate.

she met a toad who said "come with me and I'll give you shelter." so she went with the toad.

later the toad said "will you sleep in my bed?" so the princess did, but the toad remained a toad.

the princess continued to live with it because it was kind, because she was fond of it and because she was used to it.

one day, along came a handsome young prince. as the princess went off with him, she said to the toad "I did so wish you'd turned into a handsome prince," and the toad said "it's all in the mind, lady."

A MIDSUMMER NIGHT'S DREAM
PEDRO SHIMOSE trs ROBERTO MARQUEZ

You finish cleaning out the dust and the ashes, doing all the errands,
peeling the potatoes, washing, doing the dishes, throwing out the trash, finish eating leftovers in a corner of the kitchen
and go hide in your room,
look at yourself in a shattered mirror,
daub your eyebrows, makeup,
listen to soap operas, glance through "True Romance",
go to the local movie to see another Alain Delon,
plan at being a star like Marilyn or Sophia,
look at your navel,
become ecstatic looking at your navel,
move over your shadow with azaleas and gardenias,
walk over your body with a miniskirt and sunken eyes,
imagine hitting the jackpot in the lottery,
paint your dirty nails,
spell out the astrological prediction for tomorrow,
dream about your Prince Charming,
about the fairy godmother, with the magic wand,
you are the girl with the crystal slipper,
the one at the midnight ball with horses that are mice
and coaches that are pumpkins . . .
Look natita, you're pretty, but
wash your underarms and stop the foolishness,
the mistress is calling

PERSONAL POLITICAL
ROBYN ARCHER

Personal political
Personal political
What you are is what you do
The way you act is the only clue

Personal political
Personal political

You say what you want is change
But you won't change at all.
Don't you ever stop to think it's strange,
The way you're backing me up against the wall
What would life be like
In the world you'd make?
You know your cruelty stings
Until the spirit breaks.

Personal political
Personal political
Stop pushin' your blueprint down my throat
I like what you say but it's makin' me choke

Personal political
Personal political
You can't convince me by shouting me down
You talk like a saint but I don't trust your frown

Personal political
Personal political

You say what you want is good
You say what you want is true
But the way you mistreat me
Casts a shadow over you

Personal political
Personal political

A tender hearted woman out walking in the cold
Found a poor half-frozen snake layin' there in the snow.
She picked him up so tenderly and stroked his pretty skin,
'Poor thing' said the woman, 'I'm gonna take you in'
'Take me in, tender woman, take me in for heaven's sake,
Take me in' to the woman said the snake.

Well she took him home to her house and she laid him by the fire
She fed him milk and honey, she fanned the flames up higher,
She admired his pretty colours and she stroked his skin so sleek
And that tender hearted woman kept that snake there for a week.

Well the snake was gettin' better, he was preparin' for to go,
But the woman clutched him to her breast and hollered out 'Oh no'
Instead of sayin' 'thank you, baby, everything's all right'
The snake inclined his head and he gave her a vicious bite.

'You bit me, you bastard, won't you please tell me why?
You know your bite is poison, baby, and I am gonna die.'
'Oh shuddup, you silly woman' said the snake with a grin,
'You knew I was a snake, baby, when you took me in'.

MARGOT NASH
it feels like
my first big date
yet here i am
a twentysix year old
veteran of the sex war
arranging
to meet a woman
for dinner

*title from Lee Cataldi, INVITATION TO A MARXIST LESBIAN PARTY, Wild and Woolley

TWO WOMEN GAZING AT EACH OTHER
AS IF THEIR LIVES DEPENDED ON IT*
ROBYN ARCHER

Sitting in the cafe, waiting for I know not what
Lazy Sunday, one I would have forgotten
Held my coffee cup in both my hands
Stared around the restaurant, got stopped by the corner and
Within my range, how Sunday changed
There were two women gazing at each other
as if their lives depended on it, depended on it

Have you ever had that feeling that you're lonely but content
Then something comes along, out of the blue, to drive you on relentlessly

My sweet slow Sunday finely torn apart
A scene between two women enough to break your heart
Just two women gazing at each other
As if their lives depended on it, depended on it

BRIDGE: *They could have been the mistress and the wife, I suppose*
            Could have been related, sisters or so, but I didn't want to think so
            I wished they were lovers, sweet lovers

Then they began to order up mountains of coffee, toast, tomatoes, steak and eggs
(it was the biggest breakfast you ever seen)
I knew this was a hunger sprung fresh from a Sunday in bed
(You know the sort of thing I mean)
And now I read the tears and the laughter in their eyes
Felt their passion, felt my own gut heave with their lows and their highs
You could feel their sighs in the cafe, you could feel their sighs

Two women gazing at each other
As if their lives depended on it, depended on it

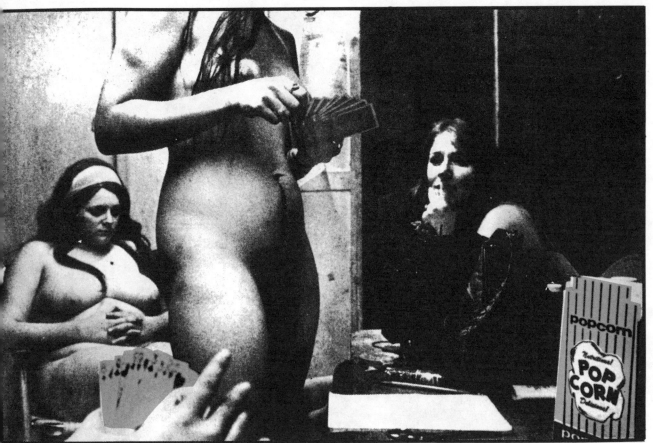

Susan Meiselas

BLUE, stripper

When I'm in here with all those chicks, we're with each other every night, we work with each other, we get our clothes off, we sit around the dressing room nude, we rap. I ignore the fact that I am gay. When I work, I work. What I do outside of work isn't anybody's business. I can control myself. If they want me to mess with them, I will; if they don't, it's understood.

SONNET 95
JOHN TRANTER

James Michener thinks of writing a guide book
to Bohemian Balmain, Sydney, Australia.
People are sick to death of the South Pacific.
He quickly flies to Balmain and has a look.
There it is, like a movie! Writers, artists!
The harbour, blue as always, the container wharves
just like it says in the novels, and the lesbians . . .
My God, the Lesbians! Bohemia Gone Mad!

This is too much for James, and he flies out.
TOP WRITER JETS OUT OF SYDNEY, AUSTRALIA!
But is that how it really happened? I like to think
of James in the Honolulu Hilton, older and sadder,
nursing a drink by the pool, nursing a broken heart,
dreaming of a pert little lesbian in Balmain.

THE OLD SOFT SCREW
ROBYN ARCHER
(SUNG)

*I could hardly believe it was happening
But everytime I looked around she was there
To hope I'd hardly dare
As we eased around, in time to that old tune.
But then I took her hand, and it was happening
O what a smiling thing to come on my holiday
So I just had to stay
And we found out, it'd been on the cards since June.*

*And I'd been finished with the other kinds of people all around
Because I couldn't learn from them I had to put them down
But then there you were, I thought, my God, it's her
Then the couch flew away and we came to ground*

*O gimme that old soft screw, I mean I like it from you
O do, o do, o do me, o do me, o do,
O gimme that old soft fuck, you know it's just my luck
To find someone as fine as you*

GIRLS IN OUR TOWN   **Vale Street 1975** *Carol Jerrems*

If a Man Could Be
LEO CORDAY/LEON CARR

If a man could be, perpetually
What he only is occasionally
A man could be, but definitely
A wonderful, wonderful thing.

If a man could do, continually
What he only does spasmodically
A man could be, indubitably
A wonderful, wonderful thing.

He's a could be good
He's a could be bad
He's a sometime make you doubt him
But here's what makes a woman mad
She's told she can't do without him.

If a man could do inspirationally
What he only does mechanically
A man could be, unequivocally
A wonderful, wonderful thing.

BOB HUDSON

The girls in our town, they just haven't a care
You see them on Saturdays, floating on air
Painting their toenails and washing their hair
Maybe tonight it'll happen

Girls in our town, they leave school at fifteen
Work at the counter, behind the machine
And spend all their money on making the scene
Yet plan on going to England

Girls in our town go to parties in pairs
Sit round the barbecue, give themselves airs
Then they go to the bathroom with their girlfriend who cares
Girls in our town are so lonely

Girls in our town are too good for the pill
But if you keep asking they probably will
Sometimes they like you, or else for the thrill
And explain it away in the morning

Girls in our town get no help from their men
No-one can let them be sixteen again
Things might get better but it's hard to say when
If they only had someone to talk to

Girls in our town can be saucy and bold
At seventeen no-one is better to hold
Then they start having kids, start getting old
Girls in our town, girls in our town

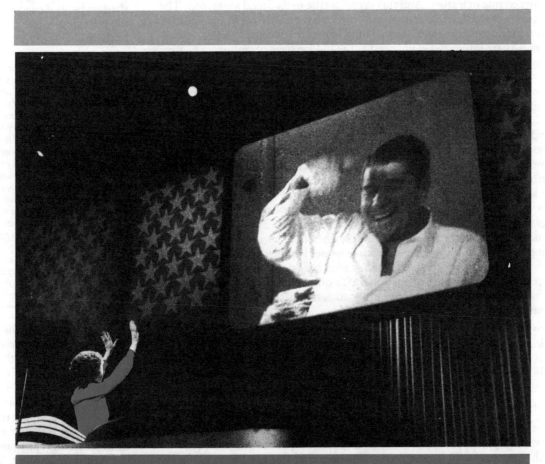

Nancy Reagan exchanging greetings with her husband's TV image

WOMEN BEHIND GREAT MEN

'BEHIND every great man stands a woman'. This used to be proclaimed with easy satisfaction by the official myth-makers of our grandparents' generation. It was meant to be a statement about the indispensability of the wife and mother, tireless helpmate of the empire builder. It was meant to celebrate what those generations saw as the complementarity of the sexes. These days, it's hard to read it as anything other than propaganda, used to reconcile women to lives of vicarious achievement, living through their husbands, children and lovers; used to ennoble housework by proximity to genius.

But at the same time the saying is a true one; it is true that what we are accustomed to calling 'history' is nothing more nor less than the doings of men, usually great ones, but men in the mass as well (peasants, armies, revolutionary forces, bankers, traders, men of the church . . .), and that half the human race has no recorded role in history. And this saying is true in its literal sense, too. The great men in history, art, literature and politics have leaned on women in all sorts of ways: for domestic comfort, sexual fulfilment, creative inspiration.

Feminists are interested in uncovering the hidden lives of women in history, re-reading the pages of the history book with an eye for the women whose lives are shadows behind the great men. But the task is made very difficult if we have preconceptions of what we will find. Since we know that at all periods in history women have had little freedom of action, it won't surprise us to find that the great heroes were married to women who seemed to do little more than sit around waiting for them to return from their exploits. Not much comfort there for modern women looking for inspiration! And it would be overcompensating to assume that, on the contrary, these were vital and courageous women, contributing at every stage to their husbands' success. On the whole, we simply don't know what their lives were like.

The only way to find the women is to look behind the men. Germaine Greer makes this point in a particularly telling way in her book *The Obstacle Race: the fortunes of women painters and their work,* when she observes that the most striking thing about the women who made names for themselves as painters before the nineteenth century is that they were nearly all related to better-known male painters. The simple explanation is that only women in this position would have had access to training and the chance to perfect their skills. Therefore, Germaine Greer argues,

'Any student of women painters . . . finds that he is actually studying the female relatives of male artists, a curious study in itself, and one which must take account of certain basic factors, some of which, such as the legal status of female relatives, the opportunity that male relatives have to confine and repress women, are obvious, while others, like the effect of filial status upon the self-image of the artist, are insidious.'

In other words, Greer found that the only way to find out about the lives of these women painters was to look at their relationships with the more (or indeed, sometimes *less*) famous men with whom they lived and worked. So in her book Greer concentrates on the sort of self-image that working always in the shadow of other male painters produced in her women painters, and goes on to argue that **because** they created in the shadow of men, they accepted a smaller version of their own abilities — and hence did not make a mark on the history of art. Because they accepted the fact that their husbands/fathers/lovers were the true geniuses, often their own work consisted of mainly doing the hackwork in the studio of the master. With the passage of time, paintings that they **were** solely responsible for became attributed to the master — so we do not have the physical evidence of these women's talents. Both the women and their works vanish in the shadow behind the great artists, while the men shine more brightly because of them.

Feminist art historians have taken Germaine Greer to task for asking the wrong questions. They say that if Greer had adopted a different definition of what great art was, she would have been able to find plenty of examples of a strong women's art tradition. They say that Greer has fallen in with definitions of art that stress the importance in art of projecting individual personality and vision, and great art as the projection of a powerful personality and a unique vision of the world. No wonder, then, that so few women's personalities emerge through great art — women were simply not permitted to impose their individual personalities. But if we concentrate on the technical skill, rather than the evidence of the artist's ego in the painting, we might rate women artists better. Part of the problem of finding great women artists is that the criteria we use for greatness only work for men.

At the risk of oversimplifying, we can look at the convenient pigeonholes into which women have been slotted — artist's muse, helpmate; interfering wife, stifling his creativity; frustrated and thwarted creative talent, trying to find an outlet through a great man's activity; dedicated biographer and promoter of the great man's talent. What do these conventional pictures of women really show when held up to a strong light?

Dorothy Wordsworth (lived 1771-1855), sister of the one poet everybody has heard of, was a small footnote in history as the devoted companion of the poet, his housekeeper, and recorder of their walking tours in England's Lake district. In fact, her own achievement as a writer entitles her to an independent place in literature.

◆

MONDAY 4TH OCTOBER 1802, my brother William was married to Mary Hutchinson. I slept a good deal of the night and rose fresh and well in the morning. At a little after 8 o'clock I saw them go down the avenue towards the church. William had parted from me upstairs. I gave him the wedding ring —with how deep a blessing! I took it from my forefinger where I had worn it the whole of the night before — he slipped it again onto my finger and blessed me fervently. When they were absent my dear little Sara prepared the breakfast. I kept myself as quiet as I could, but when I saw the two men running up the walk, coming to tell us it was over, I could stand it no long and threw myself on the bed where I lay in stillness, neither hearing or seeing anything, till Sara came upstairs to me and said 'They are coming'. This forced me from the bed where I lay and I moved I know not how straight forward, faster than my strength could carry me till I met my beloved William and fell upon his bosom. . .

The clouds beneath our feet spread themselves to the water, and the clouds of the sky almost joined them

Dear Dorothy
Living in the shadow of the man who saw daffodils.
Sister Dot who never married
      who went walking with William in the ruins on his honeymoon
         and left new bride Mary alone by the fire…
Dorothy Wordsworth whose exquisite journals
also saw daffodils
      clouds
And yet I learned that poem at ten,
And at twenty was studying 'The Romantics'
and was never informed that Dorothy wrote such
Wonderful words in her daily journal…

Just another of the legion of ill-defined
Women Behind Great Men…

SUNG
Yes she's the woman behind the great man
She belongs to that most exclusive clan
Of women who give up their birthright for the fame
Of slaving as a lackey for the great man's name
Now it never happens quite the same in reverse
Denis Thatcher and Prince Phillip don't share the same curse
The TV never comments on their shirts and ties
And they're free to live the grand life apart from their wives
And what about Maud, Maud Gonne
All that time little Willie Yeats
was sublimating his hard on for Maud in a park of randy swans.
Old Willie, who hung out for Maud
   and hung out for Maud
      and never had a fuck till he was thirty one.
But what do you ever hear about Maud
Only that W.B. Yeats had the hots for her
When she refused for the hundredth time in fifteen years
with a no, no, no again, I'll fuck but not be married
He proposed to her daughter

Revolutionary, feminist, battered wife, single mother
and all of this bravely borne in the Ireland of her choice
   not her birth

Maud's a story and a half in her own right
But what do you ever hear about Maud ?

I'd like to be the woman behind the great man
I'd stick a gun in his ribs and demand
My rightful wages as adviser to the state
The copyright on my ideas he got at the breakfast plate.

('WOMEN BEHIND GREAT MEN'
R. Archer)

ALFRED TENNYSON
**Come into the garden Maud
For the black bat night has flown
Come into the garden Maud
I am here at the gate alone,
I am here at the gate alone**

*See LUCKY EYES & A HIGH HEART:
Nancy Cardozzo*

The role of muse, creative inspiration, indispensable helpmate, is the most flattering of the pigeon-holes into which women are slotted. But it is a deadly flattery, because it confirms women in the role of selfless handmaid of genius, an essentially passive position. And when a gifted woman married to a genius asserts her own claims, often enough they are denied as illegitimate, because his is the talent which should be nurtured.

In the history of women painters blotted out by the looming shadow of their fathers, lovers, and brothers, there is one reverse case. Suzanne Valadon (lived 1865-1938) was a French woman painter with a powerful style, and powerful personality. She began to draw while working as an artist's model, and frequently used her own body as the subject of sensual nude studies. She had a son, Maurice Utrillo, also a painter of Paris street scenes, who had a young friend Andre Utter, who became his mother's lover and later husband. Suzanne painted Andre nude, in conscious defiance of tradition, which says that men may paint a nude woman, but the male body may not be taken as an object by a woman. Suzanne Valadon also completely overshadowed her young husband and her son, whose work came to resemble hers. But despite Germaine Greer's exultation in Valadon's strength of will and overwhelming sexuality, it is still probably true that for every one person who has seen a Valadon work, let alone heard of her, there are ten who can identify an Utrillo . . .
Germaine Greer, THE OBSTACLE RACE, and Margaret Walters, THE NUDE MALE,

Baudelaire, the French poet who wrote lyrically of decadence and spiritual corruption, had as his muse a black woman. As Angela Carter shows in her story *Black Venus,* the figure of the artist's muse is such a stock figure that we are hardly curious about her at all, taking for truth what the poet or artist made of her; if it was her body or beauty he celebrated, why should we seek out her personality? Curious, isn't it, that scholars will go to great lengths to reconstruct the details of an artist's chance conversations with other artists, trying to unlock the secrets of his creative impulse, while remaining so uninterested in the impact of the

Mary Leunig

STANDING FEMALE NUDE
CAROL ANN DUFFY

Six hours like this for a few francs.
Belly nipple arse in the window light,
he drains the colour from me. *Further to the right,
Madame. And do try to be still.*
I shall be represented analytically and hung
in great museums. The bourgeoisie will coo
at such an image of a river-whore. They call it Art.

Maybe. He is concerned with volume, space.
I with the next meal. *You're getting thin,
Madame, this is not good.* My breasts hang
slightly low, the studio is cold. In the tealeaves
I can see the Queen of England gazing
on my shape. Magnificent, she murmurs
moving on. It makes me laugh. His name

is Georges. He tells me he's a genius.
There are times he does not concentrate
and stiffens for my warmth. Men think of their mothers.
He possesses me on canvas as he dips the brush
repeatedly into the paint. Little man,
you've not the money for the arts I sell.
Both poor, we make our living how we can.

I ask him, why do you do this?
*Because I have to.
There's no choice.
Don't talk.*
My smile confuses him.
These artists take themselves
too seriously. At night I fill
myself with wine and dance
around the bars. When it's
finished he shows me proudly,
lights a cigarette.
I say twelve francs and get my shawl.
It does not look like me.

personality of the woman he lived with? Angela Carter creates a moving picture of a sulking West Indian prostitute, irritated by the great man's insistence that she play the jungle queen, when she herself is a sophisticated woman of the city; slowly dying of the poison the great poet gave to her — created and destroyed by his fantasy, but in the story, determinedly her own woman.

When Jiang Qing, Mao Tse-Tung's last wife, married him in 1938, after a career as a movie actress and an independent life, marked by a keen sense of the necessity for a woman to have a career, the Chinese Communist Party was only prepared to accept the arrangement on the condition that she devote all her energies to looking after Mao, and refrain from any political activity for thirty years. Forty-two years later, after intimate participation in the political events of the Chinese revolution of 1949, the formation of a new society which repudiated the feudal notions of women's subjection to men along with economic and class oppression, and the extraordinarily intense revolutionary period of the Cultural Revolution, Jiang Qing was tried and found guilty of counter-revolutionary plotting, persecution of political enemies, and usurping her late husband's power. In the courtroom she said, in answer to the charges: 'Everything I did, Mao told me to do. I was his dog; what he said to bite, I bit.'

Cynthia Lennon *John Roca/LGI*

'What would have happened had Shakespeare had a wonderfully gifted sister . . . ?'
Virginia Woolf, A ROOM OF ONE'S OWN

If not a muse, or a helpmate, or a dedicated patron, there's another role available to the woman behind the great man. Trouble — a distraction, a reckless breeder of hungry mouths who have to be fed, taking him away from his true art, a nag, disapproving of his rowdy friends and thereby thwarting his creativity, drowning him in domesticity, or worse, ill, clinging, mad, the cross he must bear. The American-English poet T. S. Eliot, a banker by profession who was supported in his art by donations from the circle of English writers, artists and intellectuals known collectively as the Bloomsbury Group, had a young wife Vivienne.

Virginia Woolf, who in much of her writing explored the barriers placed in the way of creative women (for example, her essay *A Room of One's Own*), was surprisingly unsympathetic towards her friend Tom's wife.

'She is insane,' she wrote in a letter. 'She suspects every word one says . . . "Do you keep bees?" I asked, handing her the honey. "Hornets," she replied. "Where?" I asked. "Under the bed". . . it's too sinister and sordid and depressing . . . one must simply let him drown, wrapped in swathes of dirty seaweed . . .'

Compare this chilling dismissal of another woman's marital and mental difficulties with an observation by another contemporary, the poet Edith Sitwell: 'At some point in their marriage Tom [Eliot] went mad, and promptly certified his wife.'

He did too, and she died in hospital twenty years before him, never visited

and never rescued by the great poet. One school of thought sees in this story the inevitable torments of a great man of genius, marvels at the detached clarity of the poetry produced in the midst of domestic chaos, at best pities the poor mad wife. Another way of seeing it is to observe how the structure of marriage in contemporary society is incompatible with two strong personalities both vying for the other's attention, and how the privileged claims of the artist to the greater attention can drive a woman crazy. It's a question of where you put the emphasis, and which moral you think the story stands for. The woman broken under the stress of genius is part of the myth of the artist as special being; so is the picture of the dull housebound slatternly wife, trying to drag the special being down to her level, through envy and bitterness at her own ordinariness.

See also Zelda Fitzgerald, wife of F. Scott . . .

See the play TOM AND VIV by Michael Hastings.

47

Shining like a beacon across this bleak landscape of tormented artists and suffering wives is the example of the robust Nora Joyce, born Nora Barnacle, wife of James Joyce, author of *Ulysses* and *Finnegan's Wake*, regarded as among the most difficult but rewarding books in twentieth century English literature. Nora never read any of his books, cared nothing for his fame and notoriety and said he should have stuck to singing. They loved each other.

Cory Aquino *Peter Solness/Sydney Morning Herald, 1986*

Nora Joyce *Bernice Abbott*

There is another group of women behind great men whose circumstances offer insights into the different social roles of men and women.

These are the women who carry on the great man's work after his death or imprisonment, and come to be revered as extensions of the man and what he stands for. Contemporary examples are Winnie Mandela, wife of the imprisoned leader of the African National Congress in South Africa; Benazir Bhutto, daughter of the executed prime minister of Pakistan, who now lives under house arrest in her country, a symbol of opposition and focus for hatred of the current regime; and above all, Corazon Aquino, recently elected President of the Philippines, who came to prominence only when her husband was murdered on his return from exile. The extraordinary movement called 'People's Power' which overthrew President Marcos took her as first its symbol, and then its leader.

It is fascinating to see how as women they fuse together practical politics and symbolic politics. As women they are powerful symbols of righteous anger and moral force: women are easily adapted into

Benazir Bhutto *on the 5th anniversary of her father's death A.P./John Redman, 1984*

symbols of justice. Because they are women, we do not assume that they are in it for themselves. Because opposition is dangerous, their courage as women stands out, and this courage lends dignity and moral authority to the movements they represent. (We saw the same phenomenon in the revolution which overthrew the Shah of Iran in 1979 — the revolutionary movement gained enormous credibility in the West because of the presence in the streets of Tehran of hundreds and thousands of Iranian women, protesting against the murder, torture and injustice of the regime.)

Winnie Mandela *after being released on bail. Her daughter Zinzi is at her side. A.P. 1985*

It seems that the more women are excluded from participation in politics, and the more closely confined they are to their domestic and mothering role, the more powerful and explosive is their entry as individuals onto the political stage. If a mother hates, surely the cause must be a just one, because mothers stand for life, nurturing and caring; mothers are not opportunist politicians, mothers don't lust for power . . . .

What happens when women **get** power is the subject of our next chapter — it's an altogether different story.

48

POWER

7

A MAN'S BEST FRIEND.

WOMEN AND
POWER

THE CLICHE:
rolling pin at the ready.

Prime Minister Margaret Thatcher
**THE STANDARD
'EXCEPTIONAL WOMAN':**
in control, tough, invincible.

Dynasty's Alexis Carrington Colby
THE FANTASY:
*beautiful and evil, plotting and
scheming in business and sex.*

**Taken all together these images of powerful women tell us very
interesting things about women, and about power, and the relationship
between sex and power.**

THE cliche: women as domestic bullies, tyrannising men through obsessive attention to
detail, getting their own back by nagging, spoiling a man's fun, prudish and disapproving. In
this picture, power is really only the exercise of negativity, forbidding or spoiling, not really
good, strong, taking-action-on-your-own-account power. Men who think women have this sort of
power, and resent them for it, are in fact critical of domesticity and marriage, because it is these
institutions which give women their 'power'. Blaming the victim.

Reactions to the Margaret Thatchers, Indira Gandhis, and Golda Meirs are much more complex, and very interesting. The first extremely interesting thing about these women is that nearly all of them are associated with authoritarian political styles. This is paradoxical for several reasons. In the first place, it goes against the sterotyped image of women as natural compromisers, avoiders of conflict and healers of quarrels. Although feminists don't find it particularly surprising to see an authoritarian woman, since the argument has always been that the supposedly 'feminine' attributes are dinned into women, not something you're born with, the question still remains — why is it that the sort of political party which stands for the traditional values of the family, patriotism, making it on your own merits, taking hard decisions, all of the values which have been invoked to keep women in their place — of all parties, these are the ones which have allowed women to lead them? And why are the parties of the left, which stand for social change, social justice, and equal rights, never led by women?

Quite possibly the answer lies in that description of the type of politics that these parties stand for. Conservative (or right-wing) political parties believe that the individual

and the family are the foundations of civilised society, and that individual freedom is best guaranteed when the government leaves people to their own devices as much as possible. They believe that individual effort will be rewarded, and are distrustful of the power of organised groups like trade unions (and women's movements), which they fear take away people's individual judgement and initiative.

Women like Margaret Thatcher can make a special claim to embody all the supposed virtues of hard work and dedication, and to reap the rewards promised by their party, because after all, haven't they **proved** the assertion that individualism is the best creed, by overcoming all obstacles, including that of being born a woman? And most fundamentally, the individualist creed enables these women to fight only on their own behalf, not on behalf of other women: they are not posing any philosophical challenge to their political supporters. On the whole the Margaret Thatchers believe wholeheartedly in all the traditional virtues of the family including the traditional role of women as homemakers and mothers. So for the Margaret Thatchers there is no need to fight a gender battle o insist that the division of labour between men and women in family and society is unjust. Therefore they do not antagonise their colleagues; they are truly honorary men.

This is one reason why for years in Australia, the surest way for a woman to get into parliament was to join the conservative party of the day, and why still today it is only the conservative parties which have women as elected leaders, and why the women's section of the conservative parties — i.e. the Liberal Party and National Country Party — has always been powerful. They have always been able to claim that women's interests and the interests of the party harmonised, because they have defined 'women's interests' to mean the interests of each woman as an individual, and the interests of the family. (They have not discerned any contradiction between the interests of the woman as an individual and the interests of the family.) What they want for women as mothers, wives, workers is individual respect and dignity.

Contrast this with the position of women in the parties of the left. These political parties (for example, the Australian Labor Party) are based on the trade union organisation of the working class, inheriting the politics of working class solidarity against the bosses, egalitarianism, and political action to get a better deal on social conditions, such as the cost of food, housing, low wages, lack of jobs. Now women taking feminist positions on all these social questions are trying to organise women as a group, to take up issues such as childcare, abortion rights, domestic violence against women, women's lower wages and poorer job prospects compared to

Prime Minister Indira Gandhi *Edoardo Fornaciari/Gamma, 1981*

men. Their comrades argue that they are setting up conflicts between women and men — when in fact what these feminist left-wing women are doing is pointing out that what suits the working class **family** may not always suit the working class **woman**. So left-wing women follow the tradition of their style of politics and argue for the interests of women as a group, and come up against the opposition of the older style of group politics, which took women very much for granted. Left-wing women have to struggle for a voice within their political parties because they are challenging the meaning of the fundamental principles of socialism. They are pointing to a connection between class oppression and the subjugation of women's interests to those of men.

In her book *Wigan Pier Revisited* Beatrix Campbell describes how traditional working-class politics in England's industrial towns has been 'the men's movement', with the only role for women that of a

'women's auxiliary'. Now this situation is being threatened by the new politics and new methods of organisation coming out of feminism. She talked to a woman who has been a Labour Party member since the 1960s, and a feminist since the 1970s: 'In the old days the women needed a way to meet because they were completely excluded from the men. They did a lot, but the party marginalised them, though because they serviced the lifestyle of the men they were encouraged by the men. Now many of the men who would at one time have encouraged their wives to join women's sections will do the opposite because they're frightened of the feminism, because of course it wouldn't be about men's lives.'

So women in conservative parties are able to say with conviction that being a woman is irrelevant to their elevation to the top — grit, determination and a will to succeed is all that is needed. They deny the existence of discrimination against women, and argue that women's interests and those of men are identical, within the family. Right-wing women acknowledge, along with their men, that women **as women** have no special claim to have power exercised on their behalf. Left-wing activist women are challenging the whole basis on which power is allocated in society: and they are saying, with varying degrees of conviction and discomfort (because saying it is difficult, and provokes conflict), that speaking for women is the basis of their claim to power in their parties. No wonder men find it more comfortable for the conservative women to succeed.

Once they've made it, though, the men will never allow themselves to forget that these are only women after all. Look at the terms of grudging respect applied to these women — who, after all, have turned out to be very good at running wars, as well as running countries (Margaret Thatcher's Falklands war; Golda Meir's Seven Day war; Indira Gandhi's war with Pakistan over Bangladesh). Nicknames like 'Iron Butterfly' and 'Iron Maiden' barely conceal the sneer beneath the admiration of strength. A butterfly is a useless showy thing, flapping about, flighty, inconsequential (not attributes one would readily apply to the real woman who bears the epithet — **Imelda Marcos**, wife and power behind the throne to the ex-president of the Philippines); a maiden is a stitched-up virgin, a prude. Admirers and detractors alike seek to explain these women's success in astonishingly puerile ways, invoking ideas like the alleged 'nanny complex' of the English to explain why Margaret Thatcher's bullying tones go down so well.

These explanations heap sexism on sexism. In the first place, they refuse to acknowledge the legitimacy of a woman in a position of power. They rely on metaphors which disparage women — another version of the 'nanny theory' of Thatcher's Britain is that she embodies every schoolboy's fantasy of a dominatrix, the leather clad queen of sado-masochism. Note that these explanations assume that it is **men's** fantasies which hold the key to the mystery. Don't women vote in Britain?

That is, of course, a rhetorical question. Those caricatures are expressing the truth of the situation as a masculine culture sees it. Women have no legitimate access to power; when they get there, they are playing a part not written by themselves. Either they are the token women, whose existence 'proves' that there is no discrimination against women, and who can therefore be used against other women; or they can be fitted into a delicious fantasy, slightly titillating because it has hints of danger, the sexual roles reversed.

'*Dynasty* is also a fantasy show, of course, but here we are talking more about the power fantasies of women in the 1980s. *Dynasty* is a very matriarchal kind of show, where the women, whether they're doing good or evil, are at least doing something. I think the female audience finds the show just as escapist and entertaining as *Magnum, P.I.* There's precious little pure fantasy for women on television — *Dynasty* is a women's *Star Wars* or *Raiders of the Lost Ark*. Of course, women are also the primary consumers — in a way they are the ultimate end product of the television — and *Dynasty* is the ultimate consumers' show. *Dynasty* provides women — and men too — with fantasies of power and consumption.'

Esther Shapiro, creator of the concept of Dynasty, in an interview reprinted in The Australian newspaper, March 25, 1985.

— whose power fantasies? Do women really fantasise about unscrupulous power, unearned wealth, sexual intrigue? And if television is creating this audience of female consumers, aren't the fantasies more likely to be those of the sellers, not the buyers? or at least, designed in their interests?

NO MAN'S LAND
LEE CATALDI

if you could read between the lines
I write on the blackboard
well you already understand too much
to keep the peace

between the lines I'm trying to pass
you a gun

you run
through fire don't let them catch you
in the camera's eye
you can always hide
between the lines

on Sunday
worn soldiers crawl out of trenches
throw off their muddy tin hats
and dance with their brothers
on Monday
the generals order them
to fire on each other

now and then
someone refuses and you run
as if your life depended on it
dodging the letters of the law

women
chained themselves to the railings
to be heard

between the lines you can read
every word

In 1980-81 an extraordinary story was reported around the world out of India. An illiterate peasant woman of low caste took the name Phoolan Devi and became the leader of an outlaw bandit gang, after she had been pack-raped by high caste landholders in her district. For two years she and her gang raided and terrorised rich landholders, with her as the acknowledged leader.

As Tariq Ali reports the story:

. . . it was one act in particular which won her the respect of women throughout the country. She returned to the village of Behmai, the scene of her humiliation, where she gave the following terse instruction to her followers: "Today we have to take revenge upon the Thakurs." Twenty Thakurs [upper-caste Hindus] were captured. In front of the villagers, many of whom were from a low caste like Phoolan herself, they were lined up against the wall and shot. This was the first time in the history of the region that upper-caste Hindus had been despatched in this fashion. On this episode she remained unrepentant.'

Tariq Ali, THE NEHRUS AND THE GANDHIS — AN INDIAN DYNASTY, Picador 1985. Tariq Ali notes that together, Indira Gandhi and Phoolan Devi symbolised contemporary India — 'one at the top of the pyramid of power, the other buried underneath.'

Although men calmly accept and heatedly defend the social, economic, family and sexual arrangements that ensure the continuing exploitation of women, it seems that the idea of women in control is ever-present in their heart of hearts. And in some cultures these innermost thoughts and fears are allowed to surface.

At carnival time in Catholic countries men dress as women in a parody of role reversal, to symbolise the anarchy of women in power. If women were in control, the masquerade says, the world as we know it would be turned upside down, and chaos, lawlessness and reprisals would rule. Just for the one day of the carnival, men can put themselves in women's shoes, run riot through the streets — because tomorrow the world will be back in order.

Carnival of Disorder — Basel

London Features International Ltd.

PIRATE JENNY

BERTOLT BRECHT trs Ralph Manheim and John Willett

Now you gents all see I've the glasses to wash.
When a bed's to be made I make it.
You may tip me a penny, and I'll thank you very well
And you see me dressed in tatters, and this tatty old hotel
And you never ask me how long I'll take it.
But one of these evenings there will be screams from the harbour
And they'll ask: what can all that screaming be?
And they'll see me smiling as I do the glasses
And they'll say: how she can smile beats me.
    And a ship with eight sails and
    All its fifty guns loaded
    Has tied up at the quay.

They say: get on, dry your glasses, my girl
And they tip me and don't give a damn.
And their penny is accepted, and their bed will be made
(Although nobody is going to sleep there, I'm afraid)
And they still have no idea who I am.
But one of these evenings there will be explosions from the harbour,
And they'll ask: what kind of a bang was that?
And they'll see me as I stand beside the window
And they'll ask: what has she got to smile at?
    And that ship with eight sails and
    All its fifty guns loaded
    Will lay siege to the town.

Then you gents, you aren't going to find it a joke
For the walls will be knocked down flat
And in no time the town will be razed to the ground
Just one tatty old hotel will be left standing safe and sound
And they'll ask: did someone special live in that?
Then there'll be a lot of people milling round the hotel
And they'll ask: what made them leave that place alone?
And they'll see me as I leave the door next morning
And they'll say: don't tell us she's the one.
    And that ship with eight sails and
    All its fifty guns loaded
    Will run up its flag.

And a hundred men will land in the bright midday sun
Each stepping where the shadows fall.
They'll look inside each doorway and grab anyone they see
And put him in irons and then bring him to me
And they'll ask: which of these should we kill?
In that noon day heat there'll be a hush round the harbour
As they ask which has got to die.
And you'll hear me as I softly answer: the lot!
And as the first head rolls I'll say: hoppla!
    And that ship with eight sails and
    All its fifty guns loaded
    Will vanish with me.

When Polly sings this song at her own wedding supper in Bertolt Brecht's *The Threepenny Opera*, it is her moment of ascendancy. She pulls no punches in letting the crooks in her husband Mack the Knife's gang know that there is always the possibility that she will become boss over them one day.

The power of the poetry lies in the image of Pirate Jenny singing of the day when her ship will come in, and the pirates, who are in reality her troops, will lay waste to the town, sparing no-one. It is easy to see how the song has been used ever since as a statement about the revolt of the oppressed classes against their oppressors. The song seems to state very strongly that law and order and the routines of everyday life are built upon the unrewarded labours and humiliation of other people, and that everyone who benefits by this system has a personal responsibility for its continuation, and can expect no mercy. It has always been a particularly potent and dangerous song simply because it is a woman who is suddenly revealed as the enemy within, lurking unheeded in the very heart of the social system, suddenly casting aside her subservient role, and with it all her womanly virtues, like compassion and justice. . .

One theme which has always interested feminists is the connection between women, 'masculinity' and power. 'Masculinity' is of course associated with ideas about men's dominance over women, and power over women has often been associated with other sorts of power. Women are supposed to admire powerful masculine men. So what sort of responsibility can we sheet home to the women who surround a powerful man? Should we see them as the passive playthings of dominant men, as victims: or should we insist that they share in the guilt as well as the glory?

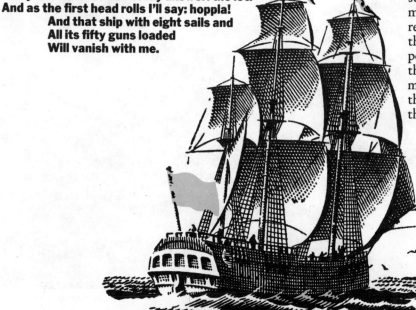

ON THE WATERGATE WOMEN

ROBIN MORGAN

Maureen Dean, wearing persimmon summer silk,
Sits smiling, silent, in the Senate Hearing Room.
Her eyelids droop. She must not doze.
She bolts upright.
But if she cannot doze, she finds she **thinks.**
She is the second wife.
The first says that he never lied.
The musings of the second are inadmissible.

Martha Mitchell, Cassandra by extension,
nurses the bruises from her beatings,
nurses her mind from the forced commitments,
waits at home, alone, with the terror that all her truths
will be seen as comic relief.

Dita Beard
has disappeared,
clutching the heart she was permitted to keep
alive, in payment for her scandal's death.

Rose Mary would
if she could, but she can't;
lips sealed by loyalty (for which, read: fear),
a faintly ridiculous scapegoat
as any Good Friday girl could have predicted.

The Committee wives watch their husbands on TV,
alone, preferably, so they can smile to themselves
at the righteous purity of such judges.

All the secretaries hunch at their IBMs,
snickering at the keys.
What they know could bring down the government.

The maids, the governesses, the manicurists,
the masseuses avert their eyes.
What they know could bring down the family.

The mistresses wait for their phones to ring.
Afraid to miss the call, they hurry
through their vomiting.

None of these witnesses would be believed.
Some do not believe themselves.

And Dorothy, Mrs. Howard Hunt, tucked into her coffin,
could hardly testify
to the cash, nestled in her lap like a rapist,
to the plane's dive through a bleached spring sky,

the taste of arsenic on her teeth,
the enormous dazzling wisdom that struck all her braincells
at the impact.
HER silence should bring down the nation.

But all the while, one woman, sitting alone
in rooms and corridors thick with deceit;
familiar, by now, with an unimaginable weariness,
having smiled and waved and hostessed her only life
into a numbness that cannot now recall
even the love
which was once supposed to make all this worthwhile —

having slept out summer in a wintry bed,
having borne children who were neither of them sons,
having, for years, stood at attention
so close to power, so powerless —

not, oh not
Thelma Catherine Patricia Ryan Nixon
blamed by the Right for her careful stupidity
blamed by the middle for her cultivated dullness
blamed by the Left for her nonexistent influence
blamed by most men for being unbeautiful
blamed by some women for being broken
blamed by her daughters for their father
blamed by her husband for her cherished mis-memory of
him as a young Quaker —

not, oh not
Thelma Catherine Patricia Ryan Nixon

who, as a young girl, loved Scarlatti,
who wanted to become an actress playing Ibsen,
who lost her own name somewhere along the way,

who now sits alone in some oversized chair,
watching with detached interest
how her sedated visions do their best
to picket before so many defilements.

This is no melodrama.
Here is no histrionic pain.

That quality of grief
could bring down
mankind.

When we look at Eva Braun, Hitler's mistress, what is of most interest to us? Do we care whether he treated her well or badly? If he treated her badly, does she count as one of his victims, or does her privileged proximity to his absolute power disqualify her from any sympathy? Should we see her as an exceptional person, or simply as a typical woman of her age and class? Surely she must have known that Hitler was evil — how could she have blinded herself to what was going on? Is that what women routinely do, love blindly? Or are women cynical, knowing that they can buy security with a no-questions-asked loving?

Why don't women expose the evil of the men they live with?

Robin Morgan's poem *On the Watergate Women* is a sustained meditation on these questions. Around the central dramatic image of the United States Senate hearings into the cover-up of the Watergate break-in ordered by President Nixon, she weaves profound insights into the lives of the women associated with the main characters. Women, she says, are the outward trappings of male power, and also the special hidden victims of that power. They are victims at the personal level, suffering beatings and sexual humiliations. And they are victims at the political level, unable to break their silence and tell what they know, forced to share the humiliation of their downfall without any real chance to influence the course of events.

But women are also in a sense accomplices in this scheme of corruption and hypocrisy, feeding men's self-esteem with their admiration and availability. No-one in this dreadful dialectic of private depravity and public corruption is entirely blameless. Women are united, whatever their class and background, in a sisterhood of powerlessness, grief and shame.

It's a very disturbing image of women's relationship to power, proposing that women are both victimised by male power and have a stake in its maintenance.

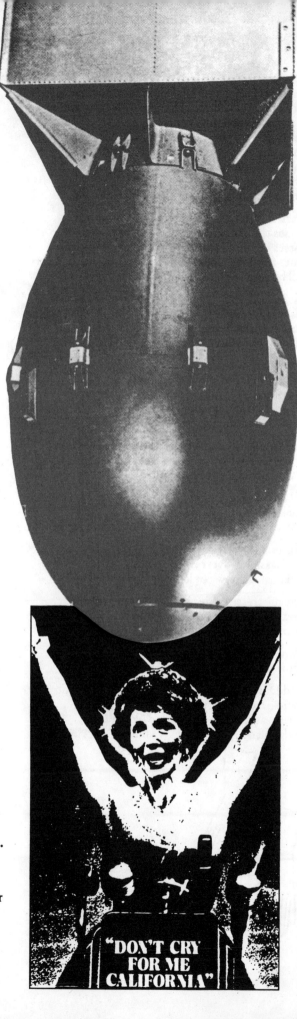

"DON'T CRY FOR ME CALIFORNIA"

THE HAND THAT ROCKS THE CRADLE BOMBS THE WORLD
ARCHER/MANSON

So Nancy's revealing her memoirs,
The first lady's getting it down
She wants to give you the tale of her life
To say that the finest thing's being a wife . . .

But look at the mongrel she's wife to,
A powerful stupid old man,
We know that there's plenty as stupid as him
But he's got all our lives in his shaky old hands . . .

And Nancy's the actress behind him
She's elegant, poised and well-dressed,
But don't you forget she's a dangerous woman
When it comes to the day when the button gets pressed . . .

'cos as we'll be dead, or slowly rotting,
She'll cuddle old Ron to her breast,
At the one time in his life, someone should point the finger
She'll be telling him, 'Dear, you knew best'

Oh the simple minded woman
Her clothes and her smiles can't cover her sin.
She praises a man who's pushing the world
To the brink of hell and asking it to jump in.

8

My night in a rut

WIFE OF A ROCK'N'ROLL STAR

KAREN WYNN-MOYLAN

Just yesterday morning, completely without warning
I was the wife of a rock 'n' roll star
There was an agent at the door rang, groupies on the floor and
They say he's gonna go far

I found that wives are an unknown breed
In a world of booze and sex and speed
Gonna be a new experience, chance to use my self-defence
Bein' the wife of a rock 'n' roll star

What will happen to love's young dream?
Will I lose my self-esteem?
Stick around for the next verse, it couldn't be much worse
Than bein' the wife of a rock 'n' roll star

Well now we're goin' on a tour
His friends say 'Whaddya need her for?'
Ah the friends of a rock 'n' roll star

He said we'd travel one day, we'll be in England Monday
Is this what's meant by gonna go far?

I'm told that wives are bad for the act
The kids like 'em single, they said it's a fact
Hiding in the dressing room, I think I'll have a breakdown soon
While he's playin' the rock 'n' roll star.

Meanwhile I'm roadie, lay and cook
Makin' joints and coffee for the group
He says we're getting rich and the press says I'm a bitch
Does divorce hurt a rock 'n' roll star?

Well he faded from the public view, took me with him too
No longer the rock 'n' roll star
We melted down gold records when we needed money quick
Even that doesn't go far

We've got a nice little cosy farm
Two kids and two goats and the air is no harm
He still practises, lying on the mattresses
And dreams he's a rock 'n' roll star

Lately I've been writing some songs
The agent says that I'm coming along,
But all the DJs, preface their airplays
With 'Here's the wife of that rock 'n' roll star'

Yoko Ono

Madonna

Patti Smith *Paul Cox/LF*

Dave Stewart and Annie Lennox
of the Eurythmics

Are girls just having fun in Rock'n'Roll? Well, a few... but if you

technological control — is still in the hands of the boys having

Cindi Lauper *LFI*

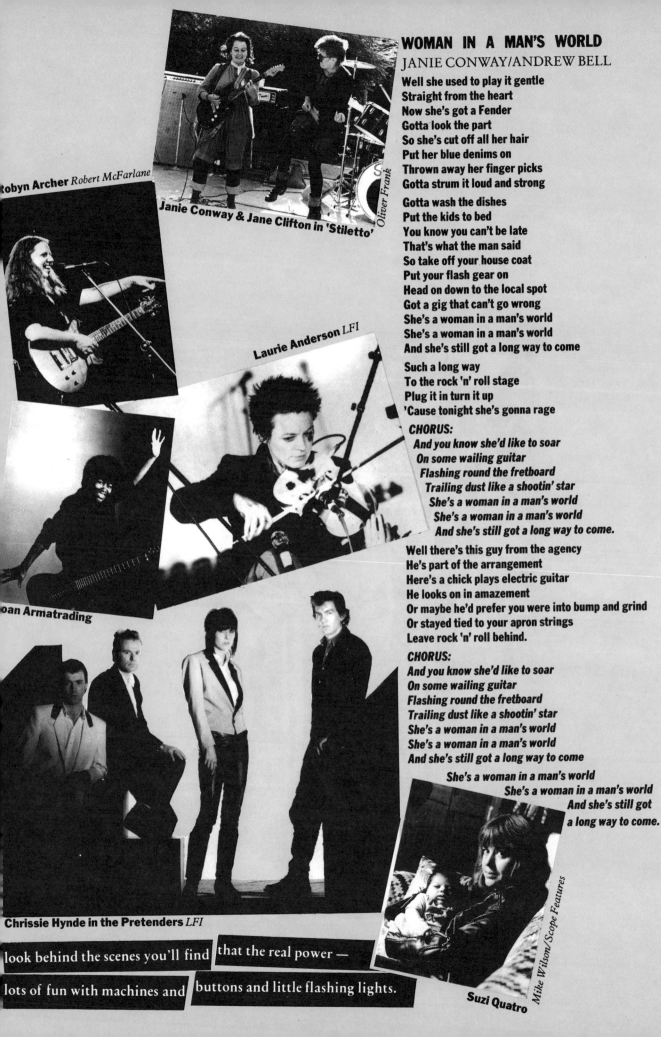

WOMAN IN A MAN'S WORLD
JANIE CONWAY/ANDREW BELL

Well she used to play it gentle
Straight from the heart
Now she's got a Fender
Gotta look the part
So she's cut off all her hair
Put her blue denims on
Thrown away her finger picks
Gotta strum it loud and strong

Gotta wash the dishes
Put the kids to bed
You know you can't be late
That's what the man said
So take off your house coat
Put your flash gear on
Head on down to the local spot
Got a gig that can't go wrong
She's a woman in a man's world
She's a woman in a man's world
And she's still got a long way to come

Such a long way
To the rock 'n' roll stage
Plug it in turn it up
'Cause tonight she's gonna rage
CHORUS:
 And you know she'd like to soar
 On some wailing guitar
 Flashing round the fretboard
 Trailing dust like a shootin' star
 She's a woman in a man's world
 She's a woman in a man's world
 And she's still got a long way to come.

Well there's this guy from the agency
He's part of the arrangement
Here's a chick plays electric guitar
He looks on in amazement
Or maybe he'd prefer you were into bump and grind
Or stayed tied to your apron strings
Leave rock 'n' roll behind.

CHORUS:
And you know she'd like to soar
On some wailing guitar
Flashing round the fretboard
Trailing dust like a shootin' star
She's a woman in a man's world
She's a woman in a man's world
And she's still got a long way to come

She's a woman in a man's world
She's a woman in a man's world
And she's still got
a long way to come.

Robyn Archer *Robert McFarlane*

Janie Conway & Jane Clifton in 'Stiletto' *Oliver Frank*

Laurie Anderson *LFI*

oan Armatrading

Chrissie Hynde in the Pretenders *LFI*

Suzi Quatro *Mike Wilson/Scope Features*

look behind the scenes you'll find that the real power —
lots of fun with machines and buttons and little flashing lights.

See SIGNED, SEALED AND DELIVERED: TRUE LIFE STORIES OF WOMEN IN POP by Sue Steward and Sheryl Garratt, and A STAR IS TORN by Robyn Archer and Diana Simmonds.

MOTHERHOOD

Through motherhood, every woman has been defined from outside herself:

mother, matriarch, matron, spinster, barren, old maid — listen to the history

of emotional timbre that hangs about each of these words. Even by default

motherhood has been an enforced identity for women, while the phrases

'childless man' and 'non father' sound absurd and irrelevant. *

IN our century there have been two great upheavals in sexual relationships, during the 1920s and again in the 1960s. In the 1920s one of the great issues around which women organised in struggle against the oppressive weight of custom, prejudice and law was that of the right to birth control. Marie Stopes in the United Kingdom set up birth control clinics, dedicated to relieving women of the burden of constant unplanned pregnancies, and at the same time giving women basic information on their own sexual and emotional needs — for which she was prosecuted for obscenity. By the 1960s 'family planning' had become part of the approved model of happy western families, with well-spaced children for married couples, and advice on sensible sexual experimentation for the young. Ironically, the 1920s saw the decline into insignificance of the women's movement which had agitated for the vote and for improvements in women's status through the first two decades of this century, while the 1960s saw the growth of a new and multi-faceted feminist movement.

So, reproductive freedom may be the one great freedom on which all the others depend, but by itself it cannot raise women's status, bring about changes in sexual relationships, reform the divorce laws, or guarantee women a decent living wage so that they can break free of economic dependence on men. But the contraceptive pill has changed the pattern of life for women — by introducing the idea that women can now choose the shape of their lives. With effective contraception a woman can decide, as most do, to compress childbearing into a few years. Instead of giving birth to several children from her early twenties to her late thirties or early forties, a woman can postpone the first child until she has finished her education, gained some years of work

This chapter explores the ways in which the social definition of womanhood in terms of motherhood affects individual women, and what feminism has to say about motherhood, mothering, and children.

experience and tested the durability of her marriage; then complete her childbearing, and re-enter the workforce in her early forties. Compared to earlier generations, many years of contemporary women's lives are 'free' from the demands of very young children.

The world is adjusting slowly and painfully to this fact of women's power to choose. The anti-feminist forces are organising their campaigns around women's right to abortion, are opposing state support for single mothers, are agitating for the retention of marriage and divorce laws which affirm traditional family roles, and most recently have turned their attacks onto new techniques of artificial conception ('test-tube babies', artificial insemination, surrogate motherhood).

Mary Leunig

* Adrienne Rich, ON LIES, SECRETS AND SILENCE

What is at stake in these great social struggles is quite simply the definition of 'woman'.

Women who decide against children are thought to be *selfish*. Single women who decide to have children alone are also thought to be selfish ... clearly there is some strong social taboo being broken by both. Women who decide against children are judged selfish on several counts: they are denying their own parents grandchildren and the satisfactions of seeing life continued through the generations; they must have too high a regard for themselves, their own sense of self and self-worth, to so lightly flout women's destiny, and substitute their own idea of a chosen destiny; and perhaps they are thought selfish because they want all the pleasures of sex without the responsibility of caring for offspring, and are content to leave all those burdens on other people. They are selfish because they assume that their own individual personality is their essential self. And there's also some thread of an idea that a woman should not put herself 'above' other women, by denying the claims of her biological body.

But the real crime, it seems, lies in the fact of *choosing*. There is, after all, some sympathy for the woman who postpones maternity for various reasons, while all along thinking that one day she will have children, then discovers that it is too late, that she is no longer fertile.

When we look at the reverse situation, the woman who decides to have a child on her own, without marrying, it becomes very clear that what makes people angry is the fact that she is making a choice about her own life — and that she expects other people to back her up in this choice.

So, a woman who decides to be a single mother is called selfish because she's not giving her baby up for adoption, thus denying it a 'proper' family environment to grow up in. And she's said to be selfish because she is giving herself the status and pleasures of motherhood without shouldering the burdens of wifehood — she's got herself a meal ticket at community expense, instead of at the expense of some man. These aren't invented arguments; they are all taken straight from a letter to a newspaper by a disgruntled citizen who didn't want his taxes to be subsidising irresponsible young women. He wasn't so much morally dismayed by the fact that sex was going on outside marriage, as he was outraged at the effrontery of women who wanted to keep their babies instead of handing them over to others, more fitted by marriage, good living and respectability, to be parents.

Clearly there are really deeply felt convictions here, under the confused thinking, which are all about motherhood as a privilege to be earned by good women, not for the unworthy and sexually irresponsible.

And there's probably resentment, too, about the impact of the women's movement, which is giving women the courage to change the rules about who is and who is not 'worthy' of motherhood.

Lesbian mothers are punished for their unfitness by having to choose between their children and the free expression of their affections. In a custody case heard by the Australian Family Court in 1980 a lesbian mother was awarded custody of the children after a bitterly contested battle with their father. The conditions laid down by the court were that she and her lover should never touch or display physical affection in front of the children, and that they should sleep apart, in separate bedrooms, with the width of the corridor between them. Not surprisingly, the 2½ year relationship survived only a few months of the tension and artificiality of this court-ordered scrutiny.

Is it fear of moral contagion that produces this sort of restriction? If so, it's an odd sort of fear, given that most homosexual men and women come from uncomplicatedly heterosexual homes.

Is a woman who gives up a child for adoption still a 'mother' in the eyes of society? The answer is probably no, even though the woman will know herself to be a mother. So motherhood is a category into which society fits some women, not simply a biological fact. It is, as Adrienne Rich describes it, 'an institution', a principle of social organisation.

Most feminist thinking about the politics of fertility has been centred on the right to free, safe abortion — the woman's right to choose. Feminists have pointed out the inhumanity of forced pregnancy and compulsory motherhood, how these concepts deny the right of a woman to decide how her own body shall be used. Feminists have argued that no-one, including the doctors, should be able to take away from a woman this fundamental right; that only the woman concerned can truly assess her own circumstances, and the effects that giving birth would have on her own sense of herself, her personality, and her hopes for the future. They have observed how the medical establishment assumes that pregnant women and those with new-born infants are incapable of rational thinking, and takes decisions about birth out of the hands of women in labour — just as it denies to women the right to choose abortion.

These insights are equally applicable to the new technologies for overcoming infertility — artificial insemination, *in vitro* fertilisation (IVF, or 'test-tube babies'), embryo transfer from one woman's womb to another's, and surrogate motherhood, where one woman gives birth for another.

There are many social and ethical issues raised by these developments, and we cannot delve into them too deeply here. But there are feminist lessons to learn from the way things are going on the artificial conception front.

The first lesson is that the challenge of overcoming infertility is seen as more important than the challenge of developing a perfectly safe and reliable form of contraception. Infinite care and patience and large sums of research money are being directed towards working out precisely how conception in the human body occurs, and how it can be emulated in the laboratory.

Contrast this with the apparent lack of concern by the makers of a brand of IUD, the Dalkon Shield, who failed to follow up persistent reports that the device was implicated in the death through septic abortion, or permanent infertility through pelvic infection, of numerous women who were using it.

Second lesson: artificial conception is a logical extension of the way the medical profession has taken over the management of childbirth and fertility generally, and made us think of women's sexuality almost entirely in terms of medical questions (the 'medicalisation of women's sexuality'). Doctors, not women, are the acknowledged experts on the functioning of the female body; because they have been given the right to control women's bodies, they have been given by extension the right to make decisions and judgments about a woman's life and social circumstances. They are permitted the absolute authority to decide which of the thousands of desperate infertile women shall be selected for artificial conception, and are being encouraged to develop criteria for choosing based on ideas about motherhood which are remarkably similar to those of the

If men could get pregnant abortion would be a sacrament not a crime

isgruntled taxpayer whose views on ingle mothers we have just quoted.

The third thing to notice is the way n which entry into a fertility program gives society the apparent right to carefully control what a woman does with her pregnant body, to protect the growing foetus she carries. The embryo becomes someone's property, o be protected by all legal means available — even when it inhabits a woman's body, which no-one may own. For example, contracts for surrogate mothers in the United States — contracts under which a woman agrees to give birth to a child for another woman — contain clauses forbidding the pregnant woman to smoke, drink, have sexual intercourse, or do anything which may be thought o jeopardise the embryo's chances.

And the public debates surrounding artificial conception and the treatment of infertility have shown how painful for many women t is not to be able to conceive. Women report feeling powerless, at the mercy of their bodies; or 'failures', having failed to achieve one of life's goals for a woman; other women felt sexually unattractive.

'n common with many women unable to conceive, [she] remembers feeling sexually dead, unattractive. Her uterus seemed a gaping empty wound. These feelings of a damaged body even made her irrational and afraid of contaminating others — that somehow, her inability to have children might be catching.

Deborah Smith, THE NATIONAL TIMES October 19 to 25, 1984.

Claims by society at large to take control over the pregnant woman's body are being taken up enthusiastically, although probably cynically, by individual men.

Many feminist writers have observed how the takeover of pregnancy and childbirth by the medical profession was a defeat for any hope of alternative female structures, in which women could take refuge from the demands of the male-centred family. In pre-industrial societies women giving birth were sequestered within a female world, cared for by women relatives and friends. Giving birth was women's business. Germaine Greer's book *Sex and Destiny* mourns both the loss of a sense of sisterhood, and the loss of control over her own life, for a woman subjected to the medical management of her fertility and pregnancy.

THE BACKYARD ABORTION WALTZ

ROBYN ARCHER

Will you remember the forties, and our wartime naughties
With the soldiers on leave with their leave-pay to spend
O a cove and his girlie could dance till the early
Morn light came, but still their fun wasn't at end.
There was always a flat, with a room at the back
Where a desperate young couple their passion could vent
O you'd grunt and you'd puff, if you got up the duff
Who'd pay for the fix-up when the leave pay was spent

CHORUS:
Let's hark back to the war, dear, I wouldn't speak false
Come and join in the backyard abortion waltz

Will you remember the Yankees, we wept in our hankies
When the gobs and marines had to go back to port
Lord, fighting them off in the parks and the gardens
Through the war, was the hardest fight us sheilas fought.
And we wept a lot more when a voice from the door
Of a doctor's rooms said, my dear, you've got clap,
And the tears turned to flood when he told you your blood
Was now bearing the child of an American chap

CHORUS:

Will you recall Betty, when she joined she was a sweaty
Little freckle-faced kid of fourteen on the run.
She'd belly-dance all day on the boards on display
Cos she thought Sideshow Alley was all so much fun
She was sixteen when the war came, lied about her age and her name
Joined the WAAF and had soldier boys with her each leave,
But her fourth backyard job cost a measly few bob
Left her dead in the gutter, it was hard to believe

CHORUS:

In 1983 a man in Queensland tried to get the Supreme Court to prohibit a woman from having an abortion. He said that she was pregnant to him, as a result of a single sexual episode, and that this gave him the right to step in to protect the 'rights' of the foetus. He wasn't intending to continue any sort of relationship with the woman, and certainly not intending to stick around to be a father to the baby when it was born. All his legal arguments centred on the 'right' of the embryo to be carried to term — a 'right' which in his view completely negated any rights the woman had to determine what should happen to her own body. Luckily the Supreme Court rejected his arguments.

But would the outcome have been different if the man and woman were married to each other, or in a long-term relationship? It might well have been, since in those circumstances the man's claims would involve arguing his own rights, not just those of an unformed embryo. Hospitals will not perform sterilisations on married women without their husband's consent ... So a woman's potential for motherhood is guarded and controlled against her own actions and wishes, in the name of society, or the ideal of marriage — and maybe, in the interests of individual men.

Although motherhood is the focus for sentiment and warm upwellings of good feeling about closeness to nature, tenderness, infinite self-sacrificing love, it is also the focus for quite deeprooted fears about women's violence. The other side of the madonna is Medea, the mythic Greek murderous mother, who killed her children when her husband left her for a younger woman. (The story comes down to us in the form of a play by Euripides, the Greek dramatist, who wrote in the fifth century BC).

Italian playwright Franca Rame, collaborator with Dario Fo, has written a modern version of *Medea*. It has the same sequence of events as the classic story of jealous desperation, the woman scorned. But Medea speaks with her own voice: her children must die because it is children who hang like wooden yokes around the necks of women, giving them no choice but to submit to the law of the fathers, which gives a man the right to seek younger flesh. Better to be remembered as a wild beast, than as a docile nanny-goat ... and Medea has no life of her own to take, since her worth to her husband lies in her children. To kill herself, she must spill their blood   *

All sorts of deeply held prejudices and subterranean fears people have about the hidden violence of mothers coalesced around the case of Lindy Chamberlain, convicted of murdering her baby daughter Azaria in the Central Australian desert in 1980. From the beginning the story was bizarre: the original coroner's inquiry substantiated Lindy Chamberlain's claim that the baby was taken from the family's tent by a dingo. But rumours that it was the mother's doing circulated from day one, along with various dark theories about her reasons for the killing, including mutterings about weird religious rituals (the family were Seventh Day Adventists). The case was reopened, another inquest held, and Lindy Chamberlain eventually found guilty and sentenced to life imprisonment. After serving three years in Darwin's Berrima gaol, she was unexpectedly and abruptly released when babies' clothing was found buried at the base of Ayers Rock — the baby's body has never been found. Yet another official inquiry into the baby's disappearance

was held in mid-1986.

The point of the story is not the mystery, but the certainty with which people take sides in the case — those who are passionately convinced of her guilt, and those who even more passionately assert her innocence. Few of the protagonists in this drawn-out drama, however, seem to recognise how much the strength of feeling is due to a clash between stereotyped images of mothers.

People who found satisfaction in the guilty verdict were reinforced in their certainties by the sight of Lindy Chamberlain in the courtroom in a bare-shouldered sundress (Darwin is a steamy/hot tropical town) — mothers, especially grieving mothers, should not be sexy, mothers don't bare their flesh, or if they do, they are bad women. By the time of the trial, Lindy Chamberlain was pregnant again. Her supporters found great comfort in this proof of her deep maternal feelings; her detractors saw only further proof of cynical manipulation of public feelings of approval and sympathy for mothers-to-be, and interpreted this pregnancy as a coolly calculated bid to cheat justice.

Kerryn Goldsworthy, writing in the Melbourne *Age* newspaper, argues persuasively that the public image of Lindy Chamberlain was an image constructed by the courts and by the media, both male-dominated institutions, and an image which was 'dominated by aspects of her femaleness. Concentrated simultaneously on her sexuality and her maternity, it challenged and violated the largely unconscious but deeply ingrained conviction that motherhood is good and female sexuality is not good and never the twain shall meet. They did meet, in the person of Lindy Chamberlain, heavily pregnant and stylishly dressed and standing trial for the murder of her baby daughter. For pregnancy is that unique and unstable condition which attests beyond doubt both to your sexuality and to your imminent maternity.'

Age 15 February 1986

Kerryn Goldsworthy argues that cases like this one provoke the polarised views they do because we are taught to revere, rather than to appreciate, motherhood. Lindy Chamberlain's 'motherliness' is the strongest thread in her supporters' defence of her. But what we need to

*MEDEA, by Dario Fo and Franca Rame, in FEMALE PARTS, translated by Stuart Hood, Pluto Plays, London 1981 — adapted by Olwen Wymark.

Michael & Lindy Chamberlain
Nigel McNeil/John Fairfax, 1982

Birth Minus 240 Days   **Birth Minus 208 Days**   **Birth Minus 176 Days**   **Birth Minus 148 Days**   **Birth Minus 116 Days**

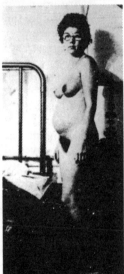
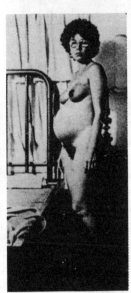
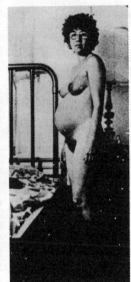

Birth Minus 91 Days   **Birth Minus 55 Days**   **Birth Minus 27 Days**   **Birth Minus 9 Hours**   **Birth Plus 4 Days**

Cynthia Cable

...ink through more carefully is why it ...so easily assumed by those ...onvinced of her guilt that a 'mother' ...a likely suspect in an unexplained ...illing. No motive, or no convincing ...otive, has ever been suggested; she ...id not appear to be depressed or ...nxious after the birth of the child. ...here is just some strong but ...narticulated feeling that mothers can ...e murderous — any mothers, not ...nly those who seem to flaunt their ...emale sexuality. And calmly ...urderous, quiet killers, not like ...ose fathers who lash out at their ...fants in fits of rage.

The laws of some countries ...ecognise that women can become ...nbearably disturbed by the ...xperience of childbirth, and have ...reated a special category of ...nfanticide' which carries a very light ...enalty for mothers who kill their babies. This is because they are assumed to be mentally unbalanced, not responsible for their actions. Lindy Chamberlain's problem was that she so insistently tried to explain her version of events, was so rational and coping. Had she been distraught and weeping, the public might have forgiven her. But part of her quality as a 'perfect mother' was precisely her ability to cope, to organise, to be a rock to her family ...

From **MOTHER IRELAND**
EDNA O'BRIEN

Countries are either mothers or fathers, and engender the emotional bristle secretly reserved for either side. Ireland has always been a woman, a womb, a cave, a cow, a Rosaleen, a sow, a bride, a harlot, and, of course, the gaunt Hag of Beare. Originally a land of woods and thickets, such as Orpheus had seen when prescribing the voyage of Jason, through a misted atmosphere. She is thought to have known invasion from the time when the Ice Age ended and the improving climate allowed deer to throng her dense forests ...

... a Hebrew woman, a lady, Caesara, niece of Noah, hearing her uncle's prophecy about a universal flood, decided to seek refuge in some foreign region, hoping to find a country as yet uninhabited and so with sin unspotted. She set out with a flock of three men and fifty women, sailing through the Red Sea, by the altars of the Philistines with the pillars of Hercules as beacons; past the treacherous coast of Spain, to Ireland, Isle of Destiny, on the shift of sustenance. Her people are the first to be interred there, the first in a long line of hardy Irish ghosts.

Bill Owens

From
ANN VERONICA
H.G. WELLS

'We are the species,' said Miss Miniver, 'men are only incidents. They give themselves airs, but so it is. In all the species of animals the females are more important than the males; the males have to please them. Look at the cock's feathers, look at the competition there is everywhere, except among humans. The stags and oxen and things all have to fight for us, everywhere. Only in man is the male made the most important. And that happens through our maternity; it's our very importance that degrades us. While we were minding the children they stole our rights and liberties. The children made us slaves, and the men took advantage of it. It's — Mrs Shalford says — the accidental conquering the essential. Originally in the first animals there were no males, none at all. It has been proved. Then they appear among the lower things' — she made meticulous gestures to figure the scale of life; she seemed to be holding up specimens, and peering through her glasses at them — 'among crustaceans and things, just as little creatures, ever so inferior to the females. Mere hangers-on. Things you would laugh at. And among human beings, too, women to begin with were the rulers and leaders; they owned all the property, they invented all the arts. The primitive government was the Matriarchate. The Matriarchate! The Lords of Creation just ran about and did what they were told.'

'But is that really so?' said Ann Veronica.

'It has been proved,' said Miss Miniver, and added, 'by American professors.'

'But how did they prove it?'

'By science,' said Miss Miniver, and hurried on, putting out a rhetorical hand that showed a slash of finger through its glove. 'And now, look at us! See what we have become. Toys! Delicate trifles! A sex of invalids. It is we who have become the parasites and toys.'

It was, Ann Veronica felt, at once absurd and extraordinarily right.

A strong theme through the writings of feminists in the early 1970s, and in the surge of feminist culture around the turn of the century, during the prolonged feminist agitation for the vote (the suffragette movement), has been a search for alternative visions of history — and therefore the hope that the future can be built differently. Writers like Elizabeth Gould Davis *(The First Sex)* asserted that archaeological evidence showed the existence of original societies which were matriarchal, in which women held political, spiritual and social power. For these writers, the history of 'civilisation' was a history of the defeat of women, and the rise of a woman-hating, aggressive masculineculture, based on the rule of the fathers — patriarchy.

It's a seductive and poetic vision, offering the hope that once again women may regain the primacy they lost to men, and be valued and revered for their closeness to nature, their nurturing and tending, their maternity. And many other feminists find much of value in the vision, even while accepting that there probably was no real historical period of matriarchal rule, and that if there were, it came about because of the economic organisation of agricultural societies, worshipping fertility goddesses and centring social life round raising children and herds. Adrienne Rich, for example, values the myth of matriarchy for its reminder that earlier societies had what she calls 'gynocentric' or woman-centred visions of the universe and the organisation of human society. She believes that women, because they are mothers, actually see the world differently from men; that because all women have a special relationship to their bodies, they are conscious of the physical world in quite different ways from men. What she means, of course, is that all women have to manage their fertility, are conscious of their role in the continuation of life, experience their bodies as potentially reproductive, with the reminder of blood. Our society is organised round a masculine vision of the world, which lacks this organic link between the physical body and experience, and hence sees the 'mind' and the 'body' as opposites, with the intellect dominant.

How does it help us to know that the ancient Greeks gradually replaced 'mother right' with 'father right'? What is proved by the fact, authenticated though it seems, that women led the early clans who lived by agriculture; that the children they brought into the world belonged to them; that they continued to determine the inherited succession even in later, highly organised kingdoms; that they were the originators of all cults, of taboo and fetish, dance, song, and many early crafts? Doesn't this harking back to an irretrievable ancient past reveal more clearly than anything else the desperate plight in which women see themselves today?

From Christa Wolf CASSANDRA : A NOVEL AND FOUR ESSAYS (Virago, 1984).

THE MOTHER ΤΤΟ

went to the mothers. she's lonely.
the little men are slowly coming back.
the Valium isn't working.
she tells me in Greek: 'they learnt
about the world
thru our language'.
'they'd spit at you, in a glass of
water'.
she serves me up a salad:
vinegar, tomatoes, oil, onions,
radishes, lettuce,
(full of the smells of spring)
'keftethes', & a plate of potatoes
boiled in sauce.
'i didn't give you Valium'
'you or Athena'
'nor Thalia too'
'i didn't give you tablets'
i watch tv. she asks me: 'what are
they saying?'
i say: 'Dr Jim Cairns has resigned'.
she cries.

MOTHERS AND DAUGHTERS

THE relationship between mothers and daughters is almost entirely absent from our literature and folklore. There are father-daughter relationships — King Lear and his three daughters in Shakespeare; Elektra, daughter of Agamemnon, who incited her brother to avenge her father's death in Greek legend — but rarely any great imaginative works dealing with the relationships between mothers and girl children. It is true that mother-in-law/ daughter-in-law stories and jokes are stock cliches for female jealousy and bitchiness, and inter-generational conflicts, but these cliches probably say more about men than about women. No doubt it is immensely flattering to men to think of themselves being fought over by their mothers and their wives, two generations of women competing with each other to provide for men's comfort.

There are probably many reasons for this failure of our culture to be interested in that intense relationship between mother and daughter. One is that because women have been historically so powerless, so dependent on the whims of men for decisions about marriage, where to live, all the details of life, that there has been little dramatic material on which to build great literary characters. Another is that the relationship between mother and daughter was bound to be one of mutual loss — the mother losing her daughter to the family of the man she marries, the daughter losing her mother to the demands of brothers, father, other male authority figures in the family. It is hard to make great moral tragedy out of the everyday disappointments of powerless people, whose lives are ruled by others. And of course, women have simply not counted as much as men; men's lives were interesting, women's lives were drab drudgery for the majority, idle frivolity for the privileged few.

In the last few years there has been a change in this pattern of neglect of mother/daughter relationships. Many women have been going back over their childhood memories and recollections of growing up in their mothers' houses, trying to find in their own lives the threads of the pattern which seems to predispose each generation of women to self-sacrificing dependence on men

CHERYL YOUNGER

This image comes from a series taken during the pregnancy and birth of my daughter. I instinctively knew this was an important time and yet felt nothing. Great warmth, laughter and pleasure welled up in me as I drove into the Coral Fruit Market that day. Here was something I could relate to after months of feeling awkward and pubescent.

and children for emotional security. Or they have been re-examining their own feelings of hostility towards their mothers, trying to work out how and why they hold their mothers responsible for continuing the oppression of women. Or from the vantage point of greater understanding, better education and greater control over their own lives, they are thinking themselves back into their mothers' experiences, to find some thread of a sisterhood of women.

A great part of the impetus for this collective re-examination of our experience as our mothers' daughters comes from the realisation that feminism not only unites women, but also deeply divides them — that sisterhood is powerful when you can achieve it, but sometimes agonisingly difficult to reach. The roots of much of women's hostility towards other women lie in the roles that women play in the family: mothers are the

guardians of their daughters' virginity on behalf of the fathers, the ones who must train their daughters to restrain their desires for independence, repress their own longings and learn to respond to the needs of others. Contemporary adult daughters are at odds with the sexual values of their mothers, and have made very different life choices — work, postponing children, divorce — to the extent that many older women feel that women's liberation is a personal attack on all they have stood for, that their daughters despise them.

Another phenomenon, going alongside this feminist-inspired re-examination of the experience of being a daughter, is a series of exposés of the real lives of the Hollywood stars,

written by disillusioned daughters. (*Mommie Dearest*, by Joan Crawford' daughter Christina, and *My Mother's Keeper*, by Bette Davis's daughter B.D. Hyman, are two recent examples which spring to mind). The motivatio for these attacks is no doubt personal and various, but their cultural message is clear. They are contributions to the myth-making about the stars, that reinforces the moral that beautiful and ambitious women who have minds of their own, and the incentive as well as the opportunity to indulge themselves make bad mothers; that the price for fame and fortune for a woman is the loss of close relationships.

As fast as one part of the culture, changed by feminism, takes up the task of rehabilitating the mother/daughter relationship, the resistance sets in, and the walls of myth are re-erected. But increasingly that myth seems shallow, short on understanding and compassion.

MOTHERING

FEMINISTS are intensely interested in the part that women as mothers play in passing on expectations about proper roles for men and women, and, sometimes despite themselves, reproducing in their own families all the conditions that lead to women's sense of frustration and oppression. Some fundamental questions required hard answers — for example, if women were as life-affirming and nurturing as the new feminist scholarship suggested they were, how come the boy children women brought up turned out aggressive and domineering? Since it was perfectly clear that women did most of the bringing-up of children, and that fathers had very little part in it, why were women passing on the wrong sets of values?

Putting it bluntly, why were feminist mothers producing the sort of men they were criticising?

The debates are still going on, and we have listed in the bibliography some of the most important books on this subject, since it is impossible to summarise all the strands of the argument.

However, there are some common themes emerging. The argument goes like this:

Mothers are the primary parent, for both boys and girls; mothers do most of the caring and teaching of their children. But mothers have different attitudes towards girls and boys. In saying this, feminists are saying something much more important than merely pointing out how mothers teach girls to be girls, by giving them dolls to play with, and teach boys to be little men, giving them bicycles to explore the world with. If it were as simple as that, girls could be brought up to be like boys by simply giving them boys' playthings. The feminist argument is much more complex — they are saying that mothers have a different emotional relationship with girl children: a relationship which is marked by disappointments and frustrations that the mother feels about her own position as a woman in a man's world.

A mother has learned through her own experience that a woman's needs are not met, unless she is prepared to translate her own needs into a desire to make other people happy — a woman's need to be needed is her only legitimate expectation. A mother's experience has taught her that she will be relied on by her family for emotional support, so that women need to learn not to be selfish, not to put themselves and their emotional needs before the needs of others. To be a proper mother to her daughter, and give her the right emotional equipment to give her a chance to be happy, a mother must restrain her daughter's desire for independence.

On the other hand, boys can be unreservedly loved, while encouraged to become independent, and to see themselves as completely separate from their mothers. A girl is seen by her mother as a sort of extension of herself, and kept close by throughout childhood. Because of their very different relationship to their mothers, girls grow up with a less confident sense of their own personalities, more attuned to seeking approval from other people. Girls carry into their adult lives their mothers' ambivalent feelings about being female in a world which does not value women as strong individuals.

This, it is argued, is the real reason why women find sisterhood so difficult to achieve — it's not as simple as saying that women are in competition for men (which in itself is a very male-centred way of seeing the world!). Women feel ambivalent about other women because their mothers could not give them a self-esteem that they themselves lacked.

I always wanted to look like my father.

Eve Kessler

TransNational

BRIEF:

WOMEN
AND WORK

'After you've caused inflation and unemployment...
it's hard to think of what to cook for dinner.'

Registered for Posting as a Publication: Category B.

9 to 5 AND THE NIGHTSHIFT

NINE TO FIVE

DOLLY PARTON

Tumble outa bed and I stumble to the kitchen
Pour myself a cup of ambition
And yawn and stretch and try to come to life
Jump in the shower and the blood starts pumpin'
Out on the streets the traffic starts jumpin'
With folks like me on the job from nine to five

Workin' nine to five, what a way to make a livin'
Barely gettin' by, it's all takin' and no givin'
They just use your mind and they never give you credit
It's enough to drive you crazy if you'll let it
Nine to five, for service and devotion
You would think that I would deserve a better promotion
Want to move ahead but the boss won't seem to let me
I swear sometimes that man is out to get me

They let you dream just to watch 'em shatter
You're just a step on the bossman's ladder
But you got dreams he'll never take away
You're in the same boat with a lot of your friends
Waitin' for the day your ship'll come in
And the tide's gonna turn and it's all gonna roll your way.

Workin' nine to five, what a way to make a livin'
Barely gettin' by, it's all takin' and no givin',
They just use your mind and you never get the credit
It's enough to drive you crazy if you'll let it
Nine to five, yeah they got you where they want you
There's a better life, and you think about it don't you
It's a rich man's game, no matter what they call it
And you spend your life puttin' money in his pocket

MOST women work, in one way or another, just as most women are housewives, in one way or another. In this chapter we are juxtaposing women who work in the ordinary paid workforce, with women who work in the sex business, on the streets as prostitutes, or in massage parlours. What we are trying to do is to draw out the connections between women's sexuality and the work they do — to find out what 'women's work' is, and why it is different from 'men's work'.

WOMEN'S WORK IS NEVER DONE — BY MEN

In the Australian workforce, for every six men, there are nearly four women. One in two Australian women are at work. Two out of every three working women are married.

These figures show as clearly as anything could, that we are entirely mistaken to think of 'the workers' as men. 'The average worker' is almost as likely to be a woman — and not just a young woman straight from school, either, but a woman with a husband and children to look after. But despite these clear figures, the public image of 'the worker' is that of a skilled tradesman or bluecollar man in a boiler suit. Why does this image persist?

71

One very important reason is that men and women do different types of work — the workforce is divided up into men's jobs and women's jobs, with not much middle ground where men and women work together doing the same sort of work.

For example, over one third of the female work force is in clerical work, and four out of five women workers are in either clerical, sales, technical, professional or service work.

And women in clerical jobs are working alongside other women, rarely alongside men — over 70% of people working in clerical jobs are women.

This tendency for women to be clustered together in just a few occupations, segregated from the male workforce, is even more pronounced in service type occupations — think of nurses, shop assistants, telephonists, front counter assistants in government offices, receptionists, food preparers, workers in laundries and dry cleaners, office juniors — all the jobs where you need to deal with people, keep a sweet temper, anticipate people's needs, clean up after other people, and generally make other people's lives and work more pleasant and streamlined.

These are the visible female occupations. There are large numbers of women workers in more traditional bluecollar work, too — process workers in factories, machinists, spraypainters in vehicle manufacturers' plants, cleaners. More than half the women workers in the manufacturing sector are at the dirty end of the work — but they are largely invisible, because of the shifts they work, starting early and finishing early, because they are migrant women, because they don't join trade unions.

Our society doesn't encourage women to think of themselves as workers. One possible factor in this process of disguising the truth is that in many ways the work that women do in the workforce is a sort of extension of the work they do in the home, when they get home from work — servicing other people's lives.

'Women's work' is, compared to men's work, regarded as unskilled or less skilled. This is so irrespective of the actual amount of difficulty in the work, or the degree of adeptness required to be good at it. The point is made in the comparison with men's jobs. Nursing is a classic example. Ever since it became an organised profession in the mid-19th century, nursing has been female, from top to bottom. Medicine is male, nursing is female. Nurses are paid less (seen as less skilled?) than motor mechanics. In fact nursing is a highly skilled, and multi-skilled occupation, with a growing degree of responsibility and decision-making. In Australia nurse training has just been taken out of the learn-on-the-job hospital environment, and made into a course of tertiary study. The professionalisation of nursing has taken place at the same time as the entry of men into nursing in growing numbers

— most notably at the top — as nursing administrators take over from the personally powerful figure of The Matron.

There's another example of an occupation changing its sex, in banking. Twenty years ago bank tellers were young men, getting their feet on the bottom rung of the career ladder. Along comes the microchip, computerisation takes the mental arithmetic out of the teller's job, and hey presto, women start to replace the boys on the front counters of the banks. The career ladder now has a different bottom rung.

Broadly speaking, the introduction of new technologies like computerisation has rapidly produced a new division of skills, again along gender lines. So, women become the data processors, while the men go into programming and software development. Because so many of women's traditional jobs are the monotonous, repetitive ones which automation and computerisation are designed to replace, the impact of new technologies is falling disproportionately on women, with effects that are only just becoming apparent. The recent 'discovery' of RSI, repetition strain injury, which afflicts keyboard operators like word processor operators, and factory process workers, is one of the most obvious adverse effects of the new technologies on women workers.

Another obvious impact is that women's jobs often lose their skill component with the introduction of new technologies, as with the example given above of the sexual division of labour between data processing and computer programming. The supervisory elements of the old job are translated into whole new jobs, which often become male jobs.

Helen, at 9a.m., at noon, at 5.15

JUDY GRAHN

Her ambition is to be more shiny
and metallic, black and purple as
a thief at midday; trying to make it
in a male form, she's become as
stiff as possible.
Wearing trim suits and spike heels,
she says "bust" instead of breast;
somewhere underneath she
misses love and trust, but she feels
that spite and malice are the
prices of success. She doesn't realise
yet, that she's missed success, also,
so her smile is something still
genuine. After a while she'll be a real
killer, bitter and more wily, better at
pitting the men against each other
and getting the other women fired.
She constantly conspires.
Her grief expresses itself in fits of fury
over details, details taking the place of meaning,
money takes the place of life.
She believes that people are lice
who eat her, so she bites first; her
thirst increases year by year and by the time
the sheen has disappeared from her black hair,
and tension makes her features unmistakably
ugly, she'll go mad. No one in particular
will care. As anyone who's had her for a boss
will know
the common woman is as common
as the common crow.

72

Women in fulltime work earn only 78 cents for every dollar earned by their male counterparts. In some sectors, the figure is as low as 67 cents in the dollar.
These figures are not affected by the fact that more women than men work part-time; but they do reflect the fact that more men than women workers have overtime payments.
Equal pay for work of equal value became official government policy in 1972.

All these figures taken together show that women are clustered together in largely all-female occupations at the bottom of the skill ladder for their part of the workforce, earning less than men. Women's work is not valued as highly as men's work — so the formula 'equal pay for work of equal value' doesn't produce equal pay for women as a result.

It is fascinating to see new divisions of labour, new definitions of 'women's work' and 'men's work' settling in with the new technologies, and all the other great transformations taking place in the workforce. For a long time it has been argued that with better education, and a growing realisation in the community that women are in the workforce to stay, girls' opportunities will improve, their ambitions increase, and the general level of women's wages increase as they move into traditional male · occupations. Equal opportunity and anti-discrimination legislation has been drawn up on this principle — that all it needed was to convince employers that prejudice against women workers was counter-productive. But why are things changing so slowly?

The answer seems to be that this all-pervasive segregation of the world of work into men's work and women's work is not just some archaic hangover from the bad old days when women were supposed to cook, bear children and observe the rituals of religion (*Kinder, kirche, kuche,* in the words of Hitler).

It appears that it is extremely important for our society to maintain and where necessary, as things change, actually recreate ironclad distinctions between women's work and men's work. This observation has led many feminist researchers to turn their attention to the links between power structures, at work, at home and in society generally, and the maintenance of the division of labour between men and women. Specifically, of course, feminist researchers are interested in the sexual power structure, the system which appears to ensure that men are advantaged over women.

Many of the links between the 'sexual power structure' and the sexual division of labour become a lot clearer when we look at the phenomenon of sexual harassment of working women.

In the last ten years or so, the issue of sexual harassment of women at work has become a feminist issue, and finally come to the attention of the authorities. Not that there is anything particularly new in the reports of men propositioning, touching up, whistling, jeering at, trying to embarrass, or indeed sexually assaulting the women who work for them — think of the old tired office jokes about the secretary sitting on the boss's lap to take dictation. But two things have changed. First, women are speaking out, resisting, instead of quietly putting up with it or leaving in rage. Second, and this may be connected with women's resistance, there seems to be more, or more intense, sexual harassment around. There is speculation that this might be because some men are feeling that the balance of power in the work environment has changed against them, as women get the support of anti-discrimination legislation, feel more confident and determined to achieve better working conditions (as we will see in chapter 14, there's a very similar argument that the apparent increase in rape is due to feminism — men feeling threatened are fighting back in the crudest way possible, reminding women that whatever they may think of themselves, to men they're just meat).

There's probably some truth in this speculation. But there are a lot of other very complicated things going on in the sexual politics of the workplace. As we have shown, some jobs are actually changing their gender, turning from women's jobs into men's jobs, or vice versa, in response to changes in the workplace due to the introduction of new technologies. While there's nothing inherent in particular types of work that makes them men's work or women's work, there is something fixed and apparently unchanging about the need for a distinction between men's and women's work. In the process of changing over, there's a real struggle for power going on — and one of the strongest weapons men have is sexual power over women.

Another factor that may be involved, and for feminists this is a very controversial area, is that whereas the question of sexuality in the office used to be very clear, with men in the positions of power, now things are becoming blurred as women join the ranks of the bosses. There is some evidence beginning to emerge which shows that many *women* don't like working for female bosses, and one of the things they don't like is the idea of another woman having control over their lives, without the possibility of mild flirtation softening the blunt fact of power. In other words, mild flirtation with a male boss has been for some women workers a sort of compensation for powerlessness; with a female boss, there's no compensation, just the stark reminder that you're not as successful as she is. If this is true, the undercurrent of sexuality in the workplace has served the same function at work, as romance has in maintaining the allure of marriage — that is, disguising the naked truth of the power structure between the sexes.

It's going to be some time before the full picture becomes clear. But what is already becoming clear is that as women try to change the rules of the workplace, move into formerly male jobs, try to get the skill level of their own work recognised as being equivalent to that of male jobs, they will be increasingly confronting and challenging the sexual politics of the workplace.

Sandy Edwards

There is no doubt that for many women that daily tension of having to negotiate, manage or avoid sexual situations at work is the price they have to pay for trying to change the rules. The choices are hard: make too much fuss, and they'll say you are neurotic, imagining sexual threats where all they meant was good-natured joking; go along with it, try to be one of the boys, and they'll say you're leading them on. Meanwhile, there's a sort of quiet guerrilla warfare being carried on by the male resistance fighters, in the form of deliberate displays of nude girlie pinups on the walls of factories, constant low level barrages of sexual innuendo, as they resist the pressures on their sense of themselves as men doing a man's work.

At the same time as they are beginning to analyse and understand the sexual politics of the workplace, feminists are taking a close look at that other traditionally female occupation, prostitution, to see how power relations, economic factors and sexuality are woven together there.

The twin images of the good girl and the prostitute, the madonna and the whore, have just about circumscribed the range of possibilities for women for centuries. Feminists have often turned the distinction on its head, in order to reveal the true position of women. So, for example, the 17th century feminist critics pointed out that the most respectable married women in their society were really engaged in a form of prostitution, having sold their bodies to a man out of dire economic necessity, having neither the education nor the opportunity to work to support themselves. Contemporary feminists are pointing out that a prostitute really is what she calls herself, a 'working girl', working to support herself and working to keep the sexual power structure intact. Contemporary feminists are pointing out that there are many subtle similarities between the sort of service work that women do as receptionists, sales assistants, secretaries, and the service role that prostitutes play. Seventeenth century feminists were drawing parallels between prostitution and the only alternative form of work then available — marriage. Contemporary feminists are drawing parallels between prostitution and other forms of work. The purpose of the comparison is the same in both cases — to draw attention to the way the sexual power structure turns women against other women, and ultimately advantages men.

In Business
ROBYN ARCHER/ANDREW BELL

They say Miss Babette's tough as nails
Well sure, she's a business girl with a head and a body
for business
She'll tell you, 'I only got into the game
'Cos a girl's gotta make a crust
So what if they bust you occasionally?
(It sure beats cleaning dunnies.)'

They say Miss Babette's happy in her work
Well sure, she's a professional taking pride in the
oldest profession
She'll tell you, 'I look great, my body's a good one
So I can sell it, take it back, sell it again
The name of the game's free enterprise
(It sure beats *giving* it away in the old "cook for you clean
for you" racket.)'

So don't come on so strong
With your movies, poems and songs
About the gold-hearted whore
You know she don't hang round here no more
I ain't no sinner, ain't no saint
Your kind of morals are only as deep as my face paint — I'm
just in business

They say Miss Babette's sick of the cops
Well sure, they turn a blind eye today; have you arrested
tomorrow
She'll tell you, 'I just want to ply my trade
This woman's part of the business sector
Legalise her and protect her, you dogs
(It sure beats being a hypocrite *all* your life.)'

They say Miss Babette's tough as nails
Well sure, she's a business girl with a head and a body for
business
She'll tell you, 'I only got into the game
'Cos a girl's gotta make a crust
You understand, I trust, that
                    — I'm just in business.'

But it is very important not to get carried away by the metaphors. Prostitution is a different kind of work, precarious, often deadly dangerous, not particularly well-paid, in which a woman literally has to put her body on the line, and for which she is despised by straight society, including most of her customers.

Most researchers who have studied prostitution have been interested in it as a deviant kind of sexual behaviour, and have been interested in understanding why some women choose the trade, why even larger numbers of men patronise the trade. They are interested in what women and men get out of it, and what the continued existence of prostitution despite the sexual revolution of the last two decades tells us about the sexual needs of men (why do they pay when they can get it for free?).

Don't Put Her Down You Helped Put Her There

HAZEL DICKENS

You pull the string
She's your plaything
You can make her or break her it's true
You abuse her
Accuse her
Turn around and use her
And forsake her any time it suits you.

Well there's more to her than powder and paint
And her peroxided bleached-out hair
Well if she acts that way it's 'cause you've had your day
Don't put her down you helped put her there.

She hangs around playin' the clown
While her soul is aching inside
She's heartbreak's child
'Cause she just lives for your smile
To build her up in a world made by men.

CHORUS

At the house down the way
You sneak and you pay
For her love her body or her shame
Then you call yourself a man
Say that you just don't understand
How a woman could turn out that way.

Well there's more to her than powder and paint
And the men she picks up at the bar
Well if she acts that way it's 'cause you've had your day
Don't put her down you helped put her there.

Well if she acts that way it's 'cause you've had your day
Don't put her down you helped put her there.

This sort of research produces what one feminist wittily describes as the 'hydraulic theory of male sexuality'*— the idea that men (but not women) are subject to urgent sexual needs, which set up a 'pressure' in society which produces prostitution.

Other researchers have concentrated on the relationship between prostitution and other work opportunities for women. Most feminist research has been along these lines, carrying on the tradition of analysis from the 17th century. What is now being done is fascinating work on the links between the economic circumstances of prostitution and the sexual circumstances of prostitution — in much the same way as the analysis of sexual harassment of working women is making the links between changing economic circumstances in the workplace, and threats to the male monopoly of power.

Eileen McLeod, in her book *Women Working: Prostitution Now*, has studied and interviewed both prostitute women and their clients. The quotations in the rest of this chapter come from that book, as do the insights into the nature of prostitution.

Clients sometimes express gratitude to prostitutes — which fits in with the widely held belief that prostitution will always exist because it answers some deep need in men. But what sort of need is it? Is it to do with a need for variety, for urgent sexual release when no more intimate relationship is possible? Are men's needs in this respect so different from those of women?

Charles: '*Men are lucky, if we've got the money we can have the pleasure of dishy young women. Girls can't have that.*'

Paul, a male prostitute: '*It's the same needs. But they (women) have to be the only one. It's unacceptable to them that they should have to be paying for it. ...I don't mean that it's love they think they're having, it is sex; but even so, they have to think they're the only one.*'

The difference here between what women want from a male prostitute and what men expect from a woman probably has a lot to do with issues of power and control in sexual relations, rather than with any innate difference between the sexual needs of men and women. Men who go with prostitutes are not at all concerned that they are only a client, because they are used to being in control; money is buying something they want, and something that has a value and a price. It's a commercial transaction. For a woman in the same situation of paying for sex, money has not bought her control of the transaction — money has just put her into the position of being able to display a need. But she has not changed the rules of the sexual game. She still needs the illusion that she's special.

Consider the way in which male street prostitutes approach women and the way women approach men. The male prostitute is snappily dressed, perhaps in a sharp suit, maybe in macho jeans and belt — at all events, he's covered. There's no standing exposed on a street corner with his buttocks flimsily covered and his shirt unbuttoned to the waist in the chill winds of the early morning. He's in control. He could simply walk away from the beat and be absolutely unremarkable, passing for a normal guy. The women are marked, exposed, not women but prostitutes, 'common' (in the original meaning of the word common, and the meaning of the legal phrase, 'a common prostitute', free to be used by everyone).

So the existence of prostitution may not be explained by saying that men have powerful sexual urges that must be satisfied; the existence of prostitution must be explained by the freedom which society grants to men to seek sexual gratification in all sorts of ways — it's a freedom granted by society, not an eternal and enduring characteristic of male sexuality. What we are looking at is power again — the power of ordinary men to have social arrangements ordered in such a way that their wants can be satisfied.

For Eileen McLeod, this aspect of prostitution comes out very clearly in the way that men talk about what they get from prostitutes that they can't get anywhere else.

David: '*The massage parlour provided almost in a sense a role reversal. Perhaps that's too strong — at least a role shift. Here is the woman doing to the man. I like that and don't get that at home.*'

Davy: '*I go there because I know I can lie down and just leave it to the girls, that's right.*'

Frederick: '*What I get from going to a prostitute is partly the freedom of not having to do things the way your wife wants you to do them... I know from my own point of view... I've felt very inadequate. She tells me in no uncertain terms which doesn't make it any better. This is something I don't have to worry about...*'

* Mary McIntosh 'Who Needs Prostitutes? The Ideology of Male Sexual Needs'.

Although most of the men Eileen McLeod interviewed were very anxious to keep their involvement with prostitutes a close secret, and said that they do not talk about it even with male friends, she discovered that 'both clients and prostitutes described men going to saunas in pairs or larger groups. Hiring or visiting prostitutes as adjuncts to business trips or conventions or to celebrate business deals emerged as an unexceptional part of business life from my interviews with clients from the echelons of upper management or business ownership.'

So prostitution exists because, among other things,

- **men can afford to pay for sexual variety without compromising their marriages**
- **going to a prostitute allows men a self centred sexual experience without the responsibility of intimacy**
- **it enables men to demonstrate their power over women**
- **for women it appears to offer the chance of self-employment without any outlays of capital, and with flexible working hours, and without entry qualifications.**

If, as these insights suggest, prostitution and women's work generally share many complex features, centred around economic, sexual and power factors, why is prostitution illegal? What should our response to prostitution be?

Well, the first observation to make is that it is intolerable that only the prostitute, and not the client, is penalised under existing laws. It is intolerable because prostitution exists to serve the interests of men, not the interests of women. It is the grossest hypocrisy for the law to pretend otherwise.

But the fact that the law penalises the prostitute and not the client may give us the answer to the question of why the trade is illegal. One tired old answer is that prostitution is made illegal to protect the institution of marriage, and thereby protect the interests of women. If that were true, adultery would still be illegal. And as many prostitutes argue, with bitter irony, the service they provide props up the institution of marriage, by giving men access to sexual variety.

All the evidence points in one direction. Prostitution is illegal because conventional society is offended by the sight of women selling their sexuality; prostitutes are bad women, preying on the sexual weakness of men. Prostitutes demean sex, cheapen women. Prostitutes are dangerous sexual creatures — or so runs the thread of official thinking.

But why should the weight of the criminal law be brought to bear to maintain a fantasised view of female sexuality for the advantage of variety-seeking men, at the expense of the liberty and dignity of the women involved? There probably is no answer to this question, which goes deep into the murky depths of the history of official attempts to control and regulate sexuality. There are all sorts of convenient rationalisations offered for continuing the criminalisation of prostitution — usually to do with controlling the offensive behaviour of the clients, protecting the safety of 'innocent women' or maintaining the amenities of the neighbourhood. None of these rationalisations bear up under the close examination. For example, the creation of red-light areas in working class districts, where women cannot afford to work indoors, in fact puts all women on the streets there at risk from men cruising in cars, propositioning and hurling abuse.

The great debate, and the ground on which feminists have to take a stand, is between legalising prostitution, and regulating it in massage parlours and designated red-light districts, or simply decriminalising prostitution, saying that it has nothing to do with the law at all, neither the criminal law, nor any other law.

Feminists are opposed to legalising prostitution, in the sense of turning it into a legal business, catering for the tourist trade and men in general, a sexual service station. This would mean accepting that women's bodies are a commodity over which society should have some say. In this case it would mean granting to the state the right to say when and where a woman could exchange sex for money. It is allowing the state to say that these women are different from other women, that prostitution is a problem about women. It would mean institutionalising the view that women's bodies are generally available to men — it would be adding one more approved avenue to them: marriage, or money. It would mean giving credence to the idea that with women, sex and being in the workforce go together, thus undermining the campaign against sexual harassment.

On the other hand, it is intolerable for the present situation to be allowed to continue. Even more than is the case with legalisation, the present laws against soliciting make it appear that the problem with prostitution is a problem with women; the laws as they stand really only protect men against the unwelcome sexual solicitations of prostitutes! Feminists sometimes toy with the satisfying idea of turning the tables, and prosecuting the clients not the women, but this would mean denying to a woman the right to use her body as she wishes.

So the lesser of the evils is decriminalisation — simply doing away with the laws which treat prostitutes as different, and what they do as criminal. Although this would seem to be condoning the state of affairs we have described as being organised to suit the interests of men, and as being against the interests of all women, compared to the alternatives it is the best option.

As a strategy, decriminalisation looks like this to feminists:

---

it recognises that prostitution is attractive to women mainly because it requires no training, the pay is comparatively good, there is the opportunity to work hours that suit childcare responsibilities. Legalisation would take away many of these features.

Unlike legalisation, decriminalisation does not create a class of recognised registered prostitute women whose function it is to relieve sexual tensions in society. Decriminalisation allows the possibility of casual work. It does not institutionalise sex for sale as a permanent feature of society.

So, as far as is possible, this strategy separates out the economically exploitative aspects of prostitution from the sexually exploitative aspects, and deals with each separately.

Feminists go after the institution of prostitution; the state goes after the individual women. That's the difference.

When the Yorkshire Ripper killed only prostitutes, there was fear; when he killed what the police and media described as an 'innocent girl', there was outrage. Question: what were the prostitutes guilty of that would warrant a death sentence?

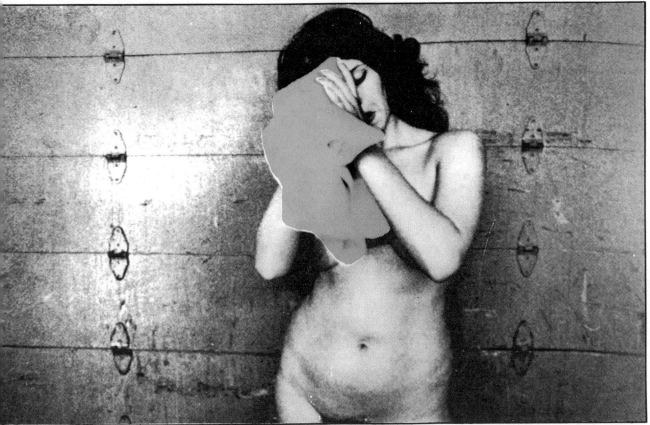

Susan Meiselas

CINDY

It's too much hassle being a girl on a girls' show. I figure a woman's place is in a house, but I ain't got no house to go to. I don't want to be equal… The only thing women are on earth for is having babies, and taking care of men and satisfying them, that's the way I feel. It's right for a woman to just be a housewife or be a stripper, it shows you're a woman. I figure if I work at it, I can get my own show and then I won't have to worry about going up there and doing it myself.

I've been working as hard as I can, and I've been saving all the money I can, and every time I turn around, someone's ripping me off. I honestly have been thinking about becoming gay, because all men want is a piece of ass and the money and they say, 'Well, chick-a-boom, you can't make me any more money, I'll see you around.'

THINGS ARE SO SLOW

BARBARA DANE

Went to work this morning, I was all set to start
The boss comes up and says something that really broke my heart
He said things are so slow, we just don't need you anymore

Went home and told my man, he didn't make a fuss
But then the finance took the car and now we're ridin' on the bus
And now we're walkin' so slow, we won't be ridin' anymore

Just one thing about it, that really blows my mind,
The boss is still sellin' what I made last week
And I can't even sell my time
Because things are so slow they just don't need it any more

We told the prime minister, we need more jobs in the nation
Do you know what that fool said? She said 'Unemployment stops inflation'
Well the woman's so slow, we just don't need her anymore

We got to get ourselves together, talk the whole thing down
Make a little plan for shakin' up the town
Because things are so slow, we just can't take it any more
Because things are so slow
We just can't make it, might have to break it, don't try to fake it
We just can't take it anymore.

This picture of women at work may not seem very familiar with its stress on the links between women's position in the sexual power structure and their economic position. But it is important to draw out these connections, not least because the media image of the women's liberation movement is that of a bunch of disgruntled middle-class women wanting a smooth ride to the top, and not willing to take account of what their sisters at the bottom of the heap really want.

At the bottom there are real wants and needs. Working women are in large proportion married women: 45% of married women with children are in the workforce. These women need good reliable childcare; the compulsory education system seems to be about the limit of state-provided childcare, even after all these years of official recognition of women's right to work.

In Factories
SANDRA WETHERALD

In summer
when the heat is on my eyes
I sign the time and come to work.
A hood is tied around my shoulders
with a rope that hanged my mother
an heirloom I prize
from time to time.
There is a clock bound to my arm.

I say: I am a time-bomb
my secret violence breeds in the summer sun
they sit in bloated cars
and blink their innocence as
blind
the sun heats down in sudden
glares
they smile vaguely as I come to work
these gentile groovers

I tick tick tick
one day I shall blow them all to death
and I, in true hatred,
shall tick myself to death beside them
I laugh insanely mine the right to madness
my eyes are secret
they never see the movement of my hands
and who could understand the anonymous
poetry
I whisper in my sleep
I am secret tick tick tick.

alarm
still in summer ticks the alarm
that reads the time
and still I walk to work.

Migrant women are triply disadvantaged, as workers, as migrants and as women.

It is the women who do the least skilled worst paid, routine and repetitive jobs.

WAITING TOO LONG
ROBYN ARCHER/ANDREW BELL

I'm thirty-six years old, not too good at English
Came from the Old Country to start a new life
Packing cardboard boxes in a tin shed in Melbourne
Underpaid as a worker, underpaid as a wife,

We've been waiting too long for the equal wages
Waiting too long for the equal rights
Bound to days of endless sweated labour
Go home to the family, sweat for them all night

I'm only sixteen and I'm working sixty hours
Glueing plastic gadgets all marked 'Made in Taiwan'
The money I make won't even keep me in sandals
The boys'd make double, so they take us young girls on

CHORUS:

You know, things might have improved for the girls on the top rung
The glossy magazines are saying 'What's all the fuss?'
But if you're looking to see the signs of equal rights
You sure ain't gonna find it by looking at us.

CHORUS:

Working women need equal pay, and equal access to all areas of the workforce, if they are to achieve the goal of economic independence. Working women need changes in the organisation of family life, for men to recognise that sharing the housework means taking responsibility for shopping, cooking, childcare, and not merely responding to pleas for help. Working women need changes in the organisation of the working day, to take account of the fact that all workers — not just female workers — have domestic responsibilities.

But we would be fooling ourselves, and demeaning the struggles that working women have made and are making to change their lives for the better, if we were to think that it is only prejudice that stands in the way of the changes that are needed. We need to see how our ideas of masculinity and femininity are shaped by, and in turn shape, the way we categorise work as suitable for women, the way in which sexuality is tied in with the power structure of the workplace, the ways in which women's role in the family and in the workplace subtly shade into each other.

Bianca Jagger *Andy Warhol*

THE LADIES WHO LUNCH

This chapter is about two kinds of responses to feminism, from two kinds of women. Those who have given this chapter their name, The Ladies Who Lunch, we will describe later in this chapter. They are opposed to feminism because they think it takes all the fun out of being a woman.

FIRST, let us look at that other women's movement, which has been growing in direct opposition to feminism. These are the Women Who Want To Be Women, the anti-feminist activists (sometimes frivolously dubbed as the Women Who Want To Be Doormats); they have the active support of fundamentalist Christian organisations, and the intellectual support of right-wing political organisations. In Australia and the United States, in particular, the movement is made up of extremely competent, articulate and sophisticated women, as well as seemingly unsophisticated, naive and artless churchwomen of indeterminate middle age. They are internationalist in their perspectives and political organisation, sending emissaries from one country to another to help fight the good fight against liberal abortion laws, pornography, liberal educational philosophies, relaxed prohibitions on male homosexuality, and, in their latest campaign, reproductive technologies and genetic experimentation (for example, test-tube babies and other techniques which involve creation of human embryos).

They are fighting on the terrain marked out by feminism, and in some cases using the language of women's liberation, but their basic assumptions about women, men, sexuality and society are the complete reverse of those of feminists.

At this point it's good to pause and take stock of the opposition, and look at the reasons why many women feel compelled to say, before making some brave statement about how they have faced and overcome pressures from men, 'I'm no women's libber, far from it, but... I believe in equality, a fair go.'

DANGER

Why does feminism seem so threatening, and sometimes such an impenetrable system of ideas, styles, ways of living that it puts women off? And how, at the same time, does it appear to the Women Who Want To Be Women to be part of a great government supported conspiracy against decent living and the future of the Christian family? What is it about feminism, or the condition of women's lives, that makes this movement for women's liberation seem to embody so many people's worst fears?

The right-wing women, the Women Who Want To Be Women, share many of the insights of feminists into women's condition, but draw completely opposite conclusions about what is to be done. So, for example, they will agree with radical feminists that the root cause of women's inferior position is male sexuality and violence, that the world is a dangerous place for a woman. But their solution is to insist on upholding the rules of the traditional marriage and family structure. In the traditional respect paid to motherhood, they see women's hope for safety. Conventional roles for women and men offer certainty for everybody, reduce the pressure on men who feel their manhood threatened by newly strident women, and thereby lower the potential for sexual violence. Conventional women's roles are important to society and civilisation, because women are the tamers of violent men, the instillers of respect for women and authority in their children, and the pivot of the family, that 'haven in a heartless world'. So in a very real sense they see any analysis of the stunting effects of traditional female roles as an attack on women's security. Theirs is a fundamentally pessimistic view of human nature, which has us hovering on the brink of barbarism, any change in the balance of forces likely to precipitate us over the edge. Men's potential for violence needs to be restrained by the virtue of good women. 'Bad' women, such as prostitutes and sexually promiscuous girls, are thrown to the wolves as a sort of hostage to fortune — these right-wing women often promote the theory that although it is regrettable, prostitution is necessary for the overall health of society because it provides 'outlets' for sexually deprived or perverted men, who would otherwise prey on 'innocent' girls and women.

Notions of innocence which should be rewarded figure prominently in the social analysis of these women, and surfaced particularly strongly in the panic over AIDS (Acquired Immune Deficiency Syndrome). One of the most consistent themes in public discussion of AIDS has been the concern that the disease will spread into 'the general population' — i.e. instead of killing mainly homosexual men it will spread to 'innocent', although sexually promiscuous, heterosexuals. Human society is seen as comprising only the basically good and decent people; others are quite literally outside society from the point of view of fundamentalist moralists. And therefore quite properly beyond the concern of the good and decent, whose own security is put at risk by having any dealings with them, their poisonous and contagious views, their life-denying lifestyles.

It's a view of human society which has many superficial resemblances to ecological theories about how living organisms coexist in nature, using ideas of fine balance, the fragility of that balance, the irreversibility of any damage done. Perhaps that is one of the reasons why this type of reaction to feminism has such a wide appeal, even to people not particularly religiously oriented — the feeling of living on the brink, of only just keeping at bay an overwhelming pessimism, is characteristic of these times of high unemployment, nuclear arms escalation, and worldwide social and political upheaval.

The link with religious feelings is easy to explain. As Andrea Dworkin says, 'religion shrouds women in real as well as magical grace', honouring motherhood, honouring

submission to the will of God, honouring obedience to clearly laid-down rules of sexual and moral conduct. Wi the proviso that it only applies to *good* women, religion does say that 'women are wonderful'. Women are the creators and nurturers of life — and that, say the Wome Who Want To Be Women, ought to be enough for any womanly woman.

And the Women Who Want To Be Women can be ve astute. They rely on ideas about female solidarity, all women sticking together, and throw these up against th supposed selfishness of feminists. With absolute accurac they point out that working conditions and wages for women are on the whole appalling, that women in the workforce will face the double day of paid work and housework, that they will be undervalued by the men th work with or for, that they will be burdened by the guilt of leaving their children with strangers, that most areas 'women's work' in the paid workforce are deadend jobs without much personal satisfaction. And this is the bargain that the feminists want you to make, they say, t give up the pleasures of a true woman's life in the family for a life of drudgery outside.

And on another tack, one which throws you complete off guard if you think of these women only as puritanica moralists, the Women Who Want To Be Women have also scored against feminism by alleging that feminism promotes joyless, loveless sex, or turns women against se and men altogether. They argue that *feminism* is earnest and moralistic, and in books like *The Total Woman* ext feminine sexual playfulness (within marriage, of course) the foundation of a happy marriage and a satisfied man.

The key to all their perceptions of the good, and campaigns against the bad, lies in whatever promotes traditional family values, respect and reverence for women, and restraint of aggressive men.

As Andrea Dworkin put it, in her book *Right Wing Women*, the movement offers women 'safety, shelter, rules, form and love' in exchange for submission and obedience to their essential feminine natures. The movement has 'succeeded in getting women as women (women who claim to be acting in the interests of womer as a group) to act effectively in behalf of male authority over women, in behalf of a hierarchy in which women ar subservient to men, in behalf of women as the rightful property of men, in behalf of religion as an expression o transcendental male supremacy. It has succeeded in getting women to act effectively against their own democratic inclusion in the political process, against thei own civil equality, against any egalitarian conception of their own worth.'

So, in the United States, the campaign by right-wing women's groups against the Equal Rights Amendment (ERA) succeeded on two main grounds. First, they argue that ERA would mean that women would be forced into conscription into the armed forces on the same basis as men. Second, they argued that ERA would force women to have abortions. How did they manage to convince a majority of voters that an amendment to the Constitution which would have enshrined women's right in the law of the land would have had the reverse effect, o taking away fundamental freedoms from women?

Basically, they were successful by arguing that the only guarantee of women's rights is a strong family-based society. They argued that the state intrudes on people's freedoms, and therefore any state-supported campaign fo women's equality is just another way for the state to take control away from families. If some selfish women campaigning for abortion rights succeed in repealing the laws against abortion, and having their right to abortion written into the law, it's just a short step further to total control of women's reproductive lives; a right to abortion will turn into compulsory abortion.

'We haven't been getting the hundreds that they do at those feminist meetings,' [she] said. 'But we have what we call the quality women — those really concerned about the family.'

'I have chosen to be a mother and this government is discriminating against me,' she said. 'There is no encouragement given to women like myself, and the role of the man as breadwinner is being constantly undermined with all this affirmative action.'

It is fascinating, but chilling too, to see how in the political thinking of the Women Who Want To Be Women, feminists — who think of themselves as being in opposition to state control of women's lives, male control of women's lives, church or medical control of women's lives — loom up as the causes of the oppression of women, the allies and agents of the state. And how the very act of *analysing* a problem somehow *creates* that problem: if feminists point out how marriage is often a state of unhappiness for women, they are blamed for that state of affairs. If feminists campaign for better treatment and childcare facilities for single mothers and their children, they are accused of forcing women into dependence on the state. In the thinking of the right-wing movement, feminists create the problems by suggesting that there are alternative ways of organising society, which do not require men and women to conform to the roles laid down for them in the traditional family structure.

Far removed from the traditional values of the Women Who Want To Be Women are the Ladies Who Lunch, the women of leisure who are the apostles of an exaggerated ideal of femininity, dedicated to fashion, style and narcissism. They are impatient with the 'stridency' of feminism, bored with the effort of hard thinking about the position of women; cynical about the motives of women who campaign for the rights of other women; and above all, determined to preserve an ideal of femininity which is all about being clever, sexy, and manipulative. They deplore the ugliness of what they think is a 'feminist look' — like not shaving your legs, or not wearing makeup. Although they are not in any sense an organised movement, their influence is great, because in a confused sort of way most women's magazines are speaking their language, while at the same time putting out a modified version of self-determination inspired by feminism.

A note on language: feminism has been fighting on the linguistic front since the beginning. One of the earliest distinctions made was between 'lady' and 'woman'. 'Lady' is typically used to describe a woman who conforms to the model of femininity current at the time — and hence, in feminist analysis, is an honorific which disguises a lack of a real respect for the woman underneath. Sometimes, too, 'lady' carries definite overtones of contempt, probably carried over from its association with the idle rich. 'Woman', on the other hand, positively resonates with strength and warm feelings, and sisterhood — even though it has a multitude of contemptuous uses too, such as 'get into the kitchen, woman!' or 'I'll get my woman to make you some dinner.' So using 'lady' in a feminist context means a deliberate irony is intended.

THE ANTI-SUFFRAGISTS
CHARLOTTE PERKINS GILMAN

Fashionable women in luxurious homes,
With men to feed them, clothe them, pay their bills,
Bow, doff the hat, and fetch the handkerchief;
Hostess or guest, and always so supplied
With graceful deference and courtesy;
Surrounded by their servants, horses, dogs —
These tell us they have all the rights they want.

Successful women who have won their way
Alone, with strength of their unaided arm,
Or helped by friends, or softly climbing up
By the sweet aid of 'women's influence':
Successful anyway, and caring naught
For any other woman's unsuccess —
These tell us they have all the rights they want.

Religious women of the feebler sort —
Not the religion of a righteous world,
A free, enlightened, upward-reaching world,
But the religion that considers life
As something to back out of! — whose ideal
Is to renounce, submit, and sacrifice,
Counting on being patted on the head
And given a high chair when they get to heaven —
These tell us they have all the rights they want.

Ignorant women — college-bred sometimes,
But ignorant of life's realities
And principles of righteous government,
And how the privileges they enjoy
Were won with blood and tears by those before —
Those they condemn, whose ways they now oppose;
Saying 'Why not let well enough alone?' —
These tell us they have all the rights they want.

And selfish women — pigs in petticoats —
Rich, poor, wise, unwise, top or bottom round,
But all sublimely innocent of thought,
And guiltless of ambition, save the one
Deep, voiceless aspiration — to be fed!
These have no use for rights or duties more.
Duties to-day are more than they can meet,
And law insures their right to clothes and food —
These tell us they have all the rights they want.

And, more's the pity, some good women, too;
Good conscientious women, with ideas;
Who think — or think they think — that women's cause
Is best advanced by letting it alone;
That she somehow is not a human thing,
And not to be helped on by human means,
Just added to humanity — an 'L' —
A wing, a branch, an extra, not mankind —
These tell us they have all the rights they want.

And out of these has come a monstrous thing,
A strange, down-sucking whirlpool of disgrace,
Women uniting against womanhood,
And using that great name to hide their sin!
Vain are their words as that old king's command
Who set his will against the rising tide.
But who shall measure the historic shame
Of these poor traitors — traitors are they all —
To great Democracy and Womanhood!

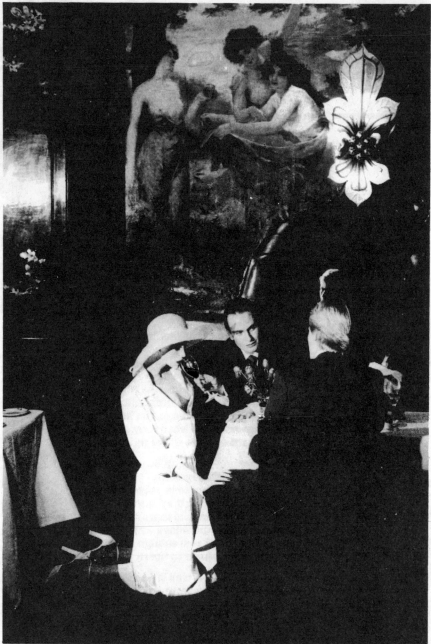

Business Lunch   *Helmut Newton*

Take fashion, for example. There are several problems with fashion. For one thing, it takes no special feminist insight to note that historically, a concern with fashionable dressing emphasises a woman's status as the property and ornament of a wealthy man —Thorstein Veblen pointed this out in his *Theory of the Leisure Class* in the 1890s. Fashion is a display of wealth, conspicuous consumption, showing that there is enough money to dress purely for pleasure, that a man's wife doesn't have to earn her own living. Well, this is less true these days, now that style and fashion have become part of everyday consumption for women.

A much more practical, as well as symbolic, difficulty with much fashionable dressing is the way it has physically constrained women. In Victorian times the classic example was corseting and bustles, the sheer bulk and weight of rigid garments immobilising the wearers.

Clothing of this type also carries all sorts of erotic messages, with the bustle emphasising the fullness of a woman's buttocks, the lacing forcing her into a fragile hourglass shape, both voluptuous and easily broken — a complex double message of fullness and vulnerability, surely appealing to the erotic sensibilities of the age, while swathing her in layers of protective covering, to preserve her modesty. For our own times, the erotic messages of the stiletto heel and the slit skirt seem pretty clear — so clear, in fact, that they can safely be parodied by the wearer. But ten years ago it was revelatory to realise, all over again, how high heels make a woman vulnerable in the street at the same time as they give a pleasing shape to calves and buttocks. 'All over again', because 19th century feminist activists had self-consciously promoted 'dress reform' as part of their campaigns for a more rational society, which would encourage women to discard their assumed frivolity and take up the duties of a citizen with all due thought and care.

(They advocated divided skirts, and looser clothing for women, and sensible knickerbockers and jackets for men. They were dismissed as cranks. Changes in clothing styles came about for other reasons, including the First World War and the introduction of bicycles, and motor cars.)

The privileges of femininity include a high permissible level of self-indulgence, in clothes, ornamentation, attention to one's body, cooking and food; as well as permission — to gossip, to care intensely about relationships, to be emotional, frivolous at times; to leave hard decisions to other people; to be evacuated first (with the children) from burning buildings or hi-jacked planes; to leave sexual initiatives to the man; to have an honourable excuse for failing to have a satisfying career. Some, if not most of these, are pleasures worth preserving; but as we have been showing, they are not unmixed privileges. There's a fine line between saying that feminine self-indulgence in clothes and appearance is a privilege, or a burden of compulsion — anxiety and guilt are to be found on both sides of that line.

So that's the third difficulty with fashion: its erotic content. Not that there's anything inherently wrong with carrying erotic messages around, but that the question of sexual identity and freedom of choice about the context of those erotic messages is, as we have seen, very problematic for women (see especially chapters 13 and 14). And its association with artificiality and female vulnerability, and stock images of femininity, makes fashion an area of confusion and anxiety for feminist women.

It's a complex area. For one thing, it's possible to see the influence of feminism on mainstream women's fashion — both in direct reflections, by more assertive styles, like the big-shouldered inverted triangle shape currently in vogue; and in a sort of indirect half-homage, half-opposition, such as the return of the '40s draped bottom, small waisted look *also* currently in vogue. So it would be fatuous to see only women's bondage and status as sex-object in the shapes of women's fashion, or to see only the desires of men and not the desires of women in the erotic and sensual messages our clothes carry. But it is even less sensible to see, as do the Ladies Who Lunch, some unambiguous expression of something called 'femininity', made by women for women, to be defended against critical analysis by kill-joy feminists. While the strong message of feminism is that women are made, not born, the even stronger message is that the lady is a pure creation of femininity, not an expression of the essence of women's natures.

So in an odd way, the anti-feminism of the Women Who Want To Be Women, and the anti-feminism of the Ladies Who Lunch, turn out to be based in fairly similar ideas about an unchanging female nature. For those who want to be Women, female nature is to do with motherhood and family; for those who want to be Ladies, it is to do with the privileges of femininity, which are bought by being pleasing to the senses of men.

The most difficult challenge thrown up by the more astute of the right-wing anti-feminists is the charge that feminists are making women suffer unnecessary guilt and anxiety about their proper role, and that all the supposed advantages of economic independence and sexual choice are illusory: that nothing could be less like freedom than living alone with small

SIZE TEN
ROBYN ARCHER

Size Ten's got boyish hips, Size Ten's got painted lips
The beauty boys are crackin' the whips over
Size Ten, try to be like them.
You'll hate yourself if you're not, mmm when you're hot you're hot,
You gotta re-arrange whatever you've got
You might even have to discard the lot
In your head, in your bed, till you're dead, you won't rate, till you emulate
Size Ten, we'll say it again
Wouldn't it be great to be in that state, Size Ten.

Mmmm, and when I look inside that mirror
Mmm, you know I don't like what I see
Mmm, I have to run and put my clothes on,
Mmm, then at last I can recognise me.

It's the size of the tit, you know it just don't fit
Into the latest dresses if you wanna make a hit
So you squeeze and you shove, honey, bit by bit
Into Size Ten, try to be like them.
And it's the shape of my thighs, they just won't compromise
Into new season's tight fitting pants
Or the image of a model in a hot romance
Such a cost, and I'm tossed, till I'm lost
Feel the frost, when you're always bein' bossed by
Size Ten, we'll say it again
Aah, wouldn't it be great to be in that state, Size Ten

Mmm, and don't I wish I could get out of it
The fears and the hatred of the body that belongs to me
Mmm, I'd really like to see it through loving eyes
The way a lover might see it and love it and tell me and let me be

This thing is causin' me a lot of confusion,
I'm gettin' to feel it's just a grand illusion
Maybe this face and body that I'm usin'
Shouldn't be like them, and nothin' like Size Ten
I'm only hittin' this old world once
And I'd have to be some kinda dunce
To want to hate and change the body I've grown
Till the one I've got already's better known to me
So I'm through, with all you, what you do
Makes me blue, always tryin' to pursue the elusive
Size Ten, we'll say it again
Aah wouldn't it be great to be in that state, Size Ten

So Women's Magazine Editor, don't tell me I'm ugly
I'm startin' to enjoy the wrinkles and the hairs
Startin' to know that lovers like the fat bits
And pretty soon this old machine o'mine'll be free from cares

You keep wantin' me to spend right to my pocket's end
On creams and powders that are meant to blend
My skin and my eyes and my hard-workin' hands
Into Size Ten, so it attracts the men.
But I'm a-tellin' you, it just won't do
Cos me and my body gonna affect a coup
Ain't gonna buy no more of your shit
This is my face and I'm gonna learn to love it.

Size Ten, Size Ten, Size Ten, Size Ten

Archives Berlei-Hestia

SIZE TEN is the theme song for a film of the same name by Susan Lambert and Sarah Gibson.

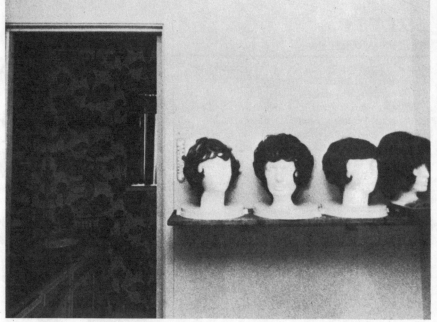
Bill Owens

Monday, Tuesday, Wednesday, Thursday... and Friday I have my hair done.

JILL MILLER
women who despise women
must live in fear of mirrors.
they hide in company with men
for camouflage.

women who despise women
have nowhere to escape to:
save private universes
with locked doors.

male words bind them helpless
gasping at the foolishness
of their female bodies.
torn twixt prostitute and saint
they spend their lives
on journeys that start
and end in limbo.

women who despise women
live alone with men for years
in ignorance of who they are.

---

children to support through working in
a labour market not attuned to
women's needs. This is part of the
claim that feminism is a tool, whether
unwitting or willing, of hard-hearted
capitalism and a society without values;
hostile to family, caring and
compassion, uninterested in children,
and at heart, life-denying. The
challenge is hard to answer, because
versions of these arguments are familiar
to feminists. And because in the re-
evaluation of feminism of the last five
years, some of the household names of
the '60s and '70s, like Betty Friedan and
Germaine Greer, have recanted their
earlier commitment to sexual politics,
arguing respectively for a broader focus
on political power for women, and a
return to a child-centred world for
women, in which power comes from
the strength of emotional bonds
between women and children.
*(Betty Friedan, THE SECOND STAGE;
Germaine Greer, SEX AND DESTINY)*

But it is important not to see
feminist victories as defeats. Women's
access to the workforce; opportunity to
plan their families; and greater sexual
freedom are good things in themselves,
even though not all women will always
want them.

And although the victories (better
contraception, some childcare, laws
against job discrimination, some
liberalisation of laws against abortion)
were undoubtedly won through the
activities of middle-class women, that
doesn't make feminism solely a middle-
class issue.

Women's oppression has many
dimensions, and is different in different
societies, and at different historical
periods.

INTRODUCTORY LETTER TO
LIFE AS WE HAVE KNOWN IT
VIRGINIA WOOLF

...Meanwhile — let me try after
seventeen years to sum up the
thoughts that passed through the
minds of your guests, who had
come up from London and
elsewhere, not to take part but to
listen — meanwhile what was it
all about? These women were
demanding divorce, education,
the vote — all good things. They
were demanding higher wages
and shorter hours —what could
be more reasonable? And yet,
though it was all so reasonable,
much of it so forcible, some of it
so humorous, a weight of
discomfort was settling and
shifting itself uneasily from side
to side in your visitors' minds. All
these questions —perhaps this
was at the bottom of it — which
matter so intensely to the people
here, questions of sanitation and
education and wages, this
demand for an extra shilling, for
another year at school, for eight
hours instead of nine behind a
counter or in a mill, leave me, in
my own blood and bones,
untouched. If every reform they
demand was granted this very
instant it would not touch one
hair of my comfortable
capitalistic head. Hence my
interest is purely altruistic, it is
thin spread and moon coloured.
There is no lifeblood or urgency
about it. However hard I clap my
hands or stamp my feet there is a
hollowness in the sound which
betrays me. I am a benevolent
spectator. I am irretrievably cut
off from the actors. I sit here
hypocritically clapping and
stamping, an outcast from the
flock...

Bianca Jagger

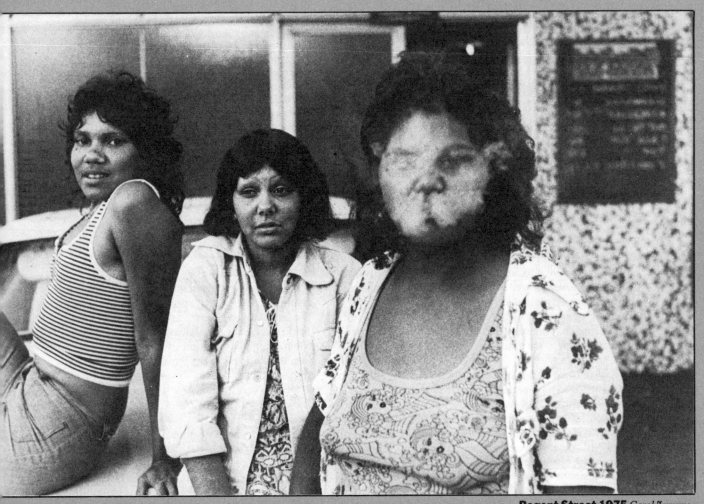

Regent Street 1975 *Carol Jerrems*

The women who live on the ground

FEMINISM and the women's liberation movement has flourished in western democratic societies such as Australia, the United Kingdom, the United States of America, Holland, Germany, France, Italy and the Scandinavian countries. In these countries, although women's real position in relation to education, jobs, equal pay, and choices about how to live their lives is as we have described it in this book, on paper at least women are equal to men before the law, have the vote and are not refused access to public life simply because they are women. Indeed, one of the reasons that feminism has taken hold in these societies is because women are basing their demands for real control over their lives on the promises held out to them as citizens equal to men. So, for example, women are saying that it is all very well to promise women equal access to desirable jobs, but that in order to deliver on that promise society has to come up with free or affordable childcare for working women.

Because of its origins in western societies feminism is often dismissed as irrelevant to the real needs of women in other societies, particularly those of the underdeveloped 'Third World' in Africa, Asia and Latin America. It is regarded as a western luxury, more relevant to individual women in advanced societies who want to get promotion at work or move into traditionally male areas in the power structure, be recognised at home as the equal of their husbands, or have the opportunities for sexual adventuring that men have. It is not seen as relevant, and sometimes seen as harmful, by the authorities in countries where the most pressing needs are for the whole population to be decently fed, clothed, housed, educated, and welded into a peaceful productive society. Against the enemies of hunger, poverty, disease, ignorance, civil war, class exploitation and exploitation of poor countries by rich countries, sexism may not seem to rank very high on the scale of social evils. And as we will see, in many parts of the world, feminism is seen as a divisive force, setting women against men, and promoting social unrest and disrespect for traditional values.

This chapter is about the relevance of feminism to women's lives in different countries, and under different sorts of social conditions, such as civil war and revolution and the experience of being an oppressed minority like the Australian Aboriginal people. It shows that feminism, at its best, is about ordinary women, and ordinary women's struggles to make their own lives in circumstances not of their own choosing, and to fight for human dignity in societies which relegate women to second-class status.

Nadine, resting on her neighbor's stoop
JUDY GRAHN

She holds things together, collects bail,
makes the landlord patch the largest holes.
At the Sunday social she would spike
every drink, and offer you half of what she knows,
which is plenty. She pokes at the ruins of the city
like an armored tank; but she thinks
of herself as a ripsaw cutting through
knots in wood. Her sentences come out
like thick pine shanks
and her big hands fill the air like smoke.
She's a mud-chinked cabin in the slums,
sitting on the doorstep counting
rats and raising 15 children,
half of them her own. The neighborhood
would burn itself out without her;
one of these days she'll strike the spark herself.
She's made of grease
and metal, with a hard head
that makes the men around her seem frail.
The common woman is as common as
a nail.

In 1978 and 1979 the streets of Iran's capital city Tehran were thronged with thousands of Iranian women risking brutal police repression to demonstrate against the hated regime of the Shah. They were not behaving like traditional Muslim women, whose life is carried on behind the four walls of the family home; they were participating in public life, on the streets, in an unprecedented way. But they were veiled, as a demonstration of their solidarity with the revolutionary Muslim spirit which was sweeping the country in opposition to the western ways of the Shah.

Before the revolution in Iran in 1979, which replaced the Shah with the Ayatollah Khomeini, great changes were taking place in women's lives. Under the regime of the Shah, corrupt and oppressive though it was, women's liberation in the western sense was given official encouragement. The Shah's sister Ashraf Pahlavi was one of the leading proponents of the United Nations Decade of Women; abortion laws and laws on divorce were liberalised, women were being encouraged to discard the traditional veil worn by Muslim women, which envelops a woman from head to feet, and to enter public life, to finish school, to make professional careers.

Since the revolution in Iran, which was brought about with such enthusiastic and courageous participation by women, strict new Islamic laws have replaced the liberal social and marriage laws of the Shah's regime. Women are now compelled to wear the veil when they appear in public; are forbidden to hold high public office (women judges were sacked, and told to find clerical jobs); are made officially inferior to men in legal and financial matters; are forbidden from entering the same schools as their brothers; and are held responsible for corrupting society through adultery, prostitution and sexually free behaviour, all of which are savagely punished as crimes.

How is this massive reversal in values to be explained? What do Iranian women stand to gain from this revolution which seems to have dashed all their hopes for equality? Why did Iranian feminists support the revolutionary movement?

How were the hopes of millions of women for a better life transformed into support for a patriarchal religious dictatorship — why was the western model for women's liberation so decisively rejected?

The answers are not obvious, and depend very much on how the question is posed. The two authors of *In the Shadow of Islam: The Women's Movement in Iran,* both feminists, disagree on the extent to which Islam, the religion, can accommodate a real concept of women's rights, and the extent to which the religion of Islam stays unchanging as it becomes the principle of government for a country. For example, one author, Nahid Yeganeh, argues that it is wrong to see Iran as an example of the inevitability of the repression of women under Islam. She points out that:

---

in three historical moments *chador* (the veil) was turned into a symbol. At the time of the Shah's compulsory unveiling, for a woman to appear without it symbolised modernity and change; during the Revolution of 1979, wearing it symbolised resistance to the Shah; and finally, at the time of the construction of the Islamic Republic, its imposition symbolised progress for the Islamic side, and regression for others.

The issue of the veil symbolises for her how women have never been able to have a real political voice of their own in Iran, and how they have all along been caught in an ongoing struggle for power between the Muslim clergy, and the secular (non-religious) state. The political movement which made the revolution had organised its forces on an appeal to Iranian nationalism, and opposition to the Americanisation of Iran under the Shah. The feminist opposition movement, which shared with women in the West an intense interest in sexual politics, and criticised the masculine domination of Iranian life, had little in common with the revolutionary movement. So women opposed to the regime became absorbed into the revolutionary movement, which was 'unwilling to tolerate a theory of women's specific oppression as women'.

So, according to Nahid Yeganeh, it is wrong to see the victory of the Ayatollah Khomeini as a defeat for Iranian feminism — it never really existed before the revolution. It is only since the revolution with the savage attacks by the authorities on women's social and economic status, that it has been possible to have a political organisation of women based on sisterhood, that is, what all women have in common. Before the revolution, feminism was only a western import, was only really relevant to westernised women in Iran.

Since the revolution, a new version of feminism has developed in Iran, according to Nahid Yeganeh. It is a Muslim feminism, which sees the westernisation of women as the greatest threat to the dignity of women and to the freedom of Iran from domination by the United States. The argument runs like this: the western woman is a sex-object, dependent on all sorts of needs and desires which are artificially promoted in order to sell things — like fashion clothes, make-up, luxury goods — which are not necessary for the economic health of Iran, but benefit foreign countries which export such goods. *

Under the old regime in Iran women had only two choices — traditional life, which meant for a woman being treated as a breeding machine, socially inferior, and allowed out into society only for religious observances; or this artificially promoted western life, which meant being exploited as a sex-object for men's pleasure, and being a slave to fashion and high living. Now, Muslim feminism is offering women a new dignity, based on a proper recognition of women's role as mothers and guardians of morality. According to this argument, the Ayatollah has a backward view of women but there is a real possibility that things will change for the better. But it is silly to get so worked up about the issue of the veil — after all, the veil does protect women from being ogled by men and allows them to go about their business unmolested.

On the other hand, *In the Shadow of Islam*'s co-author, Azar Tabari, finds that the concept of 'Muslim feminism' makes little sense. For her, Islam has nothing to offer women, because it is a religion based on patriarchal principles, in which men rule over women. When translated into politics, Islam produces a state and government which is deeply undemocratic, intolerant and totally unresponsive to expressions of popular will. All opposition is branded as 'un-Islamic' and laws are made by the clergy, not the people's representatives.

For women, all that Islam offers is a sort of sexual apartheid, in which the sexes are equal in name only, but women are forced to keep their own sphere, separate from men. For her the question of the veil is vitally important, and not just a symbolic question.

'...the veil defines the legitimate physical borders of a woman's existence in society. This seems to be related to a concept in Islamic thinking, of women as sexually active and inciting creatures, who must be controlled within strict moral and social behavioural patterns in order to protect the community from the potentially subversive influence her sexuality wields.'

---

*On this, see the next chapter of this book, on the ways in which advertising uses images of women to promote all sorts of goods.

In other words, the veil is får more than just a symbol of women's difference from men. It is an example of the way in which Islamic society controls the behaviour of all individuals in order to promote the social good, and in order to stop adultery, prostitution, jealousy, sexual violence, rape, illegitimacy, fornication . . . all of which women in their moral weakness are responsible for.

A reader for those who live in cities
BERTOLT BRECHT trans John Willett

I'm dirt. From myself
I can demand nothing but
Weakness, treachery and degradation
When one day I notice
It's getting better; the wind
Fills my sail; my time has come, I can
Become better than dirt —
I began at once.

Because I was dirt I noticed
When I'm drunk I simply
Lie down and have no idea
Who is messing me about: now I don't drink any more —
I gave it up at once.

Unfortunately
Just in order to keep alive, I had to do
Much that harmed me; I've
Wolfed down poison enough
To kill four carthorses, but
What else could I do
To stay alive? So at times I sniffed snow
Till I looked like a boneless bedspread.
Then I saw myself in the glass —
And stopped it at once.

Of course they tried to hang a dose
Of syphilis on me, but that
Was something they couldn't manage; they could only poison
    me
With arsenic: I had
Tubes in my side with
Pus flowing night and day. Who
Would ever have thought that a woman like me
Would ever make men crazy again? —
I began again at once.

I have never taken a man who did not do
Something for me, and had every man
I needed. By now I'm
Almost without feeling, almost gone dry
But
I'm beginning to fill up again, I have ups and downs, but
On the whole more ups.

I still notice myself calling my enemy
An old cow, and knowing her for my enemy because
A man looks at her.
But in a year
I'll have got over it —
I've already begun to.

I'm dirt, but everything
Must serve my purpose, I'm
Coming up, I'm
inevitable, the race of the future
Soon not dirt any more, but
The hard mortar with which
Cities are built.

(That's something I've heard a woman say.)

In these arguments about the value to women of exclusion from men, which allows women to be free from intrusive interest in their bodies and sexuality, there is an interesting echo of debates being carried on amongst feminists in our society. Educational research has showed that for girls, single-sex schooling allows them to develop their potential better than a co-educational system, in which girls have to contend with the greater amount of attention given to boys by teachers, the embarrassment of sexual scrutiny and fears of outperforming the boys. Co-education, however, is better for boys than a boys-only environment, at least as far as realising the broader goals of education, in producing socially well-adapted young people.

Women have special insights into the roots of violence in society, and special experience of the bitterness of civil wars. There are women in the fighting forces on both sides of the relentless sectarian struggles in Northern Ireland — women in the Irish Republican Army, women supporting the Ulster Unionist Party. Women on both sides have sons and husbands in prison; women supporters of the IRA are in prison going on hunger strikes to get recognition as political prisoners. Vast numbers of women in Northern Ireland are caught up every day in the violence in the streets and running through their communities, living in conditions of remorseless tension and fear, trying to keep their children away from the gangs, trying to maintain normal family life in communities split down the middle with hatred.

For a few years in the mid 1970s there was a women's peace movement in Northern Ireland, putting thousands of women into the streets in peace marches, crossing the no-go areas between the Catholic and Protestant ghettos.

A group of feminists has put together a picture of women's lives in Northern Ireland, in a book based on interviews with all sorts of Irish women on both sides of the struggle — *Only the Rivers Run Free: Northern Ireland: the Women's War*. It's a feminist analysis, which tries to draw out the connections between Irish nationalism and desires for freedom from British rule, on the one hand, and Irish women's struggles for liberation on the other. Reading this book one thing above all stands out: that so many of these brave and resourceful women have to endure as much violence and abuse from the men on 'their side', as from the British forces or the paramilitary gangs on the other side, and that the Irish Catholic and Irish Protestant churches are just about on a par for repressive policies towards women. On both sides of this war, the wives of imprisoned paramilitary fighters live in enforced chastity, watched over by their husbands' comrades. One of the worst acts of 'treachery' which a woman can commit is to be 'unfaithful' to her fighting man in prison — no matter that he beats her when he's free; while in prison he's a hero of the people, and she's a revolutionary symbol.

Rose McAllister, aged 42, pictured here with two of her four children, is an ex-Armagh prisoner who has served two terms in prison, the most recent for possession of an incendiary device. She was released in May 1980 after two years on protest for Political Status. During her first prison term she had been given Political Status.

Camerawork

Some Irish Loving — A Selection

EDNA O'BRIEN

For a country breast-fed on chastity and gullet-fed with the religion that makes Jansenism seem sportive the transgression is twice as bad. For a woman it is ten times more so. In fact considering their background I am surprised that all Irish women are not lying down on railway tracks uttering and wailing ejaculations for the oncoming train. It would be rash to hope that women have contributed as richly and as vigorously to the theme of love. But they have contributed — wild ontumely, withheld desire, craven love and a sublimated sexuality that gives rein to the most fanciful and sometimes devious images. Too often they anguish like Dido under the weight of doom, loss and rejection. Nor are they bold in their descriptions; they seldom describe him, they merely describe the feeling and the event as if it were a sacrament. Desire has gone underground and reappeared as something else.

Having seen how ideas of what women's liberation is differ so widely, depending on different social circumstances — so that we always have to ask, 'what is it that women need to be liberated from?' — are there any common threads linking women's social inferiority in all societies?

In the early 1970s feminism started to look closely at anthropological studies of the position of women in different cultures, to test the proposition that there was some common element in women's oppression. For a time a great deal of excitement was generated by a theory which seemed to explain why women's role was devalued in so many different types of society. The argument ran like this: in all cultures there seems to be a distinct separation between domestic and public life. In all human societies that we know of, women are associated with domestic life, men with public life, even though the precise boundaries between the two spheres of life may vary from one society to another, and in the same society at different times and stages in its development. But in all societies men's work, whatever it is, is valued more highly than women's. One explanation offered for this is that men's activities are associated with what we call 'culture' or civilisation; women's activities of childbearing, feeding and nurturing are associated with 'nature'. Human history, progress, is seen as the gradual winning of control over nature by means of culture — thought, science, understanding have recently replaced magic and ritual as the tools of 'culture'. Men, through their freedom from nature in the sense of responsibility for childbearing, are free to create the tools of culture. (Sherry Ortner 'Is Female to Male as Nature is to Culture?', in *Woman, Culture and Society,* edited by Michelle Zimbalist Rosaldo and Louise Lamphere, 1974.)

In a slightly different vein, Michelle Rosaldo argued a similar position:

women seem to be oppressed or lacking in value and status to the extent that they are confined to domestic activities, cut off from other women and from the social world of men. Women gain power and a sense of value when they are able to transcend domestic limits, either by entering the men's world or by creating a society unto themselves.

More recently, feminist anthropologists, applying these theoretical approaches (that is the idea that women were seen as inferior because their role is less important, 'basic') to a study of particular societies, are beginning to argue that they are overgeneralisations. Very often the earlier anthropologists, on whose work the theories were to some extent based, had failed to see some important roles carried out by women in traditional societies, being blinded by their own assumptions that the men's rituals and activities were the important ones, and that women's activities were subordinate, domestic, and supportive. Diane Bell, an Australian anthropologist, writing on her own experience of Aboriginal women's lives in *Daughters of the Dreaming,* describes a society in which concepts of male-female inequality may have little real relevance. The women she lived with in the Central Australian desert do not see themselves as male-dominated, nor excluded from important male rituals. Their world is ordered by their own important role as protectors of their people's spiritual relationship with the land. Men's and women's roles and rituals are different, but in the traditional society, women's ritual role gives them a claim to autonomy and status. White male anthropologists could not see this, partly because Aboriginal women would not reveal important rituals to men; partly because anthropologists were not looking for evidence of women's high status, having assumed on the basis of western stereotypes that women were subordinate. (Diane Bell recounts how when she first presented evidence of Aboriginal women's ritual importance to a male anthropologist, she met the response that her trouble was that she didn't believe that women could be oppressed!)

women were disadvantaged from the outset [of white settlement] because of the white male perception of them as domestic workers and sex objects. Aboriginal men have been able to take real political advantage of certain aspects of frontier society, while Aboriginal women have been seen by whites as peripheral to the political process... There was no place within the colonial order for the independent Aboriginal woman who, once deprived of her land, quickly became dependent on rations and social security.

Diane Bell's own experiences, and her understanding gained from the stories that Aboriginal women told of their lives, convince her of the need to rewrite anthropology, to write a feminist anthropology. A feminist anthropology would not accept that men are always dominant, women always inferior, but instead would look at the ways in which men and women are constantly bargaining between themselves for influence and authority. In traditional Aboriginal society the key to the relationships between men and women was their spiritual relationship to the land, in which men and women had different, but complementary functions.

But white settlement has destroyed the relationship between the people and their land, and shattered the balance of relationships between the sexes. The values of white society have replaced the values that Aboriginal people lived by, and women have been the losers. Herded into government settlements, women soon lost their traditional roles, and became dependent on their men in the white economy.

Alice Walker's novel THE COLOR PURPLE follows these themes in telling the story of a black woman's struggle for self-respect and love.

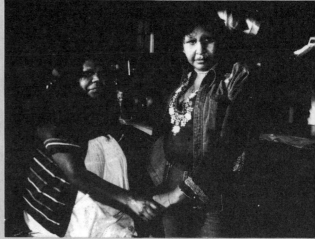

Women in Redfern 1984 *Robyn Stacey*

Kuu kuu kardiya and the women who live on the ground

LEE CATALDI

behind the microphone
pale face and hair
I was almost sure   sitting
in the same row of desks for ten years
one doesn't forget
the toss of the head

femocrat
black and gold dress   gold
handbag fat
as a bank account

meanwhile
in the draughty hall
the warlpiri women wait
their painted breasts
delicate as earth

and into
the mismanaged white festival
miraculous and powerful
quavering
fine harmonies   the certain
feathery presences

the artists stop
discuss a point of style   the song
continues   it is
a continuum sometimes
they sing it aloud

the women move lightly   brown
skin black skirts in a ring
like a windbreak
            at dawn blue
smoke from cooking fires   bodies
stirring in blankets a warm
outcrop of earth

the white woman
comes out of the house   she says
            wash the clothes
            finish the job   wipe
            the children's noses   we are
            taking these children away
            it's for their own good

the women who live on the ground
disappear into the desert
stepping lightly
out of their regulation mission bloomers
their ragged jumble sale clothing

their voices fade as water
sinks back underground

jukurra jukurra they say
taking their children with them
into the heart of that furnace
where spirits rise whiter than clay

the women are in the school
with the children who
are learning to read
yirdi they say
wirlinyirnalu yanu marluku
we hunted for kangaroo
nganimpa karnalu walyangka nyina
we live on the ground

the white woman
riding her mop like a broomstick
screams about the building
            what a waste of time   they should be
            learning to spell must and ought
            they are filthy   look
            at their noses   look
            at the dust on the floor
            at the dust on the ground

outside the school the children
write warlpiri in the dust   write
kuukuu kardiya in the dust the hot wind
blows into eyes throats noses
into all the clean clothes

the women who live on the ground
watch the white women fade
after a few years
back into their motor cars
after one or two of those seasons in which
the spirits of the secret places
open their giant lungs
and burn the houses to ash

Helmut Newton

Images

Jean Harlow

FEMINIST theory, feminist politics and feminist consciousness in this second wave of the women's movement (the first wave at the turn of the century produced the vote and women's right to enter universities and professions) have been strongly marked by a concern about representations of women. Protests and picketing at the Miss World beauty contest in London in 1969 staked this out as feminist territory, and earned the movement the reputation of being anti-pleasure, hysterical prudes. But from the beginning, feminist concern with the ways women's bodies are used in advertising, pornography, fashion magazines, art and design has been an aspect of the movement's insistence that the personal is political —that the way we live in our bodies and think about them is deeply influenced by the sexual power structure. So also are our ideas about 'pleasure' and 'beauty'; indeed, any representation of bodies and what we do with them as men and women is in some way related to our ideas about femininity and masculinity. Pictures are not just harmless abstractions from reality, but carry all sorts of messages about sexuality.

In this chapter we are looking at the feminist argument about pictures of women, and the link between advertising and pornography. The connecting idea is that women's bodies are *exploited*. In advertising women's bodies are put on display in an exploitative way, to sell goods; in pornography, women's bodies are put on display, exploited, directly for profit. Women's sexuality is taken away from them, made into the stuff of public fantasies, inextricably connected with selling — so, by extension, women themselves become commodities. Women's bodies are exploited commercially in the most direct way in prostitution — so feminist arguments are drawing a direct line between advertising images of women's bodies, pornographic images of women's bodies, and the prostitution of women's bodies.

John Berger's book *Ways of Seeing* was very influential in the early '70s. He extended the analysis of representation of women's bodies into an analysis of great paintings. Discussing the artistic tradition of the female nude, he argues that the way of presenting men and women in art is quite different, not because men and women are different but because the spectator of a painting is presumed to be a man, and the image of the woman depicted there is designed to flatter him. So female nudes are presented as if the women are naked for the viewer's pleasure; they appear to be aware of the gaze of the viewer, to be passively offering themselves to be looked at. The owner of the painting flatters himself that she is nude for him.

Berger's book remains illuminating in every sense. But his analysis is not an explicitly feminist one. The essential difference between Berger and feminist theorists like Andrea Dworkin and Susan Griffin is the strength and power that each attributes to the image. Berger says that what is wrong with these representations of women is the way private fantasy is enlisted by capitalism, in the cause of consumerism, and thereby loses its private and personal quality; even our most private thoughts become stereotyped. For Dworkin and Griffin this is also true, but is not a product of capitalist values. For them, the representation of women expresses a deep hatred of, and hostility towards women, which they argue is the essence of our culture. Looking at these pictures causes/expresses not just alienation, but *violation*.

This style of argument was dominant in feminist thinking in the early 1970s and was the basis of campaigns against particularly exploitative advertising, using stickers which said 'This ad exploits women'.

But in the late 1970s the focus broadened, and a new element entered the analysis, with increasing feminist concentration on the causes of violence against women. With all these different elements — exploitation, commercialisation, prostitution, stereotyping sexual images, and images of violence — there are now at least five distinctly different feminist positions on what pornography really is, and how feminists should deal with it.

PORNOGRAPHY IS A WEAPON

One argument concentrates on the effect of pornographic images on women. Pornography is seen as a weapon used by men to keep women in a state of submission and fear; women looking at pornographic images see a terrifying vision of how men see them — as bodies to be used, abused, tortured, humiliated; or worse, as parts of bodies — breasts, vaginas, mouths; or worst, as dead bodies, either literally lifeless, or pictured in a sexual swoon which looks more like death than pleasure. Pornography is at one end of a continuum of images and social practices which are designed to instil in women an understanding of their proper place, as sexual objects for men. It works as a weapon by being everywhere, in milder forms in advertising, in extreme forms in sex shops, so that women are confronted by these images wherever they go. In workplaces where men and women share the same physical space, pin-ups and erotic pictures are used by men to control women — by embarrassment, by forcing women to realise that it is men who in fact control the space, by reminding women that as workers they are still sexual things for men.

This line of analysis is not interested in asking questions about women's own use of pornography. Its basic assumption is that pornography is a weapon, *the* weapon of male dominance and forced female submission, so that any response a woman may have is really an expression of fear, or the compliance in her own subjection of a terrorised creature, who has no power over her own sexuality.

So the image itself wreaks violence on women, by inducing a paralysing fear, or a numbed and silenced compliance in the system of male dominance. The image doesn't just exploit, insult or degrade women, it actually has its chief effect *on* women.

PORNOGRAPHY IS A MANUAL FOR SEXUAL WARFARE

'Pornography is the theory, rape is the practice.'
— Robin Morgan

This argument sees a direct connection between pornographic images and physical violence against women: violent sexual images cause violent sexual acts. Sexual images which degrade women cause men to think of women as degraded creatures. Sometimes the argument is that the connection is very direct indeed, in the sense of saying that pornography incites men to go out and rape. More often the argument is that pornography in some way softens up society to be more inclined to violence, more tolerant of sexual practices which involve humiliation and pain for women. The essence of pornography is seen to be sadism and contempt for women, which reflects the *reality* of women's lives. Sexuality is by definition male sexuality, for women under the rule of men are like colonised people, denied any means of self-expression. And male sexuality means men possessing women, literally and metaphorically. The images of pornography faithfully reflect this reality: women gaze longingly at the camera, offering their bodies; the stories are filled with women asking for more as they are humiliated and violated, or shrinking in terror from the rapist, slasher, torturer, slave-owner. Pornography celebrates and justifies male power over women.

This position is spelled out in greatest detail in Susan Griffin's book *Pornography and Silence*. She argues that pornography expresses in extreme form a traditional cultural value of the Christian west; hatred and fear of the flesh, carnality, the forces of nature. Men fear the consequence of their own desire of women, and create sexual images which involve the humiliation of the flesh, as a means of controlling desire, and controlling women, who provoke desire. Susan Griffin calls this way of thinking, in which a fantasy is created in order to exert control over reality, the 'pornographic imagination'. This pornographic imagination is not confined to the pages of erotica, but spills over into everyday life, saturates our culture as the triumph of men over nature. So the struggle against pornography by feminists is a struggle for real human liberation from man-made culture, a struggle against a culture which preaches death and despair, a struggle for beauty in the face of horror.

This position recognises that women do participate in the continuation of this culture, by silence, by pretending to take pleasure in what revulses them, by accepting men's evaluation of them as objects, commodities. But they do so only in order to guarantee their physical survival:

'In order to survive in our bodies, to earn a living, to be accepted in society, we must sacrifice truth, we must pretend to be other than ourselves. Hence our physical survival is pitted against the survival of ourselves.'
Susan Griffin

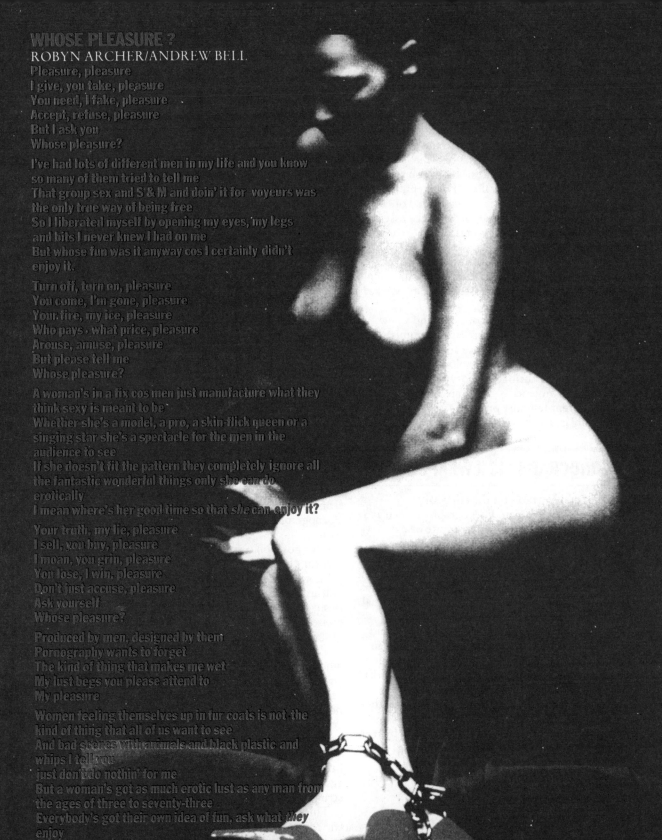

WHOSE PLEASURE ?
ROBYN ARCHER/ANDREW BELL

Pleasure, pleasure
I give, you take, pleasure
You need, I fake, pleasure
Accept, refuse, pleasure
But I ask you
Whose pleasure?

I've had lots of different men in my life and you know
so many of them tried to tell me
That group sex and S & M and doin' it for voyeurs was
the only true way of being free
So I liberated myself by opening my eyes, my legs
and bits I never knew I had on me
But whose fun was it anyway cos I certainly didn't
enjoy it.

Turn off, turn on, pleasure
You come, I'm gone, pleasure
Your fire, my ice, pleasure
Who pays · what price, pleasure
Arouse, amuse, pleasure
But please tell me
Whose pleasure?

A woman's in a fix cos men just manufacture what they
think sexy is meant to be
Whether she's a model, a pro, a skin-flick queen or a
singing star she's a spectacle for the men in the
audience to see
If she doesn't fit the pattern they completely ignore all
the fantastic wonderful things only she can do
erotically
I mean where's her good time so that *she* can enjoy it?

Your truth, my lie, pleasure
I sell, you buy, pleasure
I moan, you grin, pleasure
You lose, I win, pleasure
Don't just accuse, pleasure
Ask yourself
Whose pleasure?

Produced by men, designed by them
Pornography wants to forget
The kind of thing that makes me wet
My lust begs you please attend to
My pleasure

Women feeling themselves up in fur coats is not the
kind of thing that all of us want to see
And bad scenes with animals and black plastic and
whips I tell you
just don't do nothin' for me
But a woman's got as much erotic lust as any man from
the ages of three to seventy-three
Everybody's got their own idea of fun, ask what they
enjoy

Invite, amuse, pleasure
Don't just abuse, pleasure
The face ain't right, pleasure
But feel my bite, pleasure
Those ahs and ooohs
I ask you
Whose pleasure?

Helmut Newton

SELLING PORNOGRAPHY

Dear Woman Comrades,

I am a woman who works in a Milan newsagents and am fed up, really fed up with part of my job — dealing with the mountains of pornography and pseudo pornography that come into the kiosk every day. This morning 23 new magazines arrived and every morning is much the same. I have to sort out a heap of publications that offend women, upset me and almost make me feel sick. What can I do about it?

I can't refuse to sell them since I am a retailer and have to sell whatever the wholesaler delivers to me. I can refuse to display them, keep them off the counter but this isn't enough. I still feel that I'm selling other women and living a double life, that of the feminist and that of the newsagent earning a living. It's particularly difficult on days like today when the printers are on strike and there are no newspapers, but these damn magazines are still around, showing 'Lola With The Magic Arse' or 'Clara of the Tight Cunt' or 'The Bestial Loves of A Thirteen-Year-Old'.

I am against censorship, but can't stand selling this stuff any longer. And it isn't only old men 'or anonymous types that buy them, but comrades as well. Sometimes I hear someone asking for 'Communist Weekly' and 'Hours of Lust' please, miss." To say that I'd like to ram the papers up their arse is an understatement.

I would like the paper to start a debate on pornography, including the 'new pornography' of sadism and violence. I would like magazines that deal with love, happiness, eroticism — magazines that give joy.

One other point, I am often taken for a woman of easy virtue 'because I sell these publications. As I was once told, "Only a whore sells these boyish mags." So more than once I have had to get myself out of a fix. Not to mention the man who masturbated behind the kiosk, excited by the sight of 'my' magazines. I leave you to draw your own conclusions about the problem that may well force me to change my job.

Patrizia.

PORNOGRAPHY IS AN INDUSTRY BUILT ON THE EXPLOITATION OF WOMEN

Underlying all these cultural objections to the role that pornography plays in devaluing the image of woman, provoking violence against women, promoting contempt for women, is another basic objection to the straightforward economic exploitation of women in the porno business.

In common with the analysis of prostitution, feminists argue that the pornographic movie business institutionalises the idea that sex is a commodity that women sell, and thrives on the economic precariousness of women's lives. Because the labour market undervalues women's worth, and forces them into cycles of unemployment, women are vulnerable to the sex industry. They are being exploited as *women,* in ways that men are rarely exploited, but they are in this position because society fails to provide economic security for women who have no regular man to support them; fails to educate girls to the necessity of learning skills. What keeps pornography in circulation is the profit to be made — it is big business.

The logic of this argument suggests that a purely moral crusade against pornography is not going to succeed: outrage is no match for the power of big money.

PORNOGRAPHY IS THE IDEOLOGY OF SEXUALITY IN A SEXIST SOCIETY

Here the argument concentrates on the ways in which pornography, and sexually suggestive advertising images of women, put into public circulation ideas about female sexuality which are false, damaging to women, but by repetition have become the visual shorthand for sex itself.

For example, one of the most constant themes in pornographic imagery and advertising is the idea that women are *available.* By draping an alluring female body over the bonnet of a car, the advertiser is saying: 'If you possess this car, you will have the ability to possess this body too; both these desirable objects are available to you.' If you think about it, this idea of availability runs through most representations of women in advertising, even when the images are not particularly suggestive.

But there is another idea which goes along with this suggestion of availability, and is possibly much more damaging to women. Because women are represented as still, waiting, available, *there* for the asking, there is the suggestion that women's sexuality is entirely concentrated in their bodies, that female sexuality is all about physical responses to male desires. Women do not appear, in popular images, to have sexual selves which exist independently of men and male desires. Women are encouraged, by all these visual representations of female bodies, to see themselves as the advertisers and pornographers see them — bodies first, personalities second, when it comes to sexual attraction.

These rather complex ideas are what feminists mean by the concept of women as sex objects — it's much more than a simple idea that women are seen as objects, and includes the idea that women see themselves, to some extent at least, as objects.

And this objectifying mode of thought imposes a sort of 'Catch 22', which is hard to break free from.

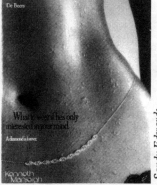

Stupid female ... but she was smart enough to know that stupidity is sexually desirable.

Sandy Edwards

PLAYUP

PLAYTHING

PLAYMATE

playmate

playaround

PLAYFUL

Helmut Newton

playball

playactor

PLAYDOUGH

PLAYDOWN

PLAYBILL

PLAYBOY

Pouts and Scowls. Rosalind Coward has analysed the meanings behind the new-look female image in fashion magazines — the scowling, fierce face, the proud, inapproachable, arrogant expression on the faces of the models. She argues that it would be quite wrong to see this change from the simpering smiles of earlier decades as any sort of positive response to feminist criticisms of images of female availability. On the contrary, she says, these scowling faces are now very reminiscent of the expressions on the faces of the women in pornographic magazines aimed at men. 'If the expression appears to say, "Fuck you," it actually reads, "Fuck me."'... We are meant to read off from the narrowing of the eyes, the perfection of the skin, the posture of the body, that this is a person confident of sexual response whether it is sought or not.' *Rosalind Coward, FEMALE DESIRE.*

It is still an image of availability, but suggests that overcoming this apparent resistance is an exciting part of sexual activity. She may be saying no, but really she's interested.

So, paradoxically, a tough image for women can actually be reinforcing even more strongly the connection between sexuality and violence.

Of course, it is the context which makes this so. A scowl on a perfectly made-up face on the front cover of a magazine devoted to teaching women how to express their femininity is very different from the scowl on the face of an angry young feminist at a 'reclaim the night' march, protesting against male violence against women.

This analysis is saying that we have to understand that pornographic images work on women too — not in the direct sense of terrorising women into submission, but by spreading and legitimising ideas about women's sexuality, so that women adopt and use these images when visualising their own sexual feelings.

and eroticism conducted by the uninhibited graph genius, Jean-Paul Goude. Once described most aptly by *Esquire* as 'The French Correction', Goude performs his art to bring nature in closer conformity to his fantasies, a collection to be found herein:

Kellie the Evangelist Stripper, Sabu, Grace Jones, Gene Kelly, Zouzou, Little Beaver, Judith Jamison, Russ Tamblyn, Toukie, Radiah, the sex circus of Eighth Avenue and the nocturnal *flore et faune* of 42nd Street.

Jean-Paul Goude is all these fantasies have in common, but even so, they form a very special community: they have been made perfect to fit the world as Goude wants it to be — there are stilts for Radiah, a new ass for Toukie, a crew cut for Grace Jones.

To account accurately for the range of his special vision, Goude's work must be considered that of painter, photographer, sculptor, musician, dancer, couturier, stage director and set designer — all of these and none of them. 'To say the truth,' Goude says, 'I see myself as an artist who uses the best means available to get a point across. What comes first is the necessity to communicate "my world". Through the use of different media I am able to show what to me is important.'

Thus he scornfully dismissed a plastic surgeon who refused to follow his design for a girlfriend's new nose. 'After all, I am the artist,' Goude says. 'What does he know?'

It is, as he says, the ultimate effect that concerns him: the extension of a limb, the padding of a flank, a nip here and a tuck there — and suddenly the fantastic people and places of Jean-Paul Goude have become his forever. Yours, too.

from the fly leaf of **Jungle Fever**
by Jean-Paul Goude

Grace Jones

1

Things happen after a badedas bath

Life is full of promise ...

2

Things happen after a badedas bath

along may come a tall dark handsome

3

Give badedas for Christmas and see what happens

...stranger...

Sandy Edwards

Robyn Stacey/Jenny Clarke

FEMINIST RESPONSES TO PORNOGRAPHY

The strongest response is anger. Anger has taken many women on to the streets in the sex-shop districts, picketing the porno cinemas, sometimes breaking into the sex shops, burning them to the ground. This anger has been very liberating, giving women a sense of their own power. It has also been the basis of very broad solidarity among women, not necessarily feminists; indeed, in the United States feminists have taken to the streets in the company of the right-wing women whose politics is opposed to everything else feminism stands for (see chapter 11).

Other feminists argue that anger alone is not an adequate response. For one thing, it tends to make one concentrate too much on the phenomenon — pornographic images, and the porn and advertising industries which purvey them — at the expense of an understanding of how these images get such wide acceptance, how they get into our own heads. Secondly, anger can cloud the judgment, so that right-wing women are eagerly embraced as sisters in the struggle. Thirdly, it turns women against other women; women who work in the sex industry feel the anger is directed at them, and condemn moral crusaders as hypocrites.

And anger obscures many difficult questions. Such as: is male violence against women sexually based — is violence, domination an inherent aspect of male sexuality, and therefore present in some way in all sexual relationships between men and women? Or has our society created this type of sexuality as part and parcel of a structure of male supremacy, in the same way as in a slave society all relationships between masters and slaves were tainted and deformed by the necessity of maintaining the power structure intact? In other words, is society sexist because our sexual behaviour is psychologically based on domination and submission — or have we created this sort of sexual behaviour pattern in order to justify and perpetuate male domination? How much do we create our own sexuality — how much does our sexuality create us?

Feminists have to find our own position on what to do about pornography. We cannot simply accept the liberal argument, that there is a distinction between public display of pornographic images, and using them in the privacy of the home. For liberals, the public display is possibly bad because it reinforces contemptuous ideas about women, and hardens people to accepting degraded images of sex, and coarsens thinking, particularly young people's thinking. Feminists argue that these links are still there even when pornography is used privately.

On the other hand, we cannot simply argue that the state should ban it. We do not accept that the state should have that sort of control over issues of sexuality such as abortion rights, access to contraception, and the free expression of sexuality by lesbians and homosexual men. As we have seen in chapter 11, anti-feminist women's groups have made a lot of headway by crusading against pornography, by appealing to women's fear of aggressive sexuality. There has to be a third way to go — a feminist campaign against exploitative sexual imagery, which still leaves room for affirmations of sexual pleasure, and the use of sexual representations which challenge conventional stereotyped thinking about female sexuality.

14

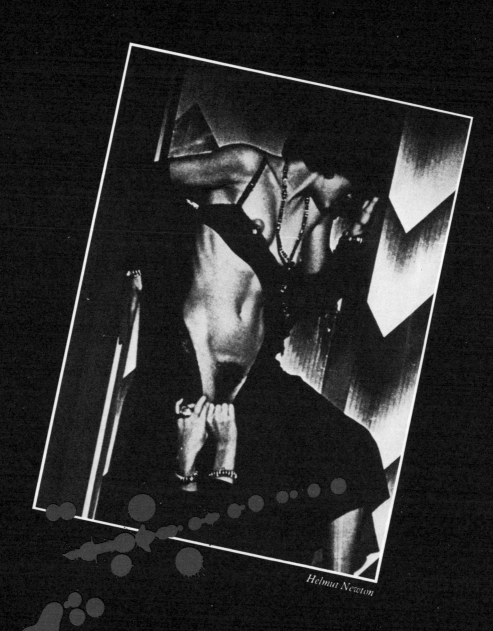

Helmut Newton

**Despite what advertisers tell you ...
Rape is NOT being worn this year!!!**

VIOLENCE

Helmut Newton

Over 60% of all homicides occur between people who know each other, often, are intimately connected

80% of child sexual assaults are perpetrated by a man known to, or in a close relationship with, the child

THE violence that women fear is of a special kind, that goes right to the heart of their sense of themselves as women. Men may fear the random and unprovoked violence of a car accident, may feel uneasy about having to one day face a challenge to their manhood in a brawl, may resent the presence of muggers on their streets. But unless they are homosexuals, they won't have to feel the dread of open spaces at night, won't fight down panic if a man stares at them hard on a deserted street, won't have to cope with front page stories about being raped and murdered in their beds by strangers — and probably won't fear deadly violence at the hands of their wives. Nor, if violence happens, in the random and casual fashion of the television crime show, will men need to examine their own motives, gnawing away at the possibility that it was all their fault, that their being there and being a man made it all happen. That their bodies, the way they moved and dressed, the way they walked, were in fact invitations to sex.

WOMAN IN TROUBLE

ANDREW BELL

Woman ! Woman in trouble !
There's danger in the alleyway
They want my love, but they'd rather bruise my face.
Woman ! Woman in trouble !
She's cryin' out to her brothers in the night
But they're all drinking at the house of Delight

I can't walk out in the streets at night
It's bad enough in the day
I see some creep walkin' up to me, and he's got something
to say
"Wanna fuck ?"

Woman ! Take it slow !
You'd better walk out on the bright side of the street
Or you might end up with your head at some guy's feet

DIALOGUE WITH MUSIC UNDER

Hey, baby, hey come on	(WHISTLE)
Hey, knockers	Oooh
Hey, look at those tits	Oooh
Oh come on	Come on
Hey	Oh, let's look at ya
Hey listen, listen	I'm lonely
I'll just	I'll just give ya a lift
I'll just	I won't ya know,
Oh come on	I'm not a moron, I'm not like one of those
Oooh	guys you read about in the papers.
Aw please	And I'm so lonely
You're so beautiful	Look it's gonna rain
And I	I'll just give ya a ride home
And I wanna	What are ya? smart or something?
Oh come on baby	Go to university or somethin
I really	do ya?
I really wanna	
talk to you	
Smart bitch	Think ya got brains?
Yah	Smart bitch
Hey legs	Hey!

Gimme a look at ya	Hey you with the tits
Aw gee	turn round
Come on	Come on
Come on	Stuck up bitch
	Wouldn't fuck her with a dog's dick !

I'd like to carry a knife in my belt
And push it in all the way
There's no use cryin' when the deed is done
Because the cops won't see it your way

Woman ! Woman in trouble !
The judge is holding your life in his hands
No matter how he tries, he still thinks like a man

Woman ! Take it in your hands !
If you can learn to hit hard and run
You might make him into the sorry one
You gotta make him into the sorry one
You gotta make him, we gotta shake him
We gotta break him into the sorry one.

In the late 1970s the women's movement concentrated attention on the sexual and physical abuse of women — that is, on rape, domestic violence, sexual harassment at work, incest — from two points of view. From one point of view, feminists were looking for remedies, looking to change the laws which made a rape trial into a trial of the victim's character, laws which failed to protect women from violence from their husbands and boyfriends, laws which allowed women to be imprisoned for murder when they struck back. From the other point of view, feminists were building a new politics, a new way of seeing the world and the relations between men and women; from this point of view feminists linked together male sexuality, male power, and the images of violence against women which saturate pornography, and provide the plot line and tension to most thrillers.

The second viewpoint, this radical feminist politics, is what most people have in mind when they call feminists 'manhaters'. The vehemence of society's response to these feminist arguments is not altogether surprising, given the amount of real anger which feminists discovered in themselves when they confronted the issues. Like the peace movement of the 1980s, the feminist campaign against male violence has an urgency about it, a feeling that this is a matter of life or death, which leads to confrontationist politics.

But there's something else there too, some raw nerve which has been touched by the feminist campaigns. It must be the way in which male aggression and male sexuality have been linked — so that some men feel that *being* male is the crime of which they are accused.

But whatever the approach, the basic message feminists have about violence against women is that it is not a matter of explaining how and why individual men come to assault individual women, but a question of how men as a sex see women as a sex. And why women endure the violence and the threat of violence is explained more by women's economic choices (or lack of them) and women's training in sexual politeness and deference to men, than it is by theories about women's supposed masochism or wish to be dominated. So for women, it's a combination of how they see themselves as a sex relative to men, and their real economic and emotional dependency in marriage and relationships.

Let us look at some prevalent images of women in relation to violent behaviour.

'it is very easy, as you know, for a girl to say after the event, "it was without my consent" … in many cases there are obvious considerations which might move her after the event to assert that: remorse, fear of pregnancy, a feeling of shame, and so on.' (judge addressing the jury in a rape case)

In a recent rape trial in England the judge declined to send the defendant to gaol, on the grounds that the victim had been guilty of 'contributory negligence', by being out alone, needing a lift home on a rainy night. There is of course no such thing as contributory negligence in a criminal case — the concept only applies to accidents.

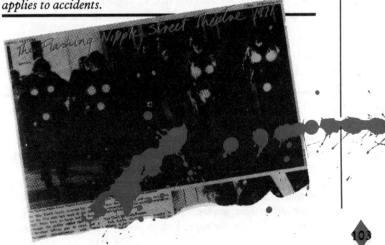

VE FREE FROM MALE AGGRESSION

RAPE IS ABOUT POWER NOT SEX

The penalties for rape are among the most severe in the criminal law. If we are to go by the language of the statute books, you would think that rape was one of the most hated crimes imaginable. Yet for many women the experience of the trial of their assailant is almost as painful and humiliating as the rape itself, with all the questioning directed at her, apparently trying to make out that she had done something to give her attacker the idea that she wanted sex with him. In many parts of the world it is standard practice for the defence lawyers in a rape case to bring to court evidence of sexual relationships the victim has had with other men, as part of an argument that if she would do it with X, wasn't it reasonable for Y to think she would do it with him. Some judges tell the jury that if the woman did not struggle, that helps to give weight to the man's claim that he thought she was consenting.

How do the victims of rape see themselves in relation to these images of their active part in precipitating the assault?

'During the actual experience of rape you will yourself to be utterly controlled, to keep the situation from ending in your death. Sometimes this attitude carries over through the reporting to the police — coolness and control — this is often seen by the police as inappropriate behaviour.'
'Sometimes the reactions of other women can be the most destructive. People ask you, why didn't you…? This saps your self-esteem, makes it clear to you that you have to take responsibility for the rape. Yes, women do have responsibilities

in relation to rape — they extend as far as making sure there is clear sexual communication, and not getting blind drunk — but why do you have to live in a fortress, and always have a companion when you go out?'

For these women, interviewed at a Rape Crisis Centre, the experience of rape, and its legal aftermath, has reminded them painfully of how difficult it is for a woman to gain any autonomy and freedom of movement for herself. From puberty girls are trained to be always watching themselves, alert for any slip in their guard that would allow a predatory male to take advantage, always aware of the sexual potential in any situation, prepared to negotiate men out of potential misunderstandings (politely of course), to manage and defuse the sexual charge in a conversation.

Rosalind Coward has pointed out how there is an odd difference between this expectation of how sexual encounters are managed, and the media image of the rapist, which reveals how there is a belief that male aggression is normal, female passivity eternal.

'in some forms of tabloid journalism it is customary to refer to women as "birds" or "sex kittens"…Men, however, accrue such epithets as "the office wolf". And those "sex offenders", in whom such newspapers are excessively interested, are referred to as "monsters" and "fiends"…Such language promotes a view of the sexes as two species: the strong species — dogs and wolves — pursue the weak — birds and kittens. When the customary limits are overstepped, men become monsters, gone too far in their natural pursuits.'

TRAFFIC
JENNIFER STRAUSS

How can I concentrate on getting there
Assaulted by some radio pontificator
Saying that rape
Is a sexual disability of women.
My rear-vision mirror tells
That tears
Are tracking a slow path
Down that woman's averted face
In the car behind.
She is the passenger: her man drives.
His mouth snicks open and shut
Above the barbs of his beard.
I try to think
That he is being kind,
But his gears grind in anger.
I am afraid that he will run me down as well;
They don't like you acquiring
The power of machines.

Some feminists, like Susan Brownmiller, author of *Against Our Will : Men, Women and Rape,* have argued that sexual violence, forcing women against their will, is the truth about patriarchal society; that violence, or the everpresent threat of violence, underpins all social institutions, and is the secret of control over women. So that actual violence by a minority of men, although officially condemned, is being carried out on behalf of all men. This is the sense in which the slogan 'all men are rapists' was used.

This theory is far too sweeping to be usefully proved or disproved. And as a general theory of the meaning of sexual violence, it is of little help when it comes to explaining why the other group who are subjected to sexual violence are homosexual males.

But it has enough of the ring of truth about it to focus people's minds on the connection between sexual violence and the unequal power relations between men and women — and to take notice of the fact that in many acts of rape the motive seems more to do with inflicting fear and humiliation, rather than sexual gratification. In the decade since Brownmiller's book was published, rape laws in many parts of the world have been changed, to include within the definition of rape assaults which do not involve the penis, and to reduce the odds against the victim at the trial by changing the rules of evidence. For example, it is no longer the case in most states of Australia that there must be some corroborating evidence (some evidence apart from the word of the victim alone) before a man may be convicted of rape. Nor may a victim's previous sexual history be used against her in quite the same free way, to discredit her and plant the suggestion that she has easy moral standards. And in some states the law has been changed to allow a husband to be prosecuted for raping his wife —which is a considerable victory for the principle that a woman's body is her own to enjoy and give as she wishes, and cannot be owned by anyone else.

THE COMPANION PLAY TO THE FATAL WEDDING

FOR HER CHILDREN'S SAKE
BY THEO. KREMER

MANAGEMENT SULLIVAN, HARRIS & WOODS

"IF YOU STRIKE MY MOTHER, I'LL SHOOT!"

TWO LOVELY BLACK EYES
CHARLES COBURN
Two lovely black eyes
O what a surprise
Only for telling a man he was wrong
Two lovely black eyes.

If looking closely at the facts and the reasons for rape gives us alarming insights into the difference between what the law says and what the law does about protecting women from male violence, looking at *domestic violence* (wife-bashing) is just plain depressing. At least in the case of rape we can see that the law is grappling with difficult concepts to do with the nature of male and female sexuality. But the failure of the law to protect women from the violence of the men they live with is simply callous — so much so, that it is justifiable to suspect that it's all about men sticking together. More palatably, and officially, the problems that lawyers find here are to do with maintaining the sanctity of marriage, the privacy of the home, and the civil liberties of the individual. But scratch a little deeper, and you soon start to encounter arguments about 'eternal human nature', like the one that says that women make themselves into victims for deep psychological reasons, or that some level of violence is inevitable in close human relationships ... inevitable, or just accepted?

Of course the phenomenon of wife-bashing has a long history, and didn't just come to light with the new wave of feminism. But before feminists started taking the lid off marriage, and insisting that personal life was political, wife-bashing was explained in terms of individual men and individual women, or at best, in terms of personality types. So it used to be associated with alcoholism (true, but that is not the whole story), or with individual women whose mothers had been bashed, and who somehow seemed to attract the bashers by their vulnerability (getting closer to the truth here), or in terms of poverty and hopelessness (not true — it happens just as often in the leafy suburbs as the decaying inner city), or an alleged working class culture of casual and expected violence. We now think that violence may be 'as typical of family relationships as love is' and that although the popular image of family violence is of Andy Capp's missus waiting up with a rolling pin, most family violence is directed at women and children first.

And still our society wants to blame the women for being the victims. If they're not being blamed for their weakness in staying with a violent man, they're being blamed for

I, Violet Roberts, wish to make application for release on licence. On March 15th, 1976, I was sentenced to life imprisonment for the murder of my husband Eric Roberts ... While I certainly do not think there is any good reason to kill *anyone,* when one suffers so much as my husband caused me to, the savage beatings, the mental torture and sexual miseries ... one lived in constant fear of him. My husband was a brutal alcoholic ... During those last 12 months, I was seldom without black eyes, bruises ... two days before the crime, he had broken a bone in one of my fingers. In addition to all the other troubles, I lost a very dear son, David, just 21 of leukemia ... I was so distraught, depressed, so very tired that night, I had not had a good night's sleep for months as every night he kept me awake with his insatiable sexual demands ... very little of my husband's behaviour was mentioned in court. I do hope you will look favourably on this, my application. I would certainly abide by whatever restrictions were placed on me, I would just be so happy to be home again.

provoking him to violence with nagging about money, or challenges to his sense of manhood. What this last piece of folk wisdom expresses is probably in fact close to the truth of the matter, when we turn the statement around, and realise that what it says is that a man needs to be in authority at home.

In many of the documented examples of sustained violence against wives, it seems that the triggering factor was often some trivial incident, like failing to be home when the man returned from work, or letting the children answer back. As Elizabeth Wilson comments,

'Far from being abnormal behaviour, the violence of men towards the women they live with should rather be seen as an extreme form of normality, an exaggeration of how society expects men to behave — as the authority figure in the family.'
Elizabeth Wilson, *WHAT IS TO BE DONE ABOUT VIOLENCE AGAINST WOMEN?*

It's hard to avoid the feeling that the instinctive reaction of law enforcers and policy-makers faced with the appalling facts of the 'normality' of domestic violence is to blame the victims, to say that the women have brought it on themselves by failing to recognise the strains on the man, or by being provocative. People who react like this are burying

Joanne Little*
BERNICE REAGON

Who is this girl, and what is she to you?
CHORUS:
Joanne Little, she's my sister
Joanne Little, she's our mama
Joanne Little, she's your lover
Joanne the woman who's gonna carry your child

I've always been told since the day I was born
Leave them no good women alone
Child you better keep your nose clean keep your butt off the street
You gonna be judged by the company you keep
Said I always walked by the golden rule
Steered clear of controversy I stayed real cool
Till along come this woman little over five feet tall
Charged and jailed with breaking the law
And the next thing I heard as it came over the news
First degree murder she was on the loose
Tell me who is this girl —
    and what is she to you?

CHORUS

Now I ain't talking bout the roaring west
This is 1975 at its most oppressive best
North Carolina state the pride of this land
Made her an outlaw hunted on every hand
Tell me what did she do to deserve this name
Killed a man who thought she was fair game
When I heard the news I screamed inside
Lost all my cool my anger I could not hide
'Cause now Joanne is you and Joanne is me
Our prison is the whole society
'Cause we live in a land that'll bring all pressure to bear on the head of a woman whose position we share
Tell me who is this girl —
    and what is she to you?

CHORUS

heir heads in the sand, perhaps out of a belief in the importance above all of keeping families together, and regarding the woman's job as being to suppress her own personality and needs, in order to avoid precipitating a violent crisis.

The bitterness of the double standard involved in this sort of thinking shows up very clearly when we look at the cases of women who have struck back, after enduring years of physical and mental, and sometimes sexual abuse, and killed the violent husband. For them the 'compassionate' law could find no defence of provocation.

The same attitudes are seen in media and bureaucratic reactions to revelations of incest involving fathers or step-fathers and young girls. For many people the issue is how to avoid breaking up the family, and the mother is blamed for allowing the situation to go unchallenged and therefore untreated, until the stage where the police are called, often when the victim reaches the age of understanding what has been happening to her, or realises that her sister is next.

By focussing attention on the 'normality' of violence within families, feminists have laid the groundwork for changes in the law or changes in police attitudes to domestic violence, which put the emphasis on removing the violent man, and offering the woman a chance to escape.

The banality of violence: victim women — the great cliche of stage and screen

So ingrained is the connection between feminine/violence/sexuality, that one of the most obvious cliches in the cinema is the following: a click of high heels down a dark street, low camera angle, deliberate footsteps coming after...we all know what's going to happen, and we know that the mad killer isn't really mad, just sexually obsessed. Why is it that this scenario is such a cliche, that it doesn't really shock us? Why is it that any film which uses this image to speak about the reality of male violence against women is described as obvious, unsubtle?

It is this quality of banality about the equation between women, violence, sex that is really the most disturbing thing, and makes it so hard to combat. People are desensitised to it, in the way that for a time it appeared that television audiences were becoming desensitised to images of horror coming out of Vietnam. See them too often, and the pictures lose their power to shock.

All of this came out in the open in a recent exchange of views about a film called *Body Double,* made by Brian de Palma. A thriller based on this conventional mode of creating suspense — the woman in danger — it was criticised by some as misogynist, woman-hating. Brian de Palma vehemently defended his film, and his artistic integrity, arguing that film-makers have to deal in the common stock of fantasy images, and that his intentions were ironic; to show up how the cliche works to create the thrill.

A more convincing, and less dubious demonstration of the power of this everyday cliche is in the films of Dutch feminist Marleen Gorris. She uses the conventional images to say that they express a deep truth about our culture, that violence is an everyday thing, that all women are vulnerable, and that all women know that when it happens it is about hatred of women. Because she was using the cliche to tell the truth, and not in the pursuit of suspense, or thrills, she was criticised as having committed the great sin of being too obvious.

Ella, in a square apron, along Highway 80

She's a copperheaded waitress, tired and sharp-worded, she hides
her bad brown tooth behind a wicked
smile, and flicks her ass
out of habit, to fend off the pass
that passes for affection.
She keeps her mind the way men
keep a knife — keen to strip the game
down to her size. She has a thin spine,
swallows her eggs cold, and tells lies.
She slaps a wet rag at the truck drivers
if they should complain. She understands
the necessity for pain, turns away
the smaller tips, out of pride, and
keeps a flask under the counter. Once,
she shot a lover who misused her child.
Before she got out of jail, the courts had pounced
and given the child away. Like some isolated lake,
her flat blue eyes take care of their own stark
bottoms. Her hands are nervous, curled, ready
to scrape.
The common woman is as common
as a rattlesnake.

Robyn Stacey

15

Hi Lindy *On the beach at Surfers Paradise is Lindy Morrison, 20, of Hawthorne, Brisbane.*

Lindy Morrisson, drummer with the Go-Betweens *Robyn Stacey*

CYCLE

This chapter is about women and their bodies: the part played in women's oppression by their hormones, the sorry saga of contraception, the experience of living as a woman inside an ageing body.

CYCLE
ROBYN ARCHER

I was not quite twelve the day I started to bleed
We went to the football: Mum, Dad, and me
They kept glancing, proud of their tomboy new-freed
And my cousin said 'Now you're a woman.'

I escaped falling pregnant though I slept with boys till
I was eighteen, I think, when I first took the pill
It meant we could go after every cheap thrill
And save having babies for later.

But when I was twenty my sisters grew strong
We rethought our roles and we learned it was wrong
To sacrifice selfhood for motherhood long
And we welcomed a childless future.

As my thirties rolled on I saw many a close friend
Obsessed by the thought of a child, to that end
They moved into communes, drew up contracts with men
Tried to make up for ten years' delaying.

Now my menopause comes, the choice can't be reversed
I live out precisely the life I rehearsed
My time's been my own with no baby to nurse
I just wonder if I'd have enjoyed it.

AT the beginning of the book we pointed out how feminism was about 'femininity', that it was a way of understanding how our society makes girls into feminine women, how a biological distinction between the sexes is transformed into a cultural and social system of 'gender'. This distinction between sex, which is a biological fact, and gender, which is a cultural and social artefact, is quite crucial to understanding feminism, and much of this book has been about how the distinction works. But now we must look at how feminism, and our culture and society, deal with the female bodies of women, to see the relationship between body, gender and women's experience.

Take menstruation, for example. Experience of menstruation, and the physical changes at the onset and cessation of menstruation (the menopause), are indisputably common to all women. And it is clearly an important common element in women's experience — think of all the autobiographical women's novels which deal movingly with the excruciating embarrassment or bewilderment of the young girl's first unexpected period, or the pride and exultation of feeling part of a great community of adult women. It's a constant experience of physicality, often romanticised by women and men alike ('Only women bleed...') or groaned over in a companionable way by women among

ON THE LIBERATING EFFECTS OF FRANKNESS —
GERMAINE GREER

'Although enlightenment is creeping into this field at its usual pace, we still have a marked revulsion for menstruation, principally evinced by our efforts to keep it secret. The success of the tampon is partly due to the fact that it is hidden...Women still buy sanitary towels with enormous discretion, and carry their handbags to the loo when they only need to carry a napkin. They still recoil at the idea of intercourse during menstruation, and feel that the blood they shed is of a special kind, although perhaps not so special as was thought when it was the liquid presented to the devil in witches' loving cups. If you think you are emancipated, you might consider the idea of tasting your menstrual blood — if it makes you sick, you've got a long way to go, baby.'

Talking about menstruation was, in the early years of the women's liberation movement, part of a strategy of de-mystifying thinking about women. Feminists showed how exaggerated coyness about menstruation was part of a definition of 'femininity' that was restrictive of women's physical freedom, part of a repressive attitude towards sex and the body, and contributed to women's anxieties about their appearance and 'personal freshness'.

To a woman who felt faintly disgusted by the whole process, society offered the soft-focus perfection of the women in the Modess ads, floating serene and unstained through grassy meadows. What a choice! Unattainable perfection, or your own weary, bloated, uncomfortable self.

Now the tampon ads have gone for the opposite stereotype of woman — active, physical, confident, ballet dancers, water skiers, sexually autonomous, rich, young women — but still the message of 'trust your tampon' is wrapped in a layer of anxiety, the reminder of how terrible it would be if it failed. Beneath the matter-of-fact tone, and the strong liberated women's images, there's still the coded message of femininity, which in this context means repress the truth about the body's function.

Raging hormones No. 1

In 1980 a young woman named Deborah Wardley applied to be taken on as a trainee airline pilot, with hundreds of hours' flying experience under her belt, and a grand determination to succeed. Her case eventually came to the High Court of Australia, on the question of whether the airline which refused her application was bound by the sex discrimination laws then in force. Although the case was always argued at the elevated level of legal principle and technicality, what was really at stake was the airline's belief that women are subject to unpredictable hormonal tides, which render them unreliable, moody, erratic, given to failures of concentration, irrationality and depression, all dangerous qualities in the cockpit of a 747. Well, yes, if a female was affected by her period in this way, she would be dangerous to have in the cockpit. But no-one had any evidence to suggest that this woman had suffered these effects of her menstrual cycle — that was never an issue. Nor was there any discussion of the legitimacy or otherwise of generalised conclusions about women's suitability for particular types of work based solely on untested assumptions about women's susceptibility to physiological changes. Knowing that the real issue was 'women's troubles' lent an air of farce to the solemn spectacle of the wigged and gowned barristers arguing points of law about employers' rights.

The airline involved had recently passed out of the hands of its founder, a business magnate fondly remembered for his description of the spokeswomen for the hostesses' union as 'those old boilers'. Deborah Wardley won her right to fly.

THE MENSTRUATION BLUES
ROBYN ARCHER

I got the menstruation, the menstruation blues
And I got 'em so hard I don't know how to lose them

I can feel my life blood flowin', flowin' down the drain
And the hardest damn thing to face is that next month it's all gonna happen again

I got a pain in my guts and my head is spinnin' around
I feel like the lowest kind of animal crawling on the ground

I can't chuck, I can't even fuck
Honey this thing has put me out of luck

No one wants to mouth around that fishy old smell
Lordy I'm so lonesome and I feel like hell

I had to spend my dope money on a bunch of fanny rags
I'm 'bout to tell you that this thing is gettin' to be one hell of a drag

HA! MINE COMES EVERY 21 DAYS!

C'MON, A BIT OF BLOOD WON'T HURT YA SON!

DON'T DISTURB DADDY, HE IS HAVING A BAD PERIOD.

Raging hormones No. 2

In 1981 two British court cases established the possibility that a woman might be able to put up pre-menstrual tension as a defence — a bit like arguing temporary insanity. In one case a woman killed her lover by running him down in her car, having discovered that he was meeting another woman. In the second case a woman threatened a policeman with a knife. She had a long list of convictions for violent behaviour, such as arson and assault, and several attempts at suicide, all occurring while she was suffering from PMT.

Arguing that PMT should be a recognised factor, like a mental condition, which reduces a woman's responsibility for crimes committed while under its influence, is very problematic. As we have seen in the last chapter, it is important for the law to recognise that explanations and excuses for human behaviour on which many legal processes, and especially the defences of provocation and self-defence, are founded are male-biased. They have been established in cases involving men, and are often simply inappropriate to women's experience. However, there's a crucial difference between saying that women's experiences are different from men's because of women's lack of resources, lack of physical power, and because of restrictive attitudes towards women; and saying that women's bodies determine their behaviour in ways that men's bodies do not.

In a study in 1981 most of the 500 participating women reported noticing some degree of physical, emotional or behavioural change in the premenstrual phase of their monthly cycle. However, it was found that the way women reacted to these changes — regarding their experience as normal and something to be put up with, or a cause for anger and irritation, or as a medical problem — depended very much on their overall personal circumstances, and how much they understood the actual physiological processes of menstruation.

WOMEN WHO KILL
ROBYN ARCHER/ANDREW BELL

A woman went talking, went interview walking
Went into the prison
She had many questions to ask of the inmates
In the women's state prison
She asked from her prepared notes, her research was sound
She asked 'what made you kill?', and this is what she found
CHORUS:
When a woman strikes, she strikes finally   (The women who kill)
When a woman waits, she waits optimall'y   (The women who kill)
This once domestic animal sits out her awful day
Just watching for the best glimpse of the throat of her prey
When a woman strikes, she strikes finally   (The women who kill)

More men mix it with crime, at any old time
You'd like to mention
It's part of the psyche of a businessman or bikie
Attack is their dimension
But a woman's long-suffering of the life that she hates
Till past the point of endurance she don't make no mistakes
CHORUS
And there's just one small addendum, it pertains to the pudendum,
It's just what was discovered,
After saving up for years the sum of bruises, anger, tears
When she wants to recover
The woman who kills waits for the monthly smell of blood
If she's gonna get you, beware those few days just before the flood.
You'd need intimate knowledge, exactly when she's gonna bleed,
This ain't no ordinary murd'rer, it's a woman who kills, Take heed!)
CHORUS

Women are at the mercy of their hormones in a much more direct way — by the practical need to find an effective and safe contraceptive.

The ultimate in contraceptives, the pill, works by pumping extra hormones through the bloodstream, with potential, but disputed side-effects which include increased risk of thrombosis and heart attack, added to the well-known but cavalierly dismissed effects of weight gain and breast tenderness. Injectable hormonal contraceptives, such as Depo-Provera, are even more controversial, since the side-effects of progestogens are potentially more serious, and the dose once given cannot be withdrawn, with the effects continuing for months. Depo-Provera is widely used by family planning organisations in the Third World, as well as by child welfare authorities in the West, for young girls whose sexual behaviour is regarded as putting them at risk of pregnancy, but who are thought too irresponsible to trust with self-administered daily methods of contraception.

As this book goes to press, thousands of women are filing lawsuits against the American pharmaceutical manufacturer A H Robins, for damages to compensate for the horrific effects of an intra-uterine device, the Dalkon Shield, which caused massive pelvic infections, sterility, and even death, because of the poor design which made it a conductor of infection into the uterus.

As we have seen in chapter 9, it has been a battle to win for women the right to control their own fertility. Now women are the victims of a male medical establishment which seems to regard a high level of discomfort and danger as an acceptable price for women to pay for that right. And as women in the West abandon hazardous hormonal methods of contraception, women in the Third World are being induced to take them up. The unwanted contraceptives are being dumped on poor countries by the rich countries which manufacture them, as a form of 'foreign aid'.

Management of fertility by manipulating hormones is making sisters of women the world over, and not for the first time. The oral contraceptive pill was secretly tested on poor and illiterate women in South America by the drug companies of the United States, with the blessing of the international family planning and aid organisations.

When we think of the loneliness of old age, we should be thinking of the loneliness of old women. Women outlive men, on average, by 7-8 years; on average, women marry men 2-3 years older than themselves. So the average woman can look forward to a widowhood of up to 10 years. Old people in our society have low status; women in our society have low status; little old ladies are the least consequential of all our citizens.

Because our thinking about women is so resolutely tied to the idea of women and children, older women are almost invisible on the agendas of social problem solvers. What happens to women when the children have left home and the husband dies?

One thing which happens is that old women end in the care of their unmarried daughters, or living with married children and their families.

My grandmother in the shower
GILLIAN COOTE

Cardigan, dun hose and spangled jiffies
Abandoned.
Spectacles too.
Eyes now unseeing,
the shower begins,
tepid and gentle
enveloping the ancient body.

Hands fumbling for baby soap
or clutching the rail
and looking frail.
Pelican-thin legs swaying
on the ansell non-slip.
Eyes seeping and sagging.
Amazing elephant folds on her buttocks
A shy eroded erotic zone.
One-two up with the breast flaps,
Give them a good scrub.

Talcum whitening the strange grey-pink
of legs of arms of back of buttock folds.
Throw it up the spout and laugh
at the last intrusion.
No regret in the air though,
all convivial and steamy
after the water-purge.

Susan Edwards, in FEMALE SEXUALITY AND THE LAW quotes a 19th century medical theory: 'man possesses his sexual organs; her sexual organs possess woman.'

NOBODY SINGS
CARYL CHURCHILL

I met an old old woman
Who made my blood run cold
You don't stop wanting sex, she said
Just because you're old
    Oh nobody sings about it
    But it happens every time.

I should be glad of the change of life
But it makes me feel so strange
All your life is being wanted
Do you want your life to change?
    Oh nobody sings about it
    But it happens every time.

Do you want your skin to wrinkle
And your cunt get sore and dry
And they say it's just your hormones
If you're angry and cry and cry
    Oh nobody sings about it
    But it happens every time.

Nobody ever saw me
She whispered in a rage
They were blinded by my beauty
Now they're blinded by my age
    Oh nobody sings about it
    But it happens all the time.

I: Me: Myself *Robyn Stacey*

In the 1984 statistical study Australian Families (the most recent study available), one in every three women over the age of 60 was living alone. One in 10 was living with an adult child. Sixty-eight % of people not living with family members were in fact women living alone.

As women are traditionally carers for their aged parents (or their husbands' aged parents), the problems of old age are women's problems in a double sense.

Women, middle-aged and old, are caught up in each other's life cycles in complex patterns of caring. Women in their fifties are often caring for aged and invalid mothers — when they are in a stage of life when they might have expected relief from the mothering role, they mother their mothers. Women in their late sixties and seventies living with daughters or daughters-in-law are often caring for young grandchildren. When an unmarried or widowed woman in her later years is caring for an old invalid mother, the isolation from work and social life can be particularly acute for both women, as the burden of care lasts over the years and takes constant attention from the carer. There is a strange parallel here with the isolation experienced by young women at home with very young children — women withdraw from social life at both extremes of their adult lives.

And because women outlive their men, it is on women that the burden of grief falls disproportionately.

THE SHOPPER
BERTOLT BRECHT Trs Michael Hamburger

I am an old woman.
When Germany had awoken
Pension rates were cut. My children
Gave me the pennies they could spare. But
I could hardly buy anything now. So at first
I went less often to the shops where I'd gone daily.
But one day I thought it over, and then
Daily once more I went to the baker's, the greengrocer's
As an old customer.
With care I picked my provisions
Took no more than I used to, but no less either
Put rolls beside the loaf and leeks beside the cabbage and
    only
When they added up the bill did I sigh
With my stiff fingers dug into my little purse
And shaking my head confessed that I didn't have enough
To pay for those few things, and shaking my head I
Left the shop, observed by all the customers.
I said to myself:
If all of us who have nothing
No longer turn up where food is laid out
They may think we don't need anything
But if we come and are unable to buy
They'll know how it is.

"JOAN OF ARC"
Special Academy Award Picture
Starring
INGRID
BERGMAN

HEROINES

From a speech on woman's sphere
LUCY STONE 1855

'I WISH that women, instead of being walking showcases, instead of begging of their fathers and brothers the latest and gayest new bonnet, would ask of them their rights.

The question of Woman's Rights is a practical one. The notion has prevailed that it was only an ephemeral idea; that it was but women claiming the right to smoke cigars in the streets, and to frequent bar-rooms. Others have supposed it a question of comparative intellect; others still of sphere. Too much has already been said and written about woman's sphere. Trace all the doctrines to their source and they will be found to have no basis except in the usages and prejudices of the age. This is seen in the fact that what is

from **LEGACY**
ROBYN ARCHER/ANDREW BELL

Legacy
The voices from the past are such a legacy,
Open up your ears, I know that you will see,
The voices from the past are such a legacy.

tolerated in woman in one country is not tolerated in another. In this country women may hold prayer meetings, etc., but in Mohammedan countries it is written upon their mosques, 'Women and dogs, and other impure animals, are not permitted to enter.' Wendell Phillips says, 'The best and greatest thing one is capable of doing, that is his sphere.' ...Leave women, then, to find their sphere. And do not tell us before we are born even, that our province is to cook dinners, darn stockings, and sew on buttons. We are told woman has all the rights she wants; and even women, I am ashamed to say, tell us so. They mistake the politeness of men for rights — seats, while men stand in this hall tonight, and their adulations; but these are mere courtesies. We want rights. The flour-merchant, the house-builder, and the postman charge us no less on account of our sex; but when we endeavour to earn money to pay all these, then, indeed, we find the difference. Women working in tailor shops are paid one third as much as men. Someone in Philadelphia has stated that women make fine shirts for twelve and a half cents apiece, that no woman can make more than nine a week, and the sum thus earned, after deducting rent, fuel etc. leaves her just three and a half cents a day for bread. Is it a wonder that women are driven to prostitution?...The present condition of woman causes a horrible perversion of the marriage relation...it is asked of a lady, 'Has she married well?' Oh, yes, her husband is rich. Woman must marry for a home...

Thus widening of woman's sphere is to improve her lot. Let us do it, and

if the world scoff, let it scoff — if it sneer, let it sneer...'

Radicals and reformers are often guilty of pretending that the struggle has no past, that up till now people have blundered along in dim incomprehension of the nature and reality of their oppression, or have lacked the knowledge or the vision to overcome it. But from the beginning, late 20th century feminism has had a strong historical sensibility, tracing continuities between the experience of womanhood in 19th century society and the present, to attempt to explain the endurance of the ideal of the housewife and mother in the face of the vast changes in every other aspect of women's social lives. Feminists have found precursors in 18th and 19th century women thinkers and social activists, such as Mary Wollstonecraft (died 1797, author of *A Vindication of the Right of Woman*); Harriet Martineau (died 1876, prolific writer on social problems and economics, advocate of free divorce and birth control); Lucy Stone, campaigner against slavery and for women's rights, who kept her maiden name on marriage; the Pankhurst women at the turn of the 20th century, leaders in the struggle for women's right to vote. These women were precursors of modern feminism because their social vision of the potential for women, and their analysis of the reasons for women's subjection, focused on factors which are still central to feminist argument — the role of women's housework in the economy of the country, the role of marriage and motherhood in denying women their full potential, he importance of women being able to support themselves, the degrading dependence of women on men, and its role in maintaining the institutions of marriage and the family, and prostitution.

But contemporary feminism is also developing a much more complex and multistranded relationship with its past. It's going beyond pointing to precursors in order to demonstrate the justice of an argument, and is making a statement about the continuity of women's experience — a continuity of struggle, and a continuity of experience in the long periods when women's intellectual breakthroughs and illuminating insights appear to have been forgotten. It's a process of looking with new eyes at our heroines, and seeing their legacy in two ways. First, seeing them as heroines, women standing against the current of their societies, women before their time, precursors of our own struggles. Second, seeing them as part of the past, a history that shapes our own sense of the possibilities for women. Their image as heroines is what this chapter is about. What does their prominence tell us about the way history is made, and women's part in the making of it?

---

*...a historical sensibility allows us to see that the makers of history are not a breed apart...that the tailoresses who struck in 1883 were no more or less solid than the typists seeking compensation for repetition strain injuries.'
Humphrey McQueen, in AUSTRALIAN SOCIETY, January 1986)*

---

*What is "common" in and to women is the intersection of oppression and strength, damage and beauty. It is, quite simply, the ORDINARY in women which will "rise" in every sense of the word — spiritually and in activism. For us, to be "extraordinary" or "uncommon" is to fail. History has been embellished with "extraordinary", "exemplary", "uncommon", and of course "token" women whose lives have left the rest unchanged. The "common woman" is in fact the embodiment of the extraordinary will-to-survival in millions of obscure women...'
Adrienne Rich, in an essay entitled 'Power and Danger: Works of a Common Woman,' in ON LIES, SECRETS AND SILENCE).*

Adrienne Rich is reminding us how the writers of history have been comfortably able to accommodate the existence of powerful, aggressive, stroppy and troublesome women, to weave their actions into a self-congratulatory picture of the march of progress, while ignoring the mundane lives of the mass of the women of their time. So how different is that from the way the mass of ordinary men have been treated by history? Quite simply, men do get a look in — as peasants, patriots, armies, rioters. The actions of men in groups are recorded, while women do not appear on the historical record *except* as isolated, singular figures. Their prominence in the pages of history implies that they are exceptional in two senses — exceptional as compared to the shadowy and dimly perceived mass of ordinary people, but, more dangerously, exceptional as compared to the completely invisible mass of women whose shadow does not even fall across the pages of history. We have no real points of comparison, to know how these women were different from their sisters. We have to believe their legends.

Joan of Arc is a fascinating historical figure — and a legend. In her book about the woman and her legend, Marina Warner makes a very telling point about how unique a figure she is. No other female hero is remembered for such a combination of military accomplishments, and saintly martyrdom. In her introduction to the book, Marina Warner warns about the difficulties facing a writer who wants to present such an unusual female figure, and talks about the various approaches taken to the story of Joan of Arc through the centuries since her death in 1431.

JOAN OF ARC : THE IMAGE OF FEMALE HEROISM
MARINA WARNER

'Joan was presented as an Amazon, or a knight of old, or a personification of virtue, because the history of individual women and of women's roles has been so thin. In the writing of female biography, it is easy to revert unconsciously to known stereotypes. Joan of Arc is a pre-eminent heroine because she belongs to the sphere of action, while so many feminine figures or models are assigned and confined to the

sphere of contemplation. She is anomalous in our culture, a woman renowned for doing something on her own, not by birthright. She has extended the taxonomy of female types; she makes evident the dimension of women's dynamism. ...Joan of Arc, in all her brightness, illuminates the operation of our present classification system, its rigidity on the one hand, its potential on the other.'

Marina Warner shows how difficult it is to unearth the 'truth' about the historical figure of Joan of Arc, the simple peasant girl who heard the voices of angels entrusting her with a divine mission to help the French king drive the invading English armies from French soil, dressed as a knight, inspired and led the troops to astonishing victories, then, captured by her enemies, was accused of witchcraft by the church authorities, and burned at the stake. Even as the flames lapped around her, she refused to give up faith in the reality of the angelic voices, and insisted on the purity and holiness of her calling and her deeds. In 1894, 463 years after her death, the Catholic Church declared her a saint. In the intervening centuries, her life and actions had rapidly taken on the proportions of a legend, and the reality of Joan's existence as a woman became obliterated under the accumulation of literary images used to describe her. Joan of Arc became a symbol. Sometimes she was seen as a modern Amazon, by writers recalling the ancient Greek stories of the race of warrior women; at other times she was seen as the embodiment of all the virtues of the age of chivalry, and the fact that she was a woman (when clearly all the knights of old were male) became just a symbol for the pure-mindedness of the mediaeval knight. During the first and second world wars, Joan of Arc became a symbol for the fighting spirit of France, brave in the face of the flames engulfing her.

As Marina Warner points out, Joan of Arc is not a figure like that of the Virgin Mary, whose virtues are lauded as the essence of femininity. Joan's femininity is less important to the legend-makers than her deeds. But there is no escaping the fact that she was a woman. As we read the different versions of the meaning of the life of Joan of Arc, we are seeing how different generations of men have dealt with the figure of an exceptional woman.

We are seeing how the imaginations of writers, priests and poets through history portray a heroic woman. Sometimes Joan appears as a figure of chastity and purity — a familiar role for female figures in paintings; we recall that in church art the Christian virtues Faith, Hope and Charity are always portrayed as serene female figures. So are the ancient Greek goddesses of music, poetry and art, the Muses.

When 20th century women look back through history for heroines, they have to pick up with the idea of Joan of Arc all these layers of symbolism, all these different pictures of womanhood.

History chooses as heroines women who succeed *in spite of,* not because of, their gender. Women who succeed in overcoming the obstacles placed in their way because they are women, who ignore the conventional restrictions on women's role, who are 'better' than their sisters. So while we admire them for their courage, we are learning the subtle lesson that to make your mark, you must dare to be different. At the same time, these historical heroines are held up as examples of womanly virtues: it gets very contradictory.

Take Florence Nightingale, for example. The Lady With the Lamp, bringer of comfort to the wounded British soldiers in the Crimea, organiser of the nursing profession, strict in her dealings with her young women nurses, courageous in her confrontations with the military chiefs who tried to curb her activities. A strong figure, a tough woman, but at the same time unbendingly Victorian in her social attitudes —and she founded the nursing profession, the very model of a 'female' career, with women always subordinate to male doctors, doing typically 'feminine' caring things, bossed about, rigidly supervised.

How do feminists assess such an ambiguous figure?

Look for the reality of her life and times, and then judge. Florence Nightingale grew up stifled by the expectation that women should be essentially idle, cultivating the arts of femininity. In all her writings she was harshly critical of women's laziness, ignorance, general incompetence and refusal to take their own lives into their hands, their lack of interest in

matters of high moral purpose. She despised her own mother and sister for these faults, and for trying to force her to be like them. Based on her own experience, she developed an analysis of the Victorian family which argued that the mother was the chief obstacle to the daughter's chances of developing her potential, by insisting on triviality (serious girls don't attract husbands...).

But there are strikingly sympathetic qualities in her, which have a modern ring. She wrote: 'The great reformers of the world turn into the great misanthropists, if circumstances or organisations do not permit them to act. Christ, if he had been a woman, might have been nothing but a great complainer.'

She also said: 'Men are angry with misery. They are irritated with

women for not being happy...To God alone may women complain, without insulting Him!'

These are genuine insights, illuminating the double bind that women of her time (mid-19th century) and class (leisured upper-class) experienced; men felt threatened and were made uncomfortable by discontented women, so that women who wished to continue to be supported by men had to continue to state how happy they were — thus supporting the continuation of a type of marriage which was making them miserable.

Florence Nightingale is being reclaimed by contemporary feminism, for this quality of insisting on the importance of acting on discontent, taking up work and self-realisation. She's a heroine, a rebellious woman.

'Passion, intellect, moral activity — these three have never been satisfied in a woman.' FLORENCE NIGHTINGALE

Sir Harry Verney, Bart., and **Miss Nightingale** *on the lawn of Claydon House, 1889*

Top Girls, British playwright Caryl Churchill's play about women, power and success, starts with a tableau of heroines and exceptional women. Marlene, head of a high-powered employment agency which specialises in getting top jobs for women, is holding a dinner party. One by one,

the guests arrive: Pope Joan, a legendary woman pope from the 9th century (her actual existence was alleged by partisans for one side in the tumultuous splits in the church; they used her as proof of how far the morality of the official church had declined; she almost certainly did not

HEROINES

ROBYN ARCHER/ANDREW BELL

Who ever said we needed heroines?
The lives of ordinary women's glory enough.
But I don't mind to keep in mind the kind of line
That certain women held

When I think of Joan of Arc
She wore her courage on her sleeve
She taught her country to believe in freedom.

When I think of Nightingale
She wore a look most severe
She saw the war out in Crimea and changed things.

And I know we all are one
No-one's free till everyone
So let's applaud the mighty deeds
But don't forget the nameless ones
The ordinary fameless ones who helped us.

When I think of you and me
We'll never deck the halls of fame
And yet the way we play the game can change things.

When I think of ripples in a pool
They spring from pebbles that you thought
You threw unthinking, yet they spread forever.

For every woman who's depressed
Who feels her life's a weary mess
Then we are all just that much less
No woman is a rock alone
We're all carved from the self-samestone of living.

Who ever said we needed heroines?
The lives of ordinary women's glory enough
But I don't mind to keep in mind the kind of line
That certain women held.

---

exist); a Victorian woman explorer/traveller (there was a long tradition of adventurous English ladies setting out alone to travel through Arabia, Japan, central Asia; genuinely intrepid, these women and their present day successors refused to allow their gender to be either help or hindrance); a mediaeval Japanese courtesan, an accomplished woman of letters and confidante of princes; and other figures from the margins of European history and story, such as Patient Griselda, the much put-upon, faithfully enduring spouse of a monster husband who tests her loyalty with impossible demands, requiring her to give up her children (shades of the requirements of Jehovah in the Old Testament); and a woman camp-follower from the Thirty Years War.

These women are Marlene's family tree; they represent ideas about the sisterhood of women, projected back through the centuries, and stand for all the ways in which women figure in history. And like Joan of Arc, they are all highly ambiguous figures, giving off contradictory messages about what it means to be female. In the play, the tableau presents images of the possibilities of women, but at the same time shows how these women would not have understood each other, would have rejected each other's choices. The play is about the difficulties facing women who try to break out of the restrictive feminine mould.

Marlene's path to success is all about the difficulty of solutions. She opts for a masculine version of self-determination, leaving behind her awkward child and turning her back on family.

So we take comfort
ENID LYONS

Two months before the new baby was born I was asked to speak at the opening of the federal election campaign (1922). At five o'clock on the day of the meeting I was totally unprepared. I had had a particularly trying day, with no time to make a note or even collect my thoughts. And now it was nearly the children's bedtime. I felt desperate. With the bath water running and the milk for the children's tea heating on the stove I sat down at the dining-table with pencil and paper.

I was tired to death. The baby on my knee was crying with fatigue, the other children were quarrelling noisily. Suddenly I burst into tears. This was not fair. No man was expected to endure such things. When Joe prepared a speech I silenced the whole house so that he could concentrate on his task.

I was still sobbing when he reached home. He agreed with all I said; he kissed my tears away, helped with the children and sent me off to the meeting to make a speech as effective of its purpose as any I have ever made. Urging women to interest themselves in public affairs, I talked politics in terms of pots and pans and children's shoes; and told how a series of breakages had left me without a single milk jug in the house; described the domestic miseries I had endured as a consequence, and relating my misfortunes to the subject of my discourse, pointed out that this was a normal condition of things in many a worker's home. Then I swept on to my peroration: 'Until every housewife in the community has at least three jugs, the Labor Party still has work to do.'

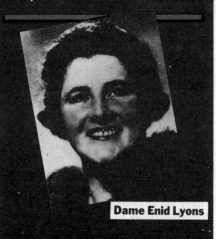

Dame Enid Lyons

117

Dame Enid Lyons

Enid Lyons became Australia's first woman representative in the federal House of Representatives in 1943, a full 43 years after the creation of the federal Parliament, and 40 years since women had first voted in federal elections (they were given the vote in Australia as a whole in 1902, although individual States had enfranchised women as early as 1894 — in South Australia). Enid Lyons first stood as a candidate for a seat in the Tasmanian Parliament in 1921. Her husband Joe Lyons was a Labor politician who changed sides in 1931, at the height of the great economic depression, and became Prime Minister of Australia at the head of an anti-Labor Nationalist Party.

In 1943 an editorial in a women's magazine heralded Dame Enid's election as that of a woman 'well fitted to pioneer an important new field for (her) sex', as a representative of an older generation who combined family life 'with an interest in public affairs'.

Cassandra

One of Florence Nightingale's manuscripts, not published during her lifetime, was titled *Cassandra*, from the Greek myth of a young woman who refused the love of Apollo, the sun-god, and was cursed with the 'gift' of futile prophecy in return. It was her fate to see the future with appalling clarity, but never to be believed. A princess of Troy, the city captured by the Greeks at the end of the Trojan wars, she foresaw the carnage of the battle and the utter destruction of the city. Florence Nightingale saw this story as symbolic of the struggle which women like herself had to wage, telling society at large, and women, one's own side, what is wrong with keeping women's lives so cramped and constrained, and failing to convince of the need for urgency. Cassandra was no false prophet; she was simply not heard.

Christa Wolf, an East German writer and poet, uses the figure of Cassandra to stand for women fighting for nuclear disarmament. Women have a special affinity with this struggle, because women as a sex have no part in the making of history, no power to influence the military machine, but as mothers bear the brunt of war, investing their whole lives in the bearing and raising of children, only to see them slaughtered. For Christa Wolf, women, symbolised by the figure of Cassandra, stand for alternative ways of organising society, and building a culture which is not besotted with power and death.

The Unilateral Blues
ROBYN ARCHER

I met a woman the other day
Said she was catchin' a train to WA
I said 'Hey lady, whatcha doin' that for?'
She said I'm gonna try to stop the nuclear war
I said 'Hey lady, you can't do that
Your neighbours'll call you a Commie rat'
She said better a rat that keeps us alive
Than a human being who's forgotten how to survive

CHORUS:
Cos I've got nothin' to lose
Sing the unilateral blues
So you get popped into a prison, hit on the head
Better off than bein' bloody dead,
Put on your travellin' shoes
Sing the unilateral blues,
And if we all join in in the anti-nuke fun
We could still be singin' in 2001

I met a politician the other day
I said why are we bound to the American way
He said when they start yellin' and things are gettin' tight
The Yanks'll help us out in the Big Bang fight
I said if they go as far as the Big Bang
We'll all be blown away and no-one gives a dang
We won't be any worse off if we just don't play
Oh Mr Politician won't you see it our way,

CHORUS

I was talkin' to my lover in bed last night
I said what do you think about the nuclear fright
Well, all the things that my sweet lover said
Sowed the seeds of a plan in my head
I said I'm gonna leap on the protest train
Yellin' bout the bombs and the nuclear rain
And if you come along for the ride with me
We could still be makin' love in 2003

CHORUS

Cassandra, the figure of myth, was thought mad by those who heard her prophecies — after all, everyone knew that Troy was invincible, enjoyed the favour of the gods; what possible harm could come to the city by allowing within its walls the great wooden horse left behind by the departing Greeks? (The wooden horse contained Greek warriors. Despite Cassandra's warnings, the horse was brought within the walls. In the dead of the night the warriors emerged, opened the gates, and let in the Greek armies).

The women who camped for five years on the muddy ground outside Greenham Common cruise missile base in England; the women who set up camp outside Pine Gap, a secret US base in the central Australian desert; the women who surrounded the NATO base in Sicily, carry on the legacy of Cassandra.

They are demonstrating a new form of protest, a women's form. They physically occupy the ground, in a women-only camp, humanising the ground which has been taken over by the war machine. Theirs is a non-violent protest, but has the moral and physical force of hundreds of women. They have evolved women's rituals, spinning webs of wool through the wire fences on the perimeter, evoking ideas of the spider spinning her shelter out of her own body, and the great web of creation. They are trying out ideas of a women's culture, women taking action on their own terms, women as a collective, without leaders and hierarchies. 'For generations the men have been leaving home to fight in wars; now the women are leaving home to fight for peace.'

Like Cassandra, they have been reviled by the press and the authorities, described as 'belligerent harpies', 'screaming destructive witches', ridiculed and castigated for living in the mud and squalor, bringing up their children away from home.

But just recently the story is being put around that the women of Greenham Common have been infiltrated by Soviet spies, who are using the camp to learn the secrets of the missile deployment within...As one of the women wryly observed, 'For years they have been telling us we were stupid women, engaged in futile exercises; now suddenly we have become super-cunning super-spies.'

But it is true that at Greenham Common women are confronting their own powerlessness, and taking their future into their own hands. Spies they are not, but subversives of a different kind.

118

he Opposition
1ARGO RANDOM

he woman in the street knows what's going on
he woman in the street's got her wits about her
itch her tent on the burial ground
obody's gonna take her alive
ot while she's got air to breathe
ot while she's got a voice to protest
he baby knows what the mama knows also
he baby ain't gonna lay down and die
he baby knows what the mama knows also
he baby ain't gonna lay down and die

HORUS:
re you
re you
re you
re you part of the opposition?

he woman in the street's got her head screwed on
he woman in the street says 'Why should I suffer?'
Makes her stand on the burial ground
he makes a louder voice with numbers
hey sing 'Women' sing 'Women all over the world'
hey sing 'Stand up, stand up and say no'.
hey sing 'Women' sing 'Women all over the world'
hey sing 'Stand up, stand up and say no'.

CHORUS

he woman in the street's got her head screwed on
he woman in the street says 'Why should I suffer?'
Makes her stand on the burial ground
he makes a louder voice with numbers
hey sing 'Women' sing 'Women all over the world'
hey sing 'Stand up, stand up and say no'.
hey sing 'Women' sing 'Women all over the world'
hey sing 'Stand up, stand up and say no'

CHORUS

BRIDGET EVANS
JUDY SMALL

There's a woman in Great Britain, Bridget Evans is her name
And she's out on Greenham Common and things will never be the same
And this is not just Bridget's fight, there's women by the score
By the hundred, by the thousand, and there'll be ten thousand more

CHORUS:
And they're fighting for their families, they're fighting for their friends
And they won't stop, no they won't stop till this nuclear madness ends
Till this nuclear madness ends

And Bridget's left her husband and her kids at home in Wales
And she hears what people say of her, that she's gone off the rails
And she says that men have left their wives and marched off to their wars
And how can her fight for humankind be any lesser cause

CHORUS

And Bridget's been to prison for they say she breached the peace
When she sat inside a sentry box and sang to the police
And her song is growing louder as it echoes off the sun
That Bridget won't leave Greenham till the battle has been won

CHORUS

There's a woman in Great Britain, Bridget Evans is her name
And she's out on Greenham Common and things will never be the same

* Liz Stanley, 'Olive Schreiner: New Women, Free Women, All Women' in *FEMINIST THEORISTS: THREE CENTURIES OF WOMEN'S INTELLECTUAL TRADITIONS*, Dale Spender, editor.

** Ann J. Lane 'Charlotte Perkins Gilman: The Personal is Political', in *FEMINIST THEORISTS*, Dale Spender (editor).

From the introduction to
Woman and Labour
OLIVE SCHREINER

One word more I should like to add, as I may not again speak or write on this subject. I should like to say to the men and women of the generations which will come after us — 'You will look back at us with astonishment! You will wonder at passionate struggles that accomplished so little; at the, to you, obvious paths to attain our ends which we did not take; at the intolerable evils before which it will seem to you we sat down passive; at the great truths staring us in the face, which we failed to see; at the truths we grasped at, but could never quite get our fingers round. You will marvel at the labour that ended in so little; —but, what you will never know is how it was thinking of you and for you, that we struggled as we did and accomplished the little we have done; that it was in the thought of your larger realisation and fuller life, that we found consolation for the futilities of our own.

What I aspired to be, and was not, comforts me.'

*Olive Schreiner (1855-1920)

Olive Schreiner was a writer, feminist and socialist, the closest friend of Eleanor Marx (Karl Marx's youngest daughter); close associate of Havelock Ellis, the pioneer sexologist. She wrote novels — *The Story of an African Farm*, based on her childhood in South Africa; essays, allegories, and a great work of feminist theory, *Woman and Labour,* in which she analyses the relationship between the state of marriage, women's participation in the labour market, prostitution, and sexual relationships between men and women. In all her writings, which were very influential at the time, but are now generally neglected, she elaborated on the way in which personal relationships expressed the social structures of oppression — including racism — within everyday life. For her, socialism and feminism were inextricably connected.

Benigna Machiavelli
CHARLOTTE PERKINS
GILMAN

I learned a lot, when I was a child, from novels and stories; even fairy stories have some point to them — the good ones. The thing that impressed me most forcibly was this: that the villains always went to work with their brains and accomplished something. To be sure they were 'foiled' in the end, but that was by some special interposition of Providence, not by any equal exertion of intellect on the part of the good people. The heroes and heroines and middle ones were mostly very stupid. If bad things happened, they practised patience, endurance, resignation, and similar virtues; if good things happened, they practised modesty and magnanimity and virtues like that, but it never seemed to occur to any of them to make things move their way. Whatever the villains planned for them to do, they did, like sheep. The same old combinations of circumstances would be worked off on them in book after book — and they always tumbled!...

'Joan (of Arc) is the dancer; we have watched her down the centuries. Her body has swayed to the music of different players, we have seen her brightening glance. Now is the time to turn from her face and her footwork, hear the music which commands the steps, analyse its measure.' — Marina Warner.

And it seemed to me, even as a very little child, that what we wanted was good people with brains, not just negative, passive, good people, but positive, active ones, who gave their minds to it.

**
Charlotte Perkins Gilman, 1860-1935 was a writer and lecturer, self-educated in economics, history and sociology, who determined at an early age to live her own life. Suffering a mental breakdown shortly after the birth of her daughter, she dragged herself back from the brink of insanity, divorced her first husband, and started her career as a writer. Her most famous books are *The Yellow Wallpaper*, a chilling short story about a woman's descent into madness, and *Women and Economics*, published in 1898. From the turn of the century to the first World War, her writings on women's rights and socialism were enormously influential.

WOMAN IN THE WINGS
MADDY PRIOR

She watches anxiously, helpless to protect
The girl in the goldfish bowl of light
The jigging marionette
And the woman in the wings, she worries when she sings
Out of key

The dancer as she twirls, oblivious and calm
With tossed curls and swirls
She will face any storm
But the woman in the wings, she fidgets with her rings
And wrings her hands

The puppet on the stage, elusive and charmed,
Battered and bruised, she collapses in the arms
Of the woman in the wings, who gently takes the strings
Leads her away

To a private dressing room, she takes the doll apart
And packs her away into the wardrobe
Till the next show starts
Then the woman in the wings, collects all her things
And goes home

The woman in the wings
Collects all her things
And goes home.

Meryl Tankard *Robert McFarlane*

The Feminist Muse:
WOMEN AND THE ARTS

FEMINISM has been an enormous creative impulse. During the late 1970s, and into the 1980s, there was an explosion of women's writing, women's publishing, women's film-making, women's art, women's theatre, women's circus, women's music; and, depending on how open the publishing and recording and film distribution industries have been at various times, a lot of this new culture has infiltrated into mainstream culture. At times it has seemed that feminist creativity has totally taken over from and eclipsed other feminist activity, and the original political activist orientation of feminist politics has been dissipated into a myriad isolated acts of artistic creation. Obviously, since we're writing this book, which builds on a cabaret, we're not inclined to agree that a feminist preoccupation with cultural activity is a bad thing — we believe that the creation of a whole different imagination is an important aspect of carrying on the feminist project of changing the gender order of society.

'Why Are There No Great Women Artists?' by Linda Nochlin in WOMAN IN SEXIST SOCIETY: STUDIES IN POWER AND POWERLESSNESS, Vivian Gornick and Barbara K. Moran, (editors) 1971.

Women have been writing utopian novels — stories set in an imagined different future, where women live in dignity and freedom, sometimes in different relationships with men, sometimes in all-female communities — since the beginning of the 20th century: Charlotte Perkins Gilman *Herland* (1920s); Monique Wittig *Les Guerilleres* (1969); Ursula le Guin *The Dispossessed* and Marge Piercy *Woman on the Edge of Time* (1970s). Compare these liberating fantasies with the bleak futures predicted for socialism by writers in the mainstream — George Orwell *Animal Farm* and *1984*; Aldous Huxley *Brave New World*.

At the same time, many women are resisting being 'categorised' as 'women writers', 'women artists', fearing that being relegated to the company of women means that they are being confined to a ghetto. So we have the depressing spectacle of admired women writers like Doris Lessing resisting identification with the surge of feminist creativity. And even for women writers of determined feminist convictions, the alacrity of the publishing industry to promote them as 'women's writers' is an irritation; no woman wants to be confined and required to speak only for women, to be denied authority on any other question.

In *How to Suppress Women's Writing* Joanna Russ reports how this problem is intensified when the woman in question is speaking both for women, and for black women. She writes: 'An example is Nzotake Shange's play *For Colored Girls Who Have Considered Suicide When the Rainbow Was Enuf*. Shange, criticised by some blacks for being anti-male, received praise from white male reviewers. As one friend commented to me sourly, "They don't think it's about them." '

But, nonetheless, women who write are *women*, as Elaine Showalter pointed out. All women writing, whatever their feelings about feminism, have to contend with the knowledge that 'women telling stories about themselves or others are not trusted; they are judged as limited, evasive, neurotic, hysterical, deceitful, immature or prejudiced — the essence of what critics call "unreliable narrators".' Women cannot claim their own experience as representative of human kind generally; but the masculine can make claims to be the universal pronoun. When a man writes about a male character with a mid-life crisis, he is understood to be making observations about human nature; when a woman writes about a woman with a mid-life crisis, she is telling the uncomprehending male half of the population what it is like to be female and facing menopause — a very particular experience. Or so runs mainstream thinking.

The 19th century practice of great women writers adopting male names to publish — George Eliot (*Middlemarch, Mill on the Floss*) was Mary Ann Evans, Charlotte Bronte first published under the name Currer Bell — was not due to social disapproval of women who wrote, but a form of resistance to this habit of denying authority to a female voice. Women were not discouraged from writing, in fact were recognised as being very good at it — but their works were seen as typically feminine in style, themes, and tone.

Feminist artists, writers, film-makers and critics throw up two responses — in fact challenges — to this habit of denying authority to the female vision and the female voice. One response is to look at the social and historical circumstances under which women have produced art and literature, to show how those circumstances have shaped both the work that the women did, and the way critics responded to it. This response aims to answer the question, 'Why have there been no great women artists?'

The second response is to reply that *all* artistic work carries with it the 'gender-markings' of its producers; that most art and literature to date have been male, made by men for consumption by a culture which 'sees' everything through the eyes of men. So the task now is to create

TO GEORGES SAND
ELIZABETH BARRETT BROWNING

I A Recognition

True genius, but true woman! dost deny
Thy woman's nature with a manly scorn,
And break away the gauds and armlets worn
By weaker women in captivity?
Ah, vain denial! that revolted cry
Is sobbed in by a woman's voice forlorn! —
Thy woman's hair, my sister, all unshorn,
Floats back dishevelled strength in agony,
Disproving thy man's name! and while before
       world thou burnest in a poet-fire,
We see thy woman-heart beat evermore
Through the large flame. Beat purer, heart, and higher,
Till God unsex thee on the heavenly shore,
Where unincarnate spirits purely aspire.

Feminist art, films, poetry and novels, which set out to subvert the male vision, and infiltrate a female vision. It's a task of teaching women, and society as a whole, to see through the eyes of women. And those women's eyes are *feminist* eyes, the vision is a feminist one. This means that the artist is in her work constantly reflecting upon how the eyes of men, the mainstream culture, would see the woman, how images of women's bodies carry all sorts of messages about masculinity and femininity, and deliberately setting out to change those messages, and substitute other images.

The difference between these two approaches could be put, rather crudely, thus: on the one hand it's a question of saying that given the same chances as men, women would produce 'great', authoritative art; on the other, it's a question of saying that women don't want those chances, because they don't want to reproduce the same old male art — their 'authoritativeness' comes from challenging all those cultural messages.

We will look at examples of both approaches in the rest of this chapter.

13 November 1983 for Christine
LEE CATALDI

these Americans   I see
floating in a tide of money
in the photo in the art magazine sent by katherine
       library I recognise myself

a well-groomed middle-aged dyke called a
'personality' who indifferent to content paints
women   birthday cakes   goats
I too could have exercised minor tyrannies of style
always buoyed up and blinded by the fronds
of inconsequence trailing like weeds and admirers

from the rocks of possession

whereas here I subject myself
to cultural dismemberment
trying to understand a people
who possess nothing
and ask everything

WOMEN ARTISTS

Germaine Greer called it *The Obstacle Race*. Women artists have been kept from greatness: by family — most of the women artists we do know of were related to male artists, in whose shadow they have remained; by love — too many gifted women have hitched their star to a male genius, and put their energies into his career and the relationship; by the condescending attitudes of men, who failed to take them seriously, gave them too easy praise, and thus inhibited their development as artists; by out and out hostility; and, according to Greer, by a series of allegedly female artistic preferences which have kept them out of the mainstream of artistic production. For example, Greer argues that there has been a tendency for women artists to concentrate on small, intricate art works, such as delicate miniatures, instead of vast works conceived on a huge scale, covering canvas with oil paint. This small scale, in Greer's view, reflected the confined circumstances of women's lives; doing things on a large scale reflects a masculine view of the world.

The arguments can be put quite differently. Instead of looking for psychological explanations for choices women artists made, we could look more closely at the physical and social circumstances under which women work.

Mama's gonna stay
ALICE GERRARD

In the early mornin' light
I creep on down the stairs
Hush you floor keep your squeakin' down
Then the smell of good hot coffee
And the silence all around
And nothin' but my thoughts
And the stirrin' of the sun
To break the sad sweet feelin' lord
Of bein' all alone.

And if I'm very still
I can drain this holy hour
And if I'm lucky
Stretch it out to two
Before the world comes crashin'
And down the stairs comes truth
And smiles and tears and ratty hair
And I can't find my shoes
And I don't know lord I don't know
If I can make it through.

But I hope you know how much I love you
'Cause I guess it ain't showin' much these days
Just old dreams of yesterday keep on gettin' in the way
Of picnic days and daisy chains
Of come on let's all go into town again
Of help you make your bed and put your clothes away
Well anyway I guess I'm gonna stay.
In the early mornin' light
I creep on down the stairs.

We could ask questions about what possibilities were open to women to be trained in their art form. For example, women were not permitted to attend classes drawing the human figure from nude models — which may itself go a long way to explaining why so many women painted landscapes and still lives (flowers and fruit), without resorting to speculation about 'essentially feminine' preferences for subjects to paint.

Or we could observe how few women in mediaeval Europe had any access to education in Latin or Greek, the languages of classical scholarship, which explains why women's literature from this period (what little there is) was written in the vernacular, that is, the common language of the country they lived in — and accordingly not treasured as literature by their own age. We don't need to speculate upon women's closeness to everyday life, or closeness to nature, to explain this 'preference' for the language of the common people. We are talking about the effects of exclusion from education — women had no other language in which to write.

Similarly with music. In the middle ages, great music was church music, composed and performed for the great liturgical rites of the church. Women were barred by their sex from holding any position in the church — how then would they be able to write music?

WOMEN PERFORMERS

In many areas of the arts which have historically excluded women from the work of composition — opera, theatre, dance, concert music, popular music, jazz — women have excelled as performers. (This may be partly due to the fact that much performance requires no more equipment than the disciplined and practised body, vocal cords, and gesture. Material barriers to practising their art were not so compelling — only the social barriers needed to be hurdled).

The question of the female body, what it stands for, how a woman lives as herself inside it, is obviously crucial for women performers.

Bette Midler *Paul Canty/L.F.*

Marilyn Monroe *Philippe Halsman*

* Angela Carter talks of Marilyn Monroe as one of a long tradition of women who have had to live out a sort of cultural stereotype as a 'blonde clown' — a mixture of wide-eyed childish vulnerability, and voluptuous

sexuality. Knowing that her loveliness and desirability provoke sexual interest for men, she must learn to deflect this interest by laughing it off, turning herself willingly into a comic creature to avoid being seen only as a sexual creature. 'She has desexed herself by acknowledging how comic her sexuality is; she is prepared to allow her tits an bum to turn into cues for raucous laughter, like a clown's red nose and baggy pants. ...She must endlessly apologise for the insulting lavishness of her physical equipment, which is a ceaseless embarrassment to her. But the laughter she invokes as a protection against the knowledge of her own sexuality is itself a form of the desecration she attempted to protect herself against by laughing at herself first of all.'

On the other hand, a male performer is not imprisoned in his body; there are fewer cultural messages in a man's body. This is not to say that male performers do not project an image of sexuality (think only of Elvis Presley!), but that the field of sexuality is wide open for the male performer to choose from. He will have authority on stage, even if he doesn't clarify his sexuality; as long as he isn't actually a screaming queen, he will have the authority of maleness, and the authority of his performance. He doesn't have to compensate for any failure to measure up to conventional images of attractiveness. He is not at risk of projecting availability — any masculine physical presence brings to mind masculine sexual prerogatives. (Demis Roussos and Placido Domingo can use their bulk in any way they want

Dolly Parton and Bette Midler strike remarkably similar attitudes towards their bodies to the Monroe strategy described by Angela Carter, but because both are working within a culture which has been touched at its edges by feminism, both are able to use their bodies in ways which Monroe could not. What they do with their

* *THE SADEIAN WOMAN, Angela Carter.*

odies carries a different meaning, because women have a ew confidence.

When Bette Midler shakes her breasts, or lets them fall heerfully out of her dress, and Dolly Parton appears in xaggerated blonde wigs, and tight sequinned bodices, ou still get the feeling that they are actually in control of he leering interest they arouse. They are able to get away vith it because there is now another cultural stereotype or a sexually independent woman — the big tough dyke, veralled and spikeheaded, hairy in the legs and armpits – which clearly doesn't apply to them. So Bette Midler nd Dolly Parton are able to project an image of ndependence from their bodies without being too hreatening.

It's a dangerous act, with the borderline between arody and pathos not always easy to discern. Midler's rag queen exaggerates the 'essence' of woman, all to do vith style, grossness, quivering flesh. She is saying to her udience 'I know that you feel comfortable with the drag ueen version of femininity, because it allows you to augh at what you might otherwise find overpowering; vell, here's the act, but remember, I'm a woman, I'm just utting this all on. It's all an act, and I'm in control. I'm urning your own fantasies back on yourselves.'

Angela Carter mourned for Marilyn Monroe: 'She is ot in control of the laughter and contempt she arouses. They are in control of her, modifying her opinion of erself, indignifying her. In herself, this lovely ghost, this ombie, or woman who has never been completely born as woman, only as a debased cultural idea of a woman, is ppreciated only for her decorative value.'

Any performer, man or woman, is going to want to be n control of the emotions aroused in the audience. For vomen performers this question of control is crucial. very time a woman appears before an audience, she has o rapidly define for the audience what sort of sexuality er character embodies, and make the distinction between er character and herself. If the performer doesn't take ontrol of our thoughts about her sexuality, we will take ontrol of her, and use the evidence of her body against her.

The newly confident feminist and women's theatre is taking up the challenge of finding ways of alerting the audience to their conventional expectations about the meanings projected by women's bodies on stage. Methods range across parody — taking the conventional 'feminine' image to extremes; very physical and confronting styles of performance, in which the sweat and effort of performance are made obvious — for example, women's circus and acrobatic performances; and plays and films *about* women's bodies and their experience of them, like Louise Page's play *Tissue*, about the loss of a breast.

SUBVERTING THE MALE GAZE

The image of the mirror is a strong theme in feminist art, and in feminist discussions about the strategies which we can use to bring women's perceptions to the centre of attention, while avoiding being categorised in the terms we are trying to reject. Mirrors reflect — just as feminists looking with new eyes at mainstream culture see women reflected there, mirrors are associated with women, women looking at themselves. Feminists are saying that women do not see 'themselves', but see a version of a self which they have prepared for men to see. Mirrors also distort, give back a splintered or warped reflection. This is what feminists are trying to do — splinter and break up traditional images of women, as a way of breaking up old expectations about women, and finding new possibilities.

One of the demonstrations at Greenham Common had women ringing the perimeter wire, holding mirrors towards the base and the lines of military police just on the other side of the wire. The men representing authority were being forced to see themselves, made to reflect upon their reflections. For once the tables were being turned; masculinity was being made to look at itself. Femininity is *always* confronted with itself, everywhere.

The questioner in black
JUDITH RODRIGUEZ

All the years of her life
she has braved the skull

All the centuries of her civilisation
she has embraced the skull

All the pores of her flesh
she has taunted the skull

Every line of her verse
looks out from the eye-sockets

At the end of the writers' dinner
she rehearses the rising

of black windy song
in the missing throat:

I am still young — nearly,
I write, I am alone,

How shall I live?
How shall I live?

Dolly Parton *Nancy Barr/L.F.I.*

Germanic Approach *Ann Noon*

DIG DEEPER

DIG DEEPER
ROBYN ARCHER/ANDREW BELL

There's a pack of women searching for a new song
There's a tactic being sought to question new wrongs
The daughters of the sixties have their own daughters now
And the theory's weary, it escapes us somehow...

So look hard at the failures and stack up the gains
As you feel the sting of backlash biting at your brain
The slogans that you used belong to ad-men now
If you want to help women, you have to learn how to
Dig deeper, dig deeper

CHORUS:
Strap an oil-rig to your breast
Sink a well into your heart
Dig deeper, dig deeper
Dredge up a woman's questions
Play a woman's part
Dig deeper, dig deeper

The moral majority want a firing squad
To deal with homosexuals in the name of their god,
Just running round in circles screaming 'Everything's wrong'
    don't help
This pack of women needs a brand new song
Dig deeper, dig deeper
Dig deeper, dig deeper

CHORUS

There's a deluge of problems, the going's still tough
But hollering VICTIM simply isn't enough
Superficial cliches won't suffice any more
There's a whole new generation knockin' at the door

Letter to Germaine
LYNN McCARTHY

Germaine, you have much to
    answer for, Germaine
You turned my body inside out
Strewed the stuffing all about, so
    help me
I can't put it all back together

I've changed, I'm a stranger to my
    friends, Germaine
They say I'm selfish, crazy now
And anyhow what right have I
To hurt the one who loves me

'What happens to the kids?' he says
'Can you afford to gamble with
    their tender age
They need you' and he's right of
    course
But they need him too

Germaine, we talk, my man and I,
    Germaine
Discussing pages of your book
'But who will clean and cook'
    he says
'And anyway, you haven't worked
    in years'

And now, Germaine, I'm trapped
    by all the rules we've made
By the rules we played
And anyway to walk away
    would hurt
The ones who love me

Germaine, where does it leave me
    now, Germaine?
You've burnt a path inside my head
Can't return to face the dead
I'll write again to tell you
    my decision.

FACING OBSCURITY

Robyn Stacey

CREDIT	DEBIT
women's movement sets up women's refuges, puts domestic violence on the political agenda	what the state gives, the state also takes away. Funding for women's refuges cut
childcare is recognised as a community responsibility, to a minimal extent funded by the state	childcare services cut, with the rolling back of the welfare state.
sex discrimination legislation in Australia, UK and USA, prohibits discrimination against women at work, etc.	laws cannot change widespread practices overnight. Individual cases won, but the system endures
affirmative action becomes thinkable; not just stopping discrimination, but trying to compensate the victims of past discrimination by changing the rules of the game — access to jobs, education	anti-feminists say that women want guaranteed quotas of jobs, etc. Claims that this is discriminatory against men, promotes mediocrity anti-feminism gets an intellectual issue to fight on
women in some places achieve more liberal abortion laws; but not yet 'free safe abortion on demand'	anti-feminism mobilises people on the issue of abortion
divorce laws in Australia changed, so that divorce becomes more like dissolving a business partnership. Women's homemaking counts as a contribution to the jointly owned property	divorced women and single mothers become the 'new poor'; despite better laws, men's superior earning power and freedom from childcare means they do better out of divorce than women do
laws against sexual harassment of women at work	
women's sexual needs recognised	
explosion of women's creativity — books, films, art, music, theatre...	feminism in danger of becoming preoccupied with cultural work, at the expense of politics
women's studies a legitimate field of study in universities	called jobs for the girls
feminism begins to change the language: 'he and she' used instead of 'he'	feminism accused of destroying the language, pursuing trivial issues, being ignorant of culture. Women are not sure whether it's an issue on which we need to take a stand
links between pornography, advertising, sexual violence against women explored publicly	a new repressiveness called for by the Women Who Want To Be Women, using links between pornography and sexual violence
women get jobs in the bureaucracy, many more women politicians	women fear their feminist politics may be compromised. Attacks on women achievers by some feminists who reject the whole 'male' system
	language and concepts of feminism co-opted by advertisers e.g. Virginia Slims cigarette ads 'you've come a long way, baby
	failure of the Equal Rights Amendment in the USA
	media proclaim feminism is dead, that it's only being kept alive by academics and stirrers, mass of women happy with their lot, insulted by claims that they are oppressed

THE SEVEN DEADLY WHIMS
NEW LIPS TO KISS
FREEDOM FROM CONVENTIONS
A NEW WORLD FOR WOMEN
NO MORE CHAPERONS
LIFE WITH A KICK IN IT
THE SINGLE MORAL STANDARD
OUR OWN LATCHKEYS

COULD GO EITHER WAY

The new technologies of reproduction — 'test-tube babies' — have raised as a social issue questions about the importance of the 'biological family', made it clear that the link between sexuality and reproduction is not a necessary one, and highlight the position of women by raising the question, 'How far may the rights of the woman to organise her own life be over-ridden by restrictions imposed on her in the cause of bringing about a successful pregnancy?'

But although these issues are now on the social agenda, and feminists are familiar with this territory, the debate could go in the direction of greater state control over women's bodies. Already, stable heterosexual marriage is the pre-requisite for entry into these medical programs.

Proliferation of management courses aimed at women, teaching how to be assertive, overcome feminine conditioning and be successful. Positive aspects are that women learn valuable skills, can go on to be role models for other women. Negative aspects are the insinuation of ideas of competitiveness and domination over others, against the spirit of co-operation and distrust of hierarchies which was feminism's model for organisation.

Feminist concerns are being talked about in the pages of magazines like *Cosmopolitan* and *Dolly* — issues of sexuality, the need for women to be autonomous, have a high opinion of their own capabilities, dress to please themselves, are staple stuff in mainstream magazines aimed at women. Negative aspects — feminism in danger of being co-opted by a consumer culture. Issues become trivialised, simplified. Feminism in danger of becoming a sort of style.

A generation of women are entering adulthood for whom the ideas of feminism are old hat, or at least familiar almost to the point of boredom. It is comforting that they will take for granted things like equal pay, and will not feel the same pressures to conformity with rigid stereotypes. But things have not changed enough. Feminism needs to inject a sense of the urgency of its politics.

THE WOMEN SIT DOWN TO PLAY II
ROBYN ARCHER/JEREMY WESLEY SMITH

The game goes on for decades
The persistence of women surpasses that of your average cowboy
And they're using a loaded pack,
So bear in mind, this deck could be dangerous.
Sometime, someone will tempt you
To gamble with this Pack of Women
                       this Deck of Dames.
If you decide to play, you could easily lose.
But be sure that
If you refuse to play, you can't win
Not now, not this game...
Do you call this a card game
Mama, it's a hard game
I'm playin' for my life, but I can feel someone messin'
There's someone looking over my shoulder
And I gotta keep reassessin'

Robert McFarlane

BIBLIOGRAPHY AND FURTHER READING

In this section we list all the references used for each chapter, giving details of the publisher of the most easily obtained edition for each book. Books which are 'edited' are usually collections of articles, or short chapters from other books, and are often a good way of finding further reading on subjects which interest you.

We have also included further reading in many chapters — these are books which add to the ideas presented in this book, or contradict them, or take feminist thinking on the various subjects off into interesting new directions. In some chapters we have listed novels which give insights into women's lives.

Chapter 1 — Introduction
Simone de Beauvoir **The Second Sex** 1949 available in Penguin
Michele Barrett **Women's Oppression Today. Problems in Marxist Feminist Analysis** Verso, 1980
Anna Coote and Beatrix Campbell **Sweet Freedom: The Struggle for Women's Liberation** Picador, 1982
Mary Daly **Gyn/Ecology: The Metaethics of Radical Feminism** Beacon Press, 1978
Hester Eisenstein **Contemporary Feminist Thought** Unwin Paperbacks, 1984
Feminist Anthology Collective **No Turning Back, Writings from the Women's Liberation Movement 1975-1980** The Women's Press, 1981
Betty Friedan **The Feminine Mystique** Dell, 1963
Angela McRobbie and Trisha McCabe **Feminism for Girls — An Adventure Story** Routledge and Kegan Paul, 1981
Kate Millett **Sexual Politics** Abacus, 1971
Juliet Mitchell **Woman's Estate** Penguin, 1971 **Women: The Longest Revolution** Virago, 1984
and Ann Oakley (editors) **The Rights and Wrongs of Women** Penguin, 1976
Robin Morgan (editor) **Sisterhood is Global** Penguin, 1985 **The Anatomy of Freedom** Martin Robertson, 1982
Ann Oakley **Subject Women** Flamingo, 1981, **Taking it like a Woman** 1984 (her story of her life; she sets out to answer the questions 'What makes someone into a feminist? What sort of person is a feminist?...)
Jane Root **Pictures of Women/Sexuality** Pandora, 1984
Sheila Rowbotham **Dreams and Dilemmas** Virago, 1983 **Hidden from History** Pluto, 1973
Gloria Steinem **Outrageous Acts and and Everyday Rebellions** Holt, Rinehart and Winston, 1983

Chapter 2 — Suburban Sonnet
Michele Barrett and Mary McIntosh **The Anti-Social Family** Verso, 1982
Pat Carlen **Women's Imprisonment — a study in social control** Routledge and Kegan Paul, 1983
Ruth Schwarz Cowan **More Work for Mother** Basic Books, 1985
Lenore Davidoff 'Landscape with Figures: home and community in English society' in Juliet Mitchell and Ann Oakley (editors), **The Rights and Wrongs of Women** Penguin, 1976. 'The Rationalisation of Housework', in Diana Leonard Barker and Sheila Allen **Dependence and Exploitation in Work and Marriage** Longman, 1976
Ann Oakley **Housewife** and **The Sociology of Housework** 1974

Chapter 3 — Woman on the Edge
Kim Chernin **The Hungry Self: Women, Eating and Identity** Times Books, 1985
Phyllis Chesler **Women and Madness** Avon, 1972
Rosalind Coward 'The Body Beautiful' and 'An Overwhelming Desire', in her book **Female Desire** Paladin, 1984
Luise Eichenbaum and Susie Orbach **Outside In... Inside Out, Women's Psychology — A Feminist Psychoanalytic Approach** Penguin, 1982
Nancy Friday **Jealousy** Morrow, 1985
Kate Grenville **Lilian's Story** George Allen and Unwin, 1985 (a novel)
Ann Jones **Women Who Kill** Fawcett Columbine, 1980
Luce Irigaray 'When the Goods Get Together' in **New French Feminisms**, edited by Elaine Marks and Isabelle de Courtivron, Schocken Books, 1981
Jill Julius Matthews **Good and Mad Women** George Allen and Unwin, 1984
Toril Moi 'Jealousy and Sexual Difference' **Feminist Review** Number 11, Summer 1982
Susie Orbach **Hunger Strike. The Anorectic Struggle as a Metaphor for Our Age** Faber, 1986

Chapter 4 — Old Maid
Mary Daly **Gyn/Ecology** Beacon Press, 1978
Barbara Ehrenreich and Deirdre English **Witches, Midwives and Nurses — A History of Women Healers** Writers and Readers Publishing Cooperative, 1973
Susan Koppelman **Old Maids. Short Stories by Nineteenth Century US Women Writers** Pandora, 1984
Martha Vicinus **Independent Women** Virago, 1985

Marina Warner **Alone of All Her Sex: The Myth and Cult of the Virgin Mary** Picador, 1985 (first published 1976)

Chapter 5 — Sexuality
Sue Cartledge and Joanna Ryan (editors) **Sex and Love: New Thoughts on Old Contradictions** The Women's Press, 1983
Barbara Ehrenreich **The Hearts of Men: American Dreams and the Flight From Commitment** Pluto, 1983 (about the male revolt against the breadwinner ethic)
Lillian Faderman **Surpassing the Love of Men** Junction Books
Jill Johnston **Lesbian Nation: The Feminist Solution** Simon and Schuster, 1974
Ann Snitow (and others, editors) **Desire: The Politics of Sexuality** Virago, 1984 (a book of readings, including Adrienne Rich's (Compulsory Heterosexuality and Lesbian Existence' and 'What We're Rollin' Around in Bed With: Sexual Silences in Feminism' by Amber Hollibaugh and Cherrie Moraga, two very influential but hard-to-come-by pieces of writing).

Chapter 6 — Women Behind Great Men
Germaine Greer **The Obstacle Race: The Fortunes of Women Painters and Their Work** Secker and Warburg, 1979
Ross Terrill **The White-Boned Demon: A Biography of Madame Mao Zedong** Heinemann, 1984
Margaret Walters **The Nude Male: A New Perspective** Penguin, 1979

Chapter 7 — Power
Tariq Ali **The Nehrus and the Gandhis — An Indian Dynasty** Picador, 1985
Beatrix Campbell **Wigan Pier Revisited** Virago, 1984

Chapter 8 — Woman in a Man's World
Robyn Archer and Diana Simmonds **A Star is Torn,** Virago, 1986
Julie Burchill **Love It Or Shove It** Century, 1985
Linda Dahl **Stormy Weather: The Music and Lives of a Century of Jazz Women** Quartet, 1985
Sue Steward and Sheryl Garratt **Signed, Sealed and Delivered: True Life Stories of Women in Pop** Pluto Press, 1984

Chapter 9 — Motherhood

Michele Barrett and Mary McIntosh **The Anti-Social Family** Verso Editions, 1982
Nancy Chodorow **The Reproduction of Mothering: Psychoanalysis and the Sociology of Gender** University of California Press, 1978
Dorothy Dinnerstein **The Mermaid and the Minotaur: Sexual Arrangements and Human Malaise** Harper and Row, 1977
Stephanie Dowrick and Sibyl Grundberg **Why Children?** The Women's Press, 1980
Hester Eisenstein **Contemporary Feminist Thought** Unwin Paperbacks, 1984 especially chapters 7, 8 and 9
Dario Fo and Franca Rame **Medea** in **Female Parts** translated by Stuart Hood, Pluto Plays, 1981
Nancy Friday **My Mother/Myself** Delacorte Press, 1977
B D Hyman **My Mother's Keeper**, Michael Joseph, 1986
Tillie Olsen **Mother to Daughter...A Reader** Virago, 1985
Adrienne Rich **Of Woman Born: Motherhood as Experience and Institution** W W Norton and Co., 1977. 'Motherhood; The Contemporary Emergency and the Quantum Leap' in **On Lies, Secrets and Silence** W W Norton and Co., 1979

Chapter 10 — 9 to 5 and the Nightshift

Beatrix Campbell 'Workplace Politics' in **Wigan Pier Revisited** Virago, 1984
Kay Daniels (editor) **So Much Hard Work: Women and Prostitution in Australian History** Fontana/Collins, 1984
Ann Game and Rosemary Pringle **Gender at Work** George Allen and Unwin, 1983
Dorothy Johnston **Tunnel Vision** Hale and Iremonger, 1984 (a novel, set in a massage parlour. Dorothy Johnston also contributes a chapter in **So Much Hard Work...**, listed above)
Mary McIntosh 'Who Needs Prostitutes? The Ideology of Male Sexual Needs' in **Women, Sexuality and Social Control** Carol Smart and Barry Smart (eds), Routledge and Kegan Paul, 1979
Catharine MacKinnon **Sexual Harassment of Working Women** Yale University Press, 1979
Eileen McLeod **Women Working: Prostitution Now** Croom Helm, 1982

Chapter 11 — The Ladies Who Lunch

Rosalind Coward 'Being Fashionable' in **Female Desire** Paladin, 1984
Andrea Dworkin **Right-Wing Women: The Politics of Domesticated Females** The Women's Press, 1983
Zillah Eisenstein 'The Sexual Politics of the new Right: Understanding the "Crisis of Liberalism" for the 1980s' in **Signs** Volume 7, Number 3, 1982
Elizabeth Wilson **Adorned in Dreams: Fashion and Modernity** Virago, 1985

Chapter 12 — The Women Who Live on the Ground

Diane Bell **Daughters of the Dreaming** McPhee Gribble/George Allen and Unwin, 1983
Eileen Fairweather, Roisin McDonough and Melanie McFadyean **Only the Rivers Run Free: Northern Ireland — The Women's War** Pluto Press, 1984
Robin Morgan (editor) **Sisterhood is Global** Penguin, 1985
Michelle Zimbalist Rosaldo and Louise Lamphere (editors) **Woman, Culture and Society** Stanford University Press, 1974
Nawal El Saadawi **The Hidden Face of Eve: Women in the Arab World** Zed Press, 1980
Azar Tabari and Nahid Yeganeh **In The Shadow of Islam — The Women's Movement in Iran** Zed Press, 1982
Alice Walker **The Color Purple** The Women's Press, 1982

Chapter 13 — Images

John Berger **Ways of Seeing** BBC/Penguin, 1972
Rosalind Coward 'Pouts and Scowls' in **Female Desire** Paladin, 1984
Andrea Dworkin **Pornography — Men Possessing Women** The Women's Press, 1981
Susan Griffin **Pornography and Silence: Culture's Revenge Against Nature** The Women's Press, 1981
Jane Root 'Who Does this Ad Think You Are?' in **Pictures of Women Sexuality** Pandora Press, 1984

Chapter 14 — Violence

Susan Brownmiller **Against Our Will: Men, Women and Rape** Simon and Schuster, 1975
Gordon Burn '...Somebody's Husband, Somebody's Son': The Story of The Yorkshire Ripper** Pan Books, 1985
Rosalind Coward 'Sexual Violence and Sexuality' in **Feminist Review 11** Summer 1982
Andrea Dworkin **Our Blood: Prophecies and Discourses on Sexual Politics** The Women's Press, 1976
Ann Jones **Women Who Kill** Fawcett Columbine, 1981
Elizabeth Wilson **What is to be done about Violence Against Women?** Penguin, 1983

Chapter 15 — Cycle

Simone de Beauvoir **Old Age** Penguin, 1977
Susan Edwards **Female Sexuality and the Law** Martin Robertson, 1981
Linda Gordon **Woman's Body, Woman's Right: A Social History of Birth Control in America** Penguin 1977
Germaine Greer **The Female Eunuch** Penguin, 1971. **Sex and Destiny** Secker and Warburg, 1984
Ruth Hall **Marie Stopes: A Biography** 1977

May Sarton **As We Are Now** and **A Reckoning** W W Norton and Co. (two novels)
Fay Weldon **Praxis** Coronet, 1978 (a novel with an old woman as the central character)

Chapter 16 — Heroines

Caroline Blackwood **On the Perimeter** Heinemann, 1984 (about Greenham women)
Judy Chicago **The Dinner Party: A Symbol of our Heritage** Anchor/Doubleday, 1979
Kay Daniels and Mary Murnane **Uphill all the Way: A Documentary History of Women in Australia** University of Queensland Press, 1980
Ruth First and Ann Scott **Olive Schreiner** Andre Deutsch, 1980
Barbara Harford and Sarah Hopkins **Greenham Common: Women at the Wire** The Women's Press, 1984
Adrienne Rich 'Power and Danger: Work of a Common Woman' in **On Lies, Secrets and Silence** W W Norton and Co., 1979
Olive Schreiner **Woman and Labour** Virago, 1979 (first published 1911)
Dale Spender **Feminist Theorists: Three Centuries of Women's Intellectual Traditions** The Women's Press, 1983. **Women of Ideas** Ark Paperbacks, 1982
Marina Warner **Joan of Arc: The Image of Female Heroism** Weidenfeld and Nicolson, 1981
Christa Wolf **Cassandra: A Novel and Four Essays** Virago, 1984

Chapter 17

Rachel Blau du Plessis 'For the Etruscans: Sexual Difference and Artistic Production — the Debate over a Female Aesthetic' in **The Future of Difference** Eisenstein and Jardine (eds), G K Hall and Co., 1980
Angela Carter **The Sadeian Woman: an exercise in cultural politics** Virago, 1979
Gisela Ecker (editor) **Feminist Aesthetics** The Women's Press, 1985
Germaine Greer **The Obstacle Race: The Fortunes of Women Painters and Their Work** Secker and Warburg, 1979
E. Ann Kaplan **Women and Film: Both Sides of the Camera** Methuen, 1983
Helene Keyssar **Feminist Theatre** Macmillan Modern Dramatists, 1984
Annette Kuhn **Women's Pictures: Feminism and Cinema** Routledge and Kegan Paul, 1982
Ellen Moers **Literary Women** Doubleday, 1976
Linda Nochlin 'Why Are There No Great Women Artists?' in **Woman in Sexist Society** Vivian Gornick and Barbara Moran (eds), 1971
Joanna Russ **How to Suppress Women's Writing** The Women's Press, 1983
Elaine Showalter **A Literature of their Own** Virago, 1978
Elizabeth Wilson **Mirror Writing** Virago, 1982 (an autobiography)

CHAPTER 1

The Women Sit Down to Play (Archer/Wesley Smith) Written for the original stage show. © Pretty Limited Music 1981.
Ida © Rosemary Florimell from **Mother I'm Rooted** ed. Kate Jennings, Outback Press 1975.

CHAPTER 2

Neurotica Suburbia (Archer) From **The Live-Could-Possibly-Be-True-One-Day Adventures of Superwoman** © Pretty Limited Music 1974.
Suburban Sonnet © Gwen Harwood From **Selected Poems**, Angus & Robertson 1975. Reproduced by permission. Recorded by Robyn Archer on the album **The Wild Girl in the Heart.**
The Housewife's Lament Trad.

CHAPTER 3

The Ballad of Dancing Doreen (McTell) Lyrics reproduced by kind permission of Essex Music of Australia Pty Ltd.
Witch Poem © Chris Sitka from **Mother I'm Rooted** ed. Kate Jennings, Outback Press 1975.
The Ballad of Lucy Jordan (Silverstein) Lyrics reproduced by kind permission of Essex Music of Australia Pty Ltd.
Steam-Yr-Letter-Open Blues (Archer) © Pretty Limited Music 1977.
Moonshine © Kate Jennings, from **Come To Me My Melancholy Baby** Outback Press 1975. Recorded by Robyn

CHAPTER 4

Spinsters © Anne Elder from **Crazy Woman.**
Not Answering © Judith Rodriguez from **Mudcrab at Gambaro's**, University of Queensland Press.
Next of Kin "If there is a 'Grandma Moses' of poetry it must be me as I have waited all my working life for the pleasure to indulge in writing and I am pleased that somebody wants to read it". © Eleanor Fassell, from **Mother I'm Rooted** ed. Kate Jennings, Outback Press 1975.
Old Maid (Archer) Written for the original stage show © 1981.
Sweet Solitary Blues (Archer) © Pretty Limited Music 1981.
Fortune Telling Patience Miss E. Whitmore-Jones from **Games of Patience.**
Coupling II (Archer) written for the original stage show © 1981.
Oracle Patience Miss E. Whitmore Jones from **Games of Patience.**
From **Gyn/Ecology** © Mary Daly, published by Beacon Press, Boston, USA; The Women's Press, London.
From **Alone of All Her Sex** by Marina Warner. Reproduced by permission of George Weidenfeld & Nicolson Ltd.
Spinster © 1961 by Sylvia Plath. Reprinted from **The Colossus and Other Poems** by Sylvia Plath, by permission (US) of Alfred A. Knopf Inc. **Collected Poems** © Ted Hughes 1967, 1981. Reproduced by permission of Olwyn Hughes. (UK)

CHAPTER 5

Snake Trad.
A Fairy Tale © Lee Cataldi, who now lives and works in Lajamanu, NT, as a guest of the Warlpiri people.
Coupling (Archer) © Pretty Limited Music 1977.
First Date © Margot Nash.
Sonnet 95 © John Tranter. First appeared in **Crying in Early Infancy: One Hundred Sonnets** published by Makar Press, Brisbane 1977.
Stephanie's Room (Baez) Lyrics reproduced by kind permission of Essex Music of Australia Pty Ltd.
Two Women Gazing at Each Other as If Their Lives Depended On It (Archer) © Pretty Limited Music 1983. Title comes from Lee Cataldi's **Invitation to a Marxist Lesbian Party.**
Old Soft Screw (Archer) © Pretty Limited Music 1971. From the album **The Ladies Choice.**
A Man Could Be a Wonderful Thing (Corday/Carr) Reproduced by permission of MCA Music (Aust) Pty Ltd.
Girls In Our Town (Hudson) MCA Music (Aust) Pty Ltd Recorded by Margret RoadKnight on the album **Margret**

A Midsummer Night's Dream by Pedro Shimose trs Roberto Marquez © 1974. Reprinted by permission of Monthly Review Press.

CHAPTER 6

Standing Female Nude © Carol Ann Duffy. Published by Anvil Press Poetry 1985.
From **The Journals** Reprinted from 'The Journal of Dorothy Wordsworth' edited by Mary Moorman (1971) by permission of Oxford University Press.
Women Behind Great Men (Archer/Bell) © Pretty Limited Music 1981. Written for the original stage show.
Maud from **Maud** Alfred, Lord Tennyson.
From **A Room of One's Own** from **A Room of One's Own** by Virginia Woolf. Reprinted by permission of the Hogarth Press.
From **The Letters of Virginia Woolf** from **The Letters of Virginia Woolf Vol 4** edited by Nigel Nicholson. Reprinted by permission of the Hogarth Press.

CHAPTER 7

On The Watergate Women from **Lady of the Beasts** by Robin Morgan © 1976 by Robin Morgan, Random House Inc., 1976. By permission of the author c/o Edite Kroll.
Pirate Jenny (Brecht/Weill) from **The Threepenny Opera** trs. Ralph Manheim and John Willett. Reproduced by permission of Methuen Ltd, London.
No Man's Land © Lee Cataldi, who now lives and works in Lajamanu, NT, as a guest of the Warlpiri people.
From **Wigan Pier Revisited** © Beatrix Campbell, Virago Press.
From an interview with Esther Shapiro (25.3.85) published in **The Australian** and reproduced by permission News Ltd.
The Hand that Rocks the Cradle Bombs The World (Archer/Manson) © Pretty Limited Music 1980.

CHAPTER 8

Woman in a Man's World (Conway/Bell) Lyrics reprinted by kind permission of Warner Bros Music Australia Pty Ltd. All rights reserved. International Copyright secured.
Wife of a Rock'n'roll Star (Wynn-Moylan) Lyrics reprinted by permission of Trafalgar Music Pty Ltd.

CHAPTER 9

The Mother © PiO from **Days of Wine and Rage** ed. Frank Moorhouse, Penguin.
From **Mother Ireland** © Edna O'Brien, published by Weidenfeld & Nicholson Ltd.
From **On Lies, Secrets & Silence** © Adrienne Rich, published by W W Norton and Co.
From **Ann Veronica** Reproduced by permission of the literary executors of the estate of H.G. Wells, and Virago Press.
From **Cassandra** by Christa Wolf, reproduced by permission of Virago Press.
Backyard Abortion Waltz (Archer) © Pretty Limited Music, 1979. From **Songs From Sideshow Alley** commissioned by and first performed at the 1980 Adelaide Festival of the Arts.
From **Some Irish Loving — A Selection** © Edna O'Brien, reproduced by permission of Weidenfeld & Nicolson Ltd.

CHAPTER 10

Nine To Five (Parton) lyrics reproduced by kind permission of Allans Music (Australia) Pty Ltd.
Things Are So Slow (Dane) © Barbara Dane/Paredon Records.
In Factories © Sandra Wetherald from **Mother I'm Rooted** ed. Kate Jennings, Outback Press 1975.
Waiting Too Long (Archer/Bell) © Pretty Limited Music 1983. Written for the Australian tour.
In Business (Archer/Bell) As above.
Helen at 9am, at noon, and at 5:15 from **The Work of a Common Woman** by Judy Grahn, St Martin's Press.
Don't Put Her Down You Helped Put Her There (Dickens) Reproduced by permission Happy Valley Music/Larrikin Music.
From **Women Working: Prostitution Now** by Eileen McLeod, 1982 Croom Helm Ltd.
From **On Lies, Secrets & Silence** © Adrienne Rich, published by W W Norton and Co.

CHAPTER 11

The Anti-Suffragists from **The Charlotte Perkins Gilman Reader** The Women's Press.
Women Who Despise Women © Jill Miller from **Mother I'm Rooted** ed. Kate Jennings, Outback Press 1975.
Size 10 (Archer) © Pretty Limited Music 1978. Commissioned as title song for the film **Size 10** directors Susan Lambert and Sarah Gibson.
Virginia Woolf's introductory letter to **Life As We Have Known It** by Margaret Llewellyn Davies. Reprinted by permission of the Hogarth Press.

CHAPTER 12

Kuu Kuu Kardiya and The Women Who Live on the Ground © Lee Cataldi, who now lives and works in Lajamanu, N.T., as a guest of the Warlpiri people.
Nadine Resting On Her Neighbour's Stoop from **The Work of a Common Woman** by Judy Grahn, St Martin's Press.

CHAPTER 13

Dear Comrades by Patrizia from **Dear Comrades**, reproduced by kind permission of the publishers, Pluto Press, London.
Girl on The Wall (Random) Reproduced by kind permission of Mushroom Music Pty Ltd.
Whose Pleasure? (Archer/Bell) © Pretty Limited Music 1983. Commissioned by Pictures of Women for their TV series **Sexuality.**
From the flyleaf of **Jungle Fever** by Jean-Paul Goude. Reprinted by permission of Xavier Moreau Inc. New York.

CHAPTER 14

Joanne Little (Reagon) Reproduced courtesy of Flying Fish Music. 'Sweet Honey In The Rock's' performance of this song is available on Flying Fish Records (FF022). 'Sweet Honey' has four other albums on Flying Fish and one on Redwood Records.
Woman In Trouble (Bell) Reprinted by permission of Wheatley Music Pty Ltd.
Two Lovely Black Eyes (Coburn) © 1896. Francis, Day and Hunter, London. For Australia and New Zealand, J. Albert & Son Pty Ltd.
Traffic Jennifer Strauss, from **Mrs Noah and the Minoan Queen** ed. Judith Rodriguez, Sisters Publishing.
Ella, in a Square Apron, Along Highway 80 from **The Work of A Common Woman** by Judy Grahn, St Martin's Press.

CHAPTER 15

Cycle (Archer) © 1981. Written for the original stage show.
Nobody Sings Caryl Churchill from her play **Vinegar Tom** Reproduced by permission of Methuen Ltd.
Menstruation Blues (Archer) © Pretty Limited Music 1973. From the album **The Ladies Choice.**
The Shopper Bertolt Brecht trs. Michael Hamburger from **Poems 1913-1956.** Reproduced by permission of Methuen Ltd.
Women Who Kill (Archer/Bell) © Pretty Limited Music 1981.

Written for the original stage show.
My Grandmother In The Shower © Gillian Coote, from **Mother I'm Rooted** ed. Kate Jennings, Outback Press 1975.
From **The Female Eunuch** by permission of Dr Germaine Greer, author of **The Female Eunuch** © 1970 Germaine Greer. Published by Grafton Books, a division of the Collins Publishing Group.

CHAPTER 16

From **On Lies, Secrets & Silence** © Adrienne Rich, published by W W Norton and Co.
From **Joan of Arc** by Marina Warner, reproduced by permission of Weidenfeld & Nicolson Ltd.
From the introduction to **Woman and Labour** Olive Schreiner, Virago Press.
The Opposition (Random) © Margo Random. 'Written in appreciation of the Greenham Common Women whose strength and courage has set an example for us all' — Margo Random.
From **So We Take Comfort** Reproduced by courtesy of the family of Dame Edith Lyons.
The Unilateral Blues (Archer) © Pretty Limited Music 1984. Written to commemorate the Cockburn Sound Peace Train protest.
Bridget Evans (Small) Reproduced by courtesy of Crafty Maid Music.
Heroines (Archer/Bell) © Pretty Limited Music 1983. Written for the Australian tour.
Woman in the Wings (Prior) Lyrics reproduced by kind permission of Festival Music (Australia).
From **Benigna Machiavelli** Charlotte Perkins Gilman, from **Benigna Machiavelli,** The Women's Press.

CHAPTER 17

To Georges Sand by Elizabeth Barratt Browning, from **Aurora Leigh and Other Poems,** The Women's Press.
Questioner in Black © Judith Rodriguez from **Mudcrab at Gambaro's,** University of Queensland Press.
From **The Sadeian Woman** © Angela Carter, Virago Press.
13 November 1983 © Lee Cataldi, who now lives and works in Lajamanu, Northern Territory, as a guest of the Warlpiri people.
Momma's Gonna Stay (Gerrard) Wynwood Music/Larrikin Music.
From **Gyn/Ecology** © Mary Daly, published by Beacon Press, Boston, USA and The Women's Press.

CHAPTER 18

Dig Deeper (Archer/Bell) © Pretty Limited Music 1981. Written for the original stage show.
Letter to Germaine (McCarthy) Reprinted by permission of MCA Music (Australia) Pty Ltd.
The Women Sit Down to Play II (Archer/Wesley Smith) © Pretty Limited Music 1981. Written for the original stage show.

ACKNOWLEDGEMENTS

CHAPTER 1

© Robert McFarlane (Judi Connelli, Jane Clifton and Michele Fawdon from **The Pack of Women,** Australian stage show), 1983
© Jochen Canobbi (**The Pack of Women** stage show, London) 1981
Robyn Stacey/Jenny Clarke **Collage with Barbie Doll**
© Preston/Tribune **Big boys don't cry**
UPI (bra burning)
Robyn Stacey/Jenny Clarke **The Moving Target** collage adapted from a photograph by Philippe Halsman

CHAPTER 2

© Bill Owens (the sink) **Suburbia** Straight Arrow Books, San Francisco.
© Bill Owens (suburbia from the air) **Suburbia**
© Mary Leunig (dreaming whilst washing the dishes) **There's No Place Like Home** Penguin 1982
© Ethel Diamond **Self-portrait as the mother of two small children** from **In/Sights: Self Portraits by Women** ed. Joyce Tenneson Cohen, Gordon Fraser Gallery Ltd. 1978
Robyn Stacey (99 Akropolis St, Sydney)

THE PICTURES

CHAPTER 3

Robyn Stacey, adapted from the cover of **She Faded into Air,** by Ethel Lina White, Popular Library Mystery (woman in doorway)
Robyn Stacey/Jenny Clarke **Laroxyl Lifts Depression**
Death in the Chair — Husband Killer Ruth Snyder, 1928 **This Fabulous Centry, 1920-30** Time Inc. New York 1969
© Robert McFarlane (Robyn Archer and Meryl Tankard from **The Pack of Women** television production) 1986
Robyn Stacey/Jenny Clarke (woman with arrows)

CHAPTER 4

Planet Comics **Supergirl**
Tom Mix and Billie Dove in **The Lucky Horseshoe,** 1925 from **The Movies** by Richard Griffith and Arthur Mayer, Spring Books, London 1957
Bette Davies from **Jezebel, Marked Woman** and **Old Maid This Fabulous Century 1930-40,** Time Inc. New York 1969
Florence Nightingale **This Fabulous Century 1940-50,** Time Inc. New York 1969
Women roller skating, from **Fashion** by Contini, Hamlyn London 1965

Nina Howell Starr **Considering Myself** from **In/Sights: Self Portraits by Women** ed. Joyce Tenneson Cohen, Gordon Fraser Gallery Ltd. 1978
Miss Hypatia Monk from **The Look: Australian Women and their Fashion** Cassell, Sydney 1976

CHAPTER 5
Rosalind Moulton, (swimming) from **In/Sights: Self Portraits by Women,** ed. Joyce Tenneson Cohen, Gordon Fraser Gallery Ltd. 1978
Robyn Stacey
Susan Meiselas **Blue — Stripper,** Camera & Cine May 1977
Mary Leunig (woman and man on couch) from **A Piece of Cake** Penguin 1986.
Carol Jerrems (1949-1980) **Vale Street 1975** Collection Australian National Gallery, Canberra

CHAPTER 6
Nancy Reagan exchanging greetings with her husband's TV image, **Newsweek** New Year issue 1984/85
Mary Leunig, (woman artist and male model) from **There's No Place Like Home,** Penguin 1982
Peter Solness (Cory Aquino) Sydney Morning Herald, 1986
Associated Press (Winnie Mandela) 1985
Bernice Abbott (Nora Joyce) **Sixty Years of Photography** by Hank O'Neal
John Redman/Associated Press (Benazir Bhutto) 1984

CHAPTER 7
Margaret Thatcher
Joan Collins
Edoardo Fornaciari (Indira Gandhi) GAMMA 1981/Scope Features (Aust)
Marlene Dietrich in **Blonde Venus,** from **This Fabulous Century 1930-40,** Time Inc. New York 1969
Suffragettes being led away, Enfield 1914' from **Fashion** by Contini, Hamlyn London 1965
Carnival of disorder, Basel' Peter Heman from **Unsere Fasnacht** Basel n.d.
London Features International Inc. (Divine)

CHAPTER 8
Oliver Frank (Janie Conway and Jane Clifton in 'Stiletto')1977
Sire (Madonna)
London Features International Ltd (Laurie Anderson)
Mike Wilson/Scope Features (Suzi Quatro and daughter)
London Features International Ltd (Cyndi Lauper)
Robert McFarlane (Robyn Archer in concert)
RCA, Ariola (Eurythmics)
Polygram (Yoko Ono)
Paul Cox/London Features International (Patti Smith)
London Features International (The Pretenders)
A and M/Festival Records (Joan Armatrading)

CHAPTER 9
P. Gillington **Venus in Measuring Glass** The Age, Melbourne 1985
Mary Leunig from **There's No Place Like Home,** Penguin 1982
Nigel McNeil/John Fairfax and Sons, (Michael and Lindy Chamberlain) 1982
Cynthia Cable **Birth Minus 240 Days...** from **The Photographer's Image** by Allinder
Bill Owens (three men on car) from **Suburbia** Straight Arrow Books, San Francisco
Cheryl Younger (self portrait) from **In/Sights: Self Portraits by Women** ed. Joyce Tenneson Cohen, Gordon Fraser Gallery Ltd. 1978
Eve Kessler **I always wanted to look like my father** from **In/Sights: Self Portraits by Women** as above

CHAPTER 10
cover **Transnational Brief: Women and Work** Tribune, Aust.
Tenosynovitis' Tribune, Australia
Sandy Edwards, (hand on bottom) and (clapper loader) both from a sexual harassment poster for the Women's Co-Ordination Unit, New South Wales government
Susan Meiselas **Cindy — Stripper,** Camera & Cine, May 1977
Oliver Strewe (women on the land)
Ruth Maddison (Assembly line workers pack potato chips), Melbourne 1974 from **For Love or Money** Megan McMurchy, Margot Oliver, Jeni Thornley, Penguin 1983

CHAPTER 11
Andy Warhol, Bianca Jagger, from **Exposures,** Grosset and Dunlap
© Bill Owens (wigs) from **Suburbia,** Straight Arrow Books
Helmut Newton, **Business lunch** from **Sleepless Nights** Quartet Books London 1978
(fashion undergarments) Archives of Berlei-Hestia, from **The Look: Australian Women and their Fashions,** Cassell Sydney 1976
(Bianca with opera glasses) from **In Vogue** by G. Howell, Allen Lane 1976

CHAPTER 12
Carol Jerrems (1949-1980) **Regent Street, 1975** Collection Australian National Gallery, Canberra
Irving Penn (veiled woman: **Vogue** front cover) from **In Vogue** by G. Howell, Allen Lane 1976
Rose McAllister Camerawork, No. 23 **Reporting Back on Ireland,** 1981,
Robyn Stacey **Women in Redfern 1984**

CHAPTER 13
Helmut Newton (woman with saddle) from **Sleepless Nights,** Quartet Books, London, 1978
Jean Harlow in **Dinner At Eight,** from **This Fabulous Century, 1930-1940,** Time Inc. New York, 1969
Helmut Newton (woman chained at the ankles) from **Sleepless Nights,** Quartet Books London 1978
© Sandy Edwards 'Stupid female... but she was smart enough to know that stupidity is sexually desirable' (de Beers ads)
Robyn Stacey/Jenny Clarke (collage of BUGA UP billboards)
© Sandy Edwards 'Life is full of promise... along may come a tall dark handsome... stranger' (Badedas ads)
Helmut Newton (playmate against cityscape) from **Sleepless Nights,** Quartet Books London 1978

CHAPTER 14
Helmut Newton (man pulling at woman's dress) from **Sleepless Nights,** Quartet Books London 1978
Helmut Newton (woman behind locked door) from **Sleepless Nights,** as above
AUS Women's Dept poster **Live Free from Male Aggression** cover of **For Her Children's Sake** from **This Fabulous Century 1870-1910** Time Inc. New York 1969
Robyn Stacey (boy with painted surfboard)
(Violet and Bruce Roberts) from a campaign handbill for their release

CHAPTER 15
Robyn Stacey (Lindy Morrisson, drummer with The Go-Betweens)
Gaynor Cardew **If God Had Given Men Periods**
Robyn Stacey **I: Me: Myself**

CHAPTER 16
© Robert McFarlane (Meryl Tankard in **The Pack of Women** television production) 1986
(Sir Harry Verney, Bart., and Miss Nightingale on the lawn of Claydon House, 1889) from **Lady in Chief** by C.W. Smith, Constable, London, 1950
© Carol-Ann Allen (mask on the wire at Greenham Common)
Dame Enid Lyons from **1,000 Famous Australians** Lansdowne-Rigby Sydney 1978
©Paul Canty/London Features International (Bette Midler) 1978
© Nancy Barr/London Features International (Dolly Parton) 1982
© Philippe Halsman (Marilyn Monroe) 1952 from **Marilyn** by Norman Mailer Grosset & Dunlap, 1973

CHAPTER 18
© Ann Noon **Germanic Approach**
Gloria Swanson publicising **Prodigal Daughters,** 1923, from **The Movies** by Richard Griffith and Arthur Mayer, Spring Books, London, 1957
Robyn Stacey/Jenny Clarke **Facing Obscurity**
© Robert McFarlane (**The Pack of Women** television production) 1986

ROBYN ARCHER is one of Australia's leading theatre talents — a singer, writer, actor and director. She was born in Adelaide, South Australia, in 1948 and now lives in Sydney. She has recorded eight albums and written or devised ten theatre shows, including **The Pack of Women** and **A Star is Torn** (with Rodney Fisher). She has written The Robyn Archer Songbook (McPhee Gribble 1980), the children's book **Mrs Bottle Burps** (Thomas Nelson 1983) and **A Star is Torn,** with Diana Simmonds, (Virago 1986).

DIANA MANSON was born in Lae, Papua New Guinea, in 1950. Since 1977 she has worked as a partner in Robyn Archer's enterprises through their company Black and Blue. She produced **The Pack of Women** in London with Dianne Robson, **Cut and Thrust** in London 1983, **Scandals** in Australia 1985 and **The Pack of Women** for television 1986.

HELEN MILLS researched and wrote the original text for this book. She was born in Adelaide in 1949 and graduated from Adelaide University with degrees in Arts and Law. She has tutored in politics and worked for the Commissioner for Equal Opportunity in South Australia, the NSW Anti-Discrimination Board and the NSW Law Reform Commission. She is currently at the Australian Broadcasting Corporation as the Director of Corporate Policy and Planning.

DEBORAH PARRY designed the book. She was born in Perth in 1956. She gained a Diploma in Graphic Design from perth Technical College. She moved to Sydney where she runs her own business, Deborah Parry Graphics, which services regular clients like RAM Magazine, the Dendy Cinema, Belvoir Street Thèatre and the Australian Film Institute.

ROBYN STACEY contributed original artwork and did picture research. She was born in Brisbane, Queensland, in 1956. She graduated from the University of Queensland with a major in Fine Arts in 1978. She is currently lecturing part-time in photography. Her own work of hand-printed photographs and studio sets has been collected by the Australian National Gallery and she is represented in all major Australian galleries.

Robert McFarlane